THE GAYANI MEDITATIONS
FOR THE CONFRATERNITY OF THE MESSAGE
BOOK ONE

The Gayan of Hazrat Inayat Khan
annotated with selections from his lectures.

Edited by Cherag Hamid Cecil Touchon

Cherag Library Publications
CheragLibrary.org

The Gayani Meditations for the Confraternity of the Message - Book One
(The Gayan of Hazrat Inayat Khan annotated with selections from his lectures.)
Edited by Cherag Hamid Cecil Touchon

ISBN: 978-0-6151-5920-1 (soft cover)

Copyright 2007 Cherag Library Publications all rights reserved

All rights reserved. No part of this document may be reproduced in any form or by any means without written permission of the publisher.

Cover Art by Cecil Touchon – digital montage of a collage on paper

Cherag Library Publications

For contact information visit us online at CheragLibrary.org

Inquiries: Staff@CheragLibrary.org

Dedication

We live in a historically potent moment so far as the Message of Hazrat Inayat Khan is concerned. I have watched as the world has become the place that Inayat Khan projected that it would become. I have looked on with amusement as traditionalists have grappled with the implications of the inevitable movement toward a world where people of all religions mingle among each other with respect and understanding and where a widening number of people are reaching out beyond the confines of the belief structures that they grew up with.

The Message of Hazrat Inayat Khan remains fresh, new and revolutionary. Its vision of humanity's purpose and future stands out as a beacon that will continue to draw an ever widening body of followers. Yet the Church of All remains a fledgling enterprise still in its infancy and in need of nurturing and development in order that it may one day serve a wider public beyond the initiatic body entrusted with preserving the Message of its founder. This book is dedicated to that wider public who is drawn to and discovers the Message though this work. To you I say; 'Welcome.'

On a more personal note, I am blessed with children who have grown up with a respect for all religious traditions and who foster a faith that transcends any particular belief system. I also dedicate this work to my beloved children Zachariah Orion Malik, Brittany Elizabeth Marie and Noor-un-nisa for whom I hope this volume will serve as a daily guidance and also eventually for their children and grandchildren.

Introduction

The purpose of the present work is to provide members of the Confraternity of the Message working to fulfill the task of becoming a Gayani with the first year of daily readings focused on the first 365 sayings of Hazrat Inayat Khan from the Gayan.

The following is an original document of the Confraternity from the 1920's that explains the idea...

This Confraternity has been formed by the Seraj-un-Munir to provide a method by which sincere and devoted members of the Universal Worship´ (Church of All) may unite in a daily form of prayer for spreading the Message.

    It is divided into two parts called:

    1. The Duty
    2. The Task

The first is obligatory upon all who join; the second is voluntary, the form of both is given below.

The Duty

- To repeat at Sunrise, or upon waking, the prayer Saum - a devotion from the Gayan, - "May the Message of God spread far and wide" (101 times*), and the prayer Pir from the Vadan and the prayer for the Universel [see morning prayers]
- To repeat at midday the prayer Salat - a devotion from the Gayan, - "Pour upon us Thy Love and Thy Light" (101 times*) and the prayer Nabi from the Vadan and the prayer for the Universel [see mid-day prayers]
- To repeat at sunset the prayer Khatum - a devotion from the Gayan - "Disclose to us Thy Divine Light" (101 times*) and the prayer Rasul from the Vadan and the prayer for the Universel [see evening prayers]
-

*the current version in the Sufi Order International is 11 times

A sacred vow to fulfill these devotions will be taken with the Seraj-un-munir, or the Seraj of the country, by the candidate for membership in the Confraternity of the Message.

NOTE: When there is a church or a chapel of the Universal Worship these devotions may all be done at one hour as a form of collective Worship; in this case the Candle of the Message [also called the Spirit of Guidence candle] should be lighted from the Center Light [commonly called the God light or candle] and the words repeated aloud by each person at the same time. The ribbon and medal of the Confraternity should be worn at a Collective Devotion, and also for the Hours.

The Task

The Task which may be undertaken voluntarily by Members of the Confraternity, is to learn by heart each day **one** sentence of the Gayan, until the entire book has been committed to memory. When the Member can inform his/her Seraj that he/she has done this, the sacred distinction of the name **Gayani** will be conferred upon him/her by the Seraj-un-Munir.

He or she may then proceed in the same manner with the Vadan, and if he/she succeeds in learning this book also, the sacred distinction of the name **Vadani** will be conferred upon him/her by the Seraj-un-Munir.

NOTE: It is not necessary that the Books be learned in such a way that any part can be remembered at any time, although this should be the ideal before the one who undertakes this sacred task, but each verse must be learned thoroughly at the time when it is studied.

Details in the Construction of this Work

Numbering System

Several versions of the Gayan were consulted in the creation of the present work including an early undated version published by the Sufi Movement identical in structure to the 2nd edition as used in ORIGINAL TEXTS: SAYINGS 1 PART 1 from COMPLETE WORKS OF PIR-O-MURSHID

HAZRAT INAYAT KHAN. This work employed a numbering system for the sayings within each sections of the Gayan but did not number the sayings for the Gayan as a whole.

In the Complete Sayings of Hazrat Inayat Khan, (ISBN: 0930872398 Sufi Order Publications, New Lebanon, NY, 1978) the Gayan was numbered as a part of the whole collection of sayings but a number of sayings were either missing or placed in a different location as compared to the early versions of the Gayan as used by ORIGINAL TEXTS: SAYINGS 1 PART 1.

Therefore it was decided to maintain the original structure of the Gayan and to then renumber the Gayan as a whole in conjunction with the section-based numbering system used in ORIGINAL TEXTS: SAYINGS 1 PART 1 in order to provide a stable reference system for the construction of this work.

Selected Readings

The readings that attend the sayings were researched and selected using a database of Inayat Khan's works called Sufiwork. While not perfect, this search tool proved invaluable in finding the materials that best suited each reading. In the early days of the computer, the entirety of the database was entered by volunteers around the United States when a call was put out to Mureeds to help convert the various publications to a digital format. So, naturally typing errors and small mistakes found their way into the database. It became evident, for instance, that a number of the sayings from the Gayan were actually missing from the database and occasionally sayings were run together as if connected. However through a careful study, I was able to edit the database and include the missing sayings. Additionally, I numbered the sayings directly in the database in order to insure that all sayings as appeared in early editions of the Gayan were present and accounted for.

The database used for the selected readings included all of the esoteric papers through Sangitha 2, the 14 volumes of the Sufi Message, the Gathekas, the Religious and Social Gathekas, the Ziraat Papers, the Supplementary (Dutch) Papers, the Message Papers and the Addresses to the Cherags.

While searching, an attempt was first made to find an exact occurrence of each saying in the materials, if not found, searches were done using unique phrases within the sayings to find a compatible reading and if none of those occurrences seemed appropriate then topical search terms were used to find a complimentary reading. In all cases the intention was to find a reading that would amplify or illuminate or contextualize Inayat Khan's sayings in relation to his lectures.

It was found that, at times, sayings were inspired or even lifted directly from the lectures, sometimes Inayat Khan referred to already published sayings while lecturing, sometimes a saying was completely unique and seemed to have no hint of a reference in the lectures but may have been the inspiration of a private moment so that it was occasionally difficult to find corroborating material. In most cases however there were contextually related materials to be found in the lectures. Often Inayat Khan followed certain themes and used certain motifs that from time to time were elaborated on in different lectures making it possible to find a number of suitable readings from which to select.

Use of This Work

This book is intended to serve as an aide to the aspiring Gayani. Therefore the daily prayers are also included in this volume so that one can read them and then proceed to one of the daily meditations with the intent of committing to memory the saying of the day.

It is also common for students to use this book to select a page by chance to provide guidance on a problem or question. The Sufi does not believe anything happens by chance.

The Morning Prayers

Invocation

Toward the One,
The Perfection of Love,
Harmony and Beauty, the Only Being,
united with all the illuminated souls,
who form the embodiment of the Master
The Spirit of Guidance.

Saum

Praise be to Thee, Most Supreme God,
Omnipotent, Omnipresent, All-pervading, the Only Being.
Take us in Thy Parental Arms, raise us from the denseness of the earth,
Thy Beauty do we worship, to Thee do we give willing surrender.
Most Merciful and Compassionate God, the Idealized Lord of the whole humanity,
Thee only do we worship, and towards Thee Alone do we aspire.
Open our hearts towards Thy Beauty, illuminate our souls with Divine Light,
O Thou, the Perfection of Love, Harmony and Beauty,
All-powerful Creator, Sustainer, Judge and Forgiver of our shortcomings,
Lord God of the East and of the West,
of the worlds above and below,
and of the seen and unseen beings.
Pour upon us Thy Love and Thy Light,
give sustenance to our bodies, hearts and souls,
use us for the purpose that Thy Wisdom chooseth,
and guide us on the path of Thine Own Goodness.
Draw us closer to Thee every moment of our life,
until in us be reflected Thy Grace, Thy Glory, Thy Wisdom, Thy Joy and Thy Peace. Amen

Pir-O-Murshid Inayat Khan -- A Prayer of the Gayatri

"May the Message of God reach far and wide"

- Recited eleven times.

Pir

Inspirer of my mind, consoler of my heart, healer of my spirit,
Thy presence lifteth me from earth to heaven, Thy words flow as the sacred

river,
Thy thought riseth as a divine spring, Thy tender feelings awaken sympathy in my heart.
Beloved Teacher, thy very being is forgiveness.
The clouds of doubt and fear are scattered by thy piercing glance,
All ignorance vanishes in thy illuminating presence;
A new hope is born in my heart by breathing thy peaceful atmosphere.
O inspiring Guide through life's puzzling ways, In thee I feel abundance of blessing. Amen

Prayer for the Universel

O Thou, Who art the Maker, Molder and Builder of the Universe,
Build with Thy own hands, the Universel,
Our temple for Thy divine message of Love, Harmony and Beauty.

The Mid-day Prayers

Invocation

Toward the One,
The Perfection of Love,
Harmony and Beauty, the Only Being,
united with all the illuminated souls,
who form the embodiment of the Master
The Spirit of Guidance.

Salat

Most Gracious Lord, Master, Messiah and Saviour of humanity, we greet Thee with all humility.
Thou art the First Cause and the Last Effect, the Divine Light and the Spirit of Guidance, Alpha and Omega.
Thy Light is in all forms, Thy Love in all beings:in a loving mother, in a kind father, in an innocent child, in a helpful friend, and in an inspiring teacher.
Allow is to recognize Thee in all Thy Holy Names and Forms: as Rama, as Krishna, as Shiva, as Buddha; let us know Thee as Abraham, as Solomon, as Zarathustra, as Moses, as Jesus, as Muhammed, and in many more Names and Forms, known and unknown to the world.
We adore Thy Past, Thy Presence deeply enlightens our being, and we look for Thy Blessing in the future, O Messenger, Christ, Nabi, the Rasul of God! Thou whose heart constantly reaches upwards, Thou comest on earth with a Message, as a dove from above when dharma decayeth, and speakest the word that is put in thy mouth, as the light filleth the crescent moon.
Let the star of the Divine Light shining in thy heart be reflected in the hearts of thy devotees.
May the Message of God reach far and wide, illuminating and making the whole of humanity as one single family in the Parenthood of God. Amen

Pir-O-Murshid Inayat Khan -- A Prayer of the Gayatri

"Pour upon us Thy Love and Thy Light".

- Recited eleven times.

Nabi

A torch in the darkness, a staff during my weakness,
A rock in the weariness of life, Thou, my Master, makest earth a paradise.
Thy thought giveth me unearthly joy,

Thy light illuminateth my life's path,
Thy words inspire me with divine wisdom,
I follow in thy footsteps, which lead me to the eternal goal.
Comforter of the broken hearted, Support of those in need,
Friend of the lovers of truth, Blessed Master, thou art the Prophet of God.
Amen

Prayer for the Universel

O Thou, Who art the Maker, Molder and Builder of the Universe,
Build with Thy own hands, the Universel,
Our temple for Thy divine message of Love, Harmony and Beauty.

The Evening Prayers

Invocation

Toward the One,
The Perfection of Love,
Harmony and Beauty, the Only Being,
united with all the illuminated souls,
who form the embodiment of the Master
The Spirit of Guidance.

Khatum

O Thou, Who art the Perfection of Love, Harmony and Beauty, The Lord of Heaven and Earth,
Open our hearts, that we may hear Thy Voice, which constantly cometh from within;
Disclose to us Thy Divine Light, which is hidden in our souls, That we may know and understand life better.
Most Merciful and Compassionate God, give us Thy Great Goodness,
Teach us Thy Loving Forgiveness,
Raise us above the distinctions and differences which divide us,
Send us the Peace of Thy Divine Spirit, And unite us all in Thy Perfect Being.
Amen

"Disclose to us Thy Divine Light".

- Recited eleven times.

Rasul

Warner of coming dangers,
Wakener of the world from sleep,
Deliver of the Message of God, Thou art our Savior.
The sun at the dawn of creation,
The light of the whole universe,
The fulfillment of God's purpose,
Thou, the life eternal, we seek refuge in thy loving enfoldment.
Spirit of Guidance, Source of all beauty, and Creator of harmony,
Love, Lover and Beloved Lord, Thou art our divine ideal. Amen

Prayer for the Universel

O Thou, Who art the Maker, Molder and Builder of the Universe,
Build with Thy own hands, the Universel,
Our temple for Thy divine message of Love, Harmony and Beauty.

Additional Prayers

Prayer for New Year

O Thou who abidest in our hearts,
most Merciful and Compassionate God,
Lord of Heaven and Earth,
we forgive others their trespasses and ask Thy forgiveness of our shortcomings.
We begin the New Year with pure heart and clear conscience, with courage and hope.
Help us to fulfill the purpose of our lives under Thy divine guidance. Amen

GAYAN

(Gayan: Song)

Notes from the Unstruck Music

ALAPAS

(Alapa: God speaking to man.)

GAYAN 001 - ALAPA-01 - When a glimpse of Our image is caught in man, when heaven and earth are sought in man, then what is there in the world that is not in man? If one only explores him, there is a lot in man.

Man shows in his life traces of all the conditions through which the clay that makes his body has gone. There are atoms of his body which represent the mineral kingdom, the vegetable kingdom and the animal kingdom; all these are represented in him. Not only his body but his mind shows the reflection of all the kingdoms through which it has passed. For the mind is the medium between heaven and earth. Man experiences heaven when conscious of his soul; he experiences the earth when conscious of his body. Man experiences that plane which is between heaven and earth when he is conscious of his mind. Man shows by his stupidity the mineral kingdom which is in him, thick and hard; he shows by his pliability the vegetable kingdom, by his productive and creative faculties which bring forth the flowers and fruits of his life from his thoughts and deeds.

Man shows the traces of the animal kingdom in him by his passions, emotions, and attachments, by his willingness for service and usefulness. And if one were to say what represents the human in him, the answer is all things, all the attributes of earth and heaven; the stillness, hardness and strength of the stone; the fighting nature, the tendency to attachment from the animals; the fruitfulness and usefulness of the vegetable kingdom; the inventive, artistic, poetical and musical genius of the sphere of the jinn; the beauty, illumination, love, calm and peace of the angelic planes. All these put together make man. The human soul consists of all, and thus culminates in that purpose for which the whole creation has taken place.

MORAL CULTURE - THE SOUL, WHENCE AND WHITHER? –
Manifestation

GAYAN 002 - ALAPA-02 - If you will go forward to find Us, We will come forward to receive you.

At every step forward that the soul takes on the path it naturally comes closer to God, and coming closer to God means inheriting or drawing towards oneself the qualities of God. In other words the soul sees more, hears more, comprehends more, and enjoys more, because it lives a greater, a higher life.

THE PATH OF INITIATION AND DISCIPLESHIP – Three Aspects of Initiation

GAYAN 003 - ALAPA-03 - Give Us all you have, and We shall give you all We possess.

There is another side to love, and that is selfishness, and the lover must escape from this. The true lover says, 'I will give everything, I will endure all things, all tortures, all torments that may have to be faced in life. I will bow in humility before whatever befalls me. I will give all that I have. I will bear all things, believe all things, hope for all things, and endure all things.' But the other side of love says, 'Are you crazy? Have you lost your senses? You are foolish. Why this complaining? See how happy the beloved is. Be happy like him, and be in his exalted position, instead of in this humility and degradation. Enter into this greatness and not into that destruction!' Then he proceeds to reason, and at length he understands. The one thing leads to destruction, the other promises safety. But in destruction there is the hand of God, while in safety there is the hand of Satan. All things that are selfish are taught by that power and by that knowledge which is the enemy of mankind. Satan is an enemy because he leads man away from the purpose of his life. He seeks to make the lover change places with the beloved and say, 'Your position is better than mine; now I would like to be like you'. And perhaps he will wait all' his life to gain that coveted position, and it never comes because the beloved would not surrender the wealth when the chance was there.

IN AN EASTERN ROSE GARDEN - Love, Harmony, and Beauty

GAYAN 004 - ALAPA-04 - In man We have designed Our image; in woman We have finished it.

Then, if we look at it from another point of view, we shall see that duality is in fact nothing but unity, in other words that two is one; and the most interesting point in this is that as soon as we see two, each of the two at once takes a different and particular position in our view. This is clear with man and woman, but also our right hand and our left hand each shows a particular power and a particular function, and the right foot and the left foot each has its peculiar place in life. The right foot is distinctly different from the left foot, and also the sight of the two eyes is not the same. One eye is always better and stronger than the other, or at least different from the other, and if there were no difference the eyes would not be a proper instrument for seeing. If there were no difference between the power and strength of man's left side and his right side, he could not live.

Philosophy, Psychology, Mysticism – Philosophy – The Law of Rhythm

GAYAN 005 - ALAPA-05 - In man We have shown Our nature benign; in woman We have expressed Our art divine.

There is nothing for which a man will so blindly sacrifice all he possesses as for the woman he loves. He can be seen discarding his standards of thought and understanding, his family and friends, and his position for the sake of her whom he loves. And one feels that Adam must gladly have left paradise, if Eve did but smile and say it was her pleasure to walk on earth.

Woman's beauty touches man more than all other beauty. The colors, the delicacy, and fragrance of flowers, the radiance and light of jewels, are but a background for her. It seems to him that all nature was created to prepare for her being. And he finds no subject so beautiful for his art as a beautiful rendering of two youthful human figures, male and female.

But how shall he describe her whom he loves? For when he is conscious of beauty, it is then that he closes his lips.

As the ocean cannot be emptied into a vessel made by human hands, so beauty cannot be captured within the limits of human definitions. There is the beauty of the pine tree, a beauty of straightness and uprightness; and again there is the beauty of the sweeping branches of the willow. Or again a curve added to the beauty of steadiness of form sometimes doubles that loveliness. What can explain this diversity? Beauty of movement, of gesture, of feature, of expression, of voice, all escape explanation, which is indeed but a limited thing.

How calmly the mountains and hills seem to be waiting for some day that is to come; if you go near to them and listen they seem to tell you this. How eagerly the trees and plants seem to be expecting some day, some hour; the hour that shall be the fulfillment of their desire. The same desire, intense and pronounced, is still seen in birds and in animals; but its fulfillment is in man. The same aspiration which works through all aspects of life and has brought forth such varying fruits culminates in humanity, and prepares through humanity a path that reaches up to the height called divinity, which is the perfection of beauty.

THE ART OF PERSONALITY - LIFE'S CREATIVE FORCES: RASA SHASTRA - Beauty

GAYAN 006 - ALAPA-06 - God is the answer to every question.

Every musician knows how difficult it is to keep his violin in tune, especially when it is shaken wherever he has to move in the crowd. The heart, therefore, is incomparably more susceptible to get out of tune. It is therefore that the seers and mystics sought solitude, and kept themselves away from the crowd; but the Prophet, by his natural mission, is placed in the midst of the crowd. It is the problem of life in the crowd which he has to solve, and yet not solve it intellectually, as everyone wishes to do, but spiritually, by keeping that instrument, the heart, in proper tune to the Infinite, that he may get the answer for all questions arising at every moment of the day.

It is therefore that even the presence of the Prophet is the answer to every question: without having spoken one word, the Prophet gives the answer; but if a mind, restless and confused, cannot hear it, then that mind receives the answer in words. The answer of the Prophet uproots every question; but the answer always comes from the heart of the Prophet without his even having been asked a question. For the Prophet is only the medium between God and man; therefore the answer is from God. It is not true that the Prophet answers a question because he reads the mind; it is the mind of the one who asks the question that strikes, in the inner plane, the divine bell, which is the heart of the Prophet; and God, hearing the bell, answers. The answer comes in a manner as if words were put into the mouth of the Prophet.

The Prophet, therefore, need not think on the question he is asked; it is all automatic, so that the question draws out of him the answer. This rule is not applied only to individuals, but to the multitude. A thousand people listening to a Prophet at the same time, and each having a different question in his mind, the question of every one of them has been answered. So the true character of the sacred scriptures is that even the book answers the question, if a person opens it automatically in order to find out a solution to a certain problem. Imagine, if the book answers, then one could expect more from the Prophet; for the soul of the Prophet is the living book: his heart is the sacred scripture.

THE UNITY OF RELIGIOUS IDEALS – The Spiritual Hierarchy - The Attunement of the Prophet

GAYAN 007 - ALAPA-07 - Make God a reality, and God will make you the truth.

But the process that the wise consider best for the seeker after truth to adopt is the process of first idealizing God and then realizing God. In other words: first make God, and God will make you. As you read in the Gayan, 'Make God a reality, and God will make you the truth.'

Vol. 4 Healing and the Mind World - THE MIND-WORLD Chapter XIII

And for man to say that in this manner or in that manner the message comes, or for man to analyze that the message must come in this form or in that form, is the greatest mistake. I do not mean to say that the prophets did not hear the Voice of God, for God can talk louder than thunder. I do not mean to say that the prophet did not talk with God, as Moses did on Mount Sinai, because the personality of God can be more concrete in the eyes of the prophet than any other person existing in the world when once he is in communion with God. As you will read in the Gayan, "Make God a reality, and God will make you the truth."

THE MESSAGE PAPERS "Superhuman" and Hierarchy August 10, 1926

One might say, how can one love God, God whom one does not know, does not see? But the one who says this wants to take the second step instead of the first; he must first make God a reality, and then God will make him the truth. This stage is so beautiful; it makes the personality so tender and gentle; it gives such patience to the worshipper of God; and together with this gentleness and patience he becomes so powerful and strong that there is nothing that he will not face courageously: illness, difficulties, loss of money, opposition--there is nothing that he is afraid of.

PHILOSOPHY, PSYCHOLOGY, MYSTICISM – MYSTICISM IN LIFE - The Path to God

GAYAN 008 - ALAPA-08 - God made man, and man made good and evil.

There is no doubt that there is always a reason behind a reason, a higher reason. And when one arrives at this higher reason one begins to unlearn, as it is called by the mystics, all that one has once learnt. One unlearns and one begins to see quite the opposite. In other words, there is no good which has not a bad side to it, and nothing bad which has not a good side to it. No one rises without a fall, and no one fails without the promise of a rise. One sees death in birth, and birth in death. It sounds very strange, and it is a peculiar idea; but all the same it is a stage. When one rises above what is called reason one reaches that reason which is at the same time contradictory. This also explains the attitude of Christ. When a criminal was taken to him he had no other attitude towards him but that of the forgiver. He saw no evil there. That is looking from a higher reason. And if we penetrate the thousand veils of reason we can touch the reason of all reasons, and we can come to an understanding that the outer reasons cannot give. And by that we understand all beings: those who are in the right and those who are in the wrong. It is said that the Apostles in one moment were inspired to speak in many languages. It was not the English language, the Hindustani or Chinese language; it was the language of every soul. When a person has reached that state of mind in which it touches the essence of reason then it communicates with every soul. It is not a great thing to know thirty languages; a person may know a hundred languages, but if he does not know the heart of man he knows nothing.

Healing and the Mind World – Mental Purification – The Control of the Mind

GAYAN 009 - ALAPA-09 - If the Almighty God chooseth, He hath power sufficient to turn thy shield into a poisoned sword, and even thine own hand into the hand of thine adversary.

There is generally a tendency seen in those treading the spiritual path to feel discouraged at having bad impressions upon their heart of their own faults and shortcomings. And they begin to feel that they are too unworthy to have anything to do with things of a sacred nature. But it is a great error, in spite of all the virtue humility has in it. When one acknowledges something wrong in oneself one gives that wrong a soul out of one's own spirit, and by withdrawing from all that is good and beautiful, spiritual and sacred, instead of developing the spirit of rejecting all errors, in time one becomes a receptacle of what is wrong. He goes on disapproving and yet collecting errors, so producing within himself a perpetual conflict that never ends. When man becomes helpless before his infirmities he becomes a slave to his errors, he feels within himself an obedient servant to his adversary.

The greater the purity developed in the heart the greater becomes the power of man. As great the power of man within himself so great becomes his power on others. A hair's breadth can divide power from weakness, which appear to have as wide a gulf between them as between land and sky.

Gatha III – Everyday Life – Reject the Impression of Errors and Shortcomings

GAYAN 010 - ALAPA-10 - Give all you have, and take all that is given to you.

Q. What is the best way in education to develop that feeling in children? A. I think people at home are more responsible for it than at school. Because this is the first work of home. But if at home such education is given and at school it is spoiled then of course there is a disharmony.

For instance I will give you an example. A nurse was telling the children that: "You must keep your toy; you must not take away the toy of another child", when they were quarrelling over one another's toys. The nurse taught them: "No, each of you have your own. The other one has not the right to touch the toys of the other." It was just, but it was not love.

Then another one came who knew about it and who said to each child: "No, all the toys belong to all of you. And the best thing is to give one's toys to the other, that you play with each other's toys. Do you not like to see your brother or sister playing with your toy? You ought to be delighted to see that your brother or sister is playing with it."

Well, that is the feeling that must be developed. This crude way in which sometimes people want to work up high ideals by troubling and fighting, that is not the way. The best way is the way of love, of harmony, of sympathy. And for that feeling must be developed instead of thought. The present generation has made a great advancement in thought. But that is not enough. Now what is needed is that battery which stands behind thought, and that is feeling.

THE SUPPLEMENTARY PAPERS – PHILOSOPHY - PSYCHOLOGY II - Science and Psychology

GAYAN 011 - ALAPA-11 - Your great enemies are those who are near and dear to you, but your still greater enemy is your own self.

…the Sufi is tolerant when harmed by another, thinking that the harm has come from himself alone. He uses counterpoint by blending the undesirable talk of the friend and making it into a fugue.

He overlooks the fault of others, considering that they know no better. He hides the faults of others, and suppresses any facts that would cause disharmony. His constant fight is with the naf, the root of disharmony and the only enemy of man. By crushing this enemy man gains mastery over himself; this wins for him mastery over the whole universe, because the wall standing between the self and the Almighty has been broken down.

Gentleness, mildness, respect, humility, modesty, self denial, conscientiousness, tolerance and forgiveness are considered by the Sufi as the attributes which produce harmony within one's own soul as well as within that of another. Arrogance, wrath, vice, attachment, greed and jealousy are the six principal sources of disharmony. Nafs, the only creator of disharmony, becomes more powerful the more it is gratified, the more it is pleased. For the time being it shows its satisfaction at having gratified its demands, but soon after it demands still more until life becomes a burden. The wise detect this enemy as the instigator of all mischief, but everybody else blames another for his misfortunes in life.

THE MYSTICISM OF SOUND AND MUSIC - THE MYSTICISM OF SOUND - Harmony

Gayan-012, Alapa-12 - Whichever path you choose, the right or the wrong, know that there is at the back always a powerful hand to help you along it.

Since God is almighty, the wise see the Hand of God in the greater power, manifesting either through an individual or by a certain condition or situation, and instead of struggling too much against the difficulties in life, and instead of moaning over the losses which cannot be helped, they are resigned to the Will of God.

In short, every plan that a person makes, and his desire to accomplish that plan, is often an outcome of his personal will; and when his will is helped by every other will that he comes in contact with in the path of the attainment of a certain object, then he is helped by God. As every will goes in the direction of his will and so his will becomes strengthened, often a person accomplishes something which perhaps a thousand people could not have been able to accomplish. Then there is another person who has a thought, a desire, and finds opposition from every side; everything seems to go wrong, and yet he has the inner urge which prompts him to go on in the path of attainment. There also is the Hand of God behind his back, pushing him on, forward in his path, even though there might seem oppositions in the beginning of his strife--but all is well that ends well.

The Unity of Religious Ideals – The Will, Human and Divine

Gayan-013, Alapa-13 - O peace-maker, before trying to make peace throughout the world, first make peace within thyself!

Life is a continual battle. Man struggles with things that are outside him, and so he gives a chance to the foes who exist in his own being. Therefore the first thing necessary in life is to make peace for the time being with the outside world, in order to prepare for the war which is to be fought within oneself. Once peace is made within, one will gain by that sufficient strength and power to be used through the struggle of life within and without.

THE ART OF PERSONALITY - CHARACTER AND PERSONALITY - Character-Building

Gayan-014, Alapa-14 - Man! Thou art the master of life, here and in the hereafter.

It would not be an exaggeration if one called the mind a world; it is the world that man makes and in which he will make his life in the hereafter, as a spider weaves his web to live in. Once a person thinks of this problem he begins to see the value of the spiritual path. The soul learns on the path in which it is trained not to be owned by the mind, but to own it; not to become a slave of the mind, but to master it.

The Soul, Whence and Whither? – Manifestation

Gayan-015, Alapa-15 - Out of space there arose light, and by that light space became illuminated.

The light from which all life comes exists in three aspects, namely the aspect which manifests as intelligence, the light of the abstract, and the light of the sun. The activity of this one light functions in three different aspects. The first is caused by a slow and solemn activity in the eternal Consciousness which may be called consciousness or intelligence. It is intelligence when there is nothing before it to be conscious of, when there is something intelligible before it, the same intelligence becomes consciousness. A normal activity in the light of intelligence causes the light of the abstract at the time when the abstract sound turns into light. This light becomes a torch for the seer who is journeying towards the eternal goal. The same light in its intense activity appears as the sun.

No person would readily believe that intelligence, abstract light and the sun are one and the same - yet language does not contradict itself, and all three have always been called by the name of light. These three aspects of the one light form the idea that lies behind the doctrine of the Trinity, and that of Trimurti which existed thousands of years before Christianity among the Hindus, and which denotes the three aspects of the One: the One being three.

Substance commences to develop from radiance to atom, but before this it exists as a vibration. What man sees he accepts as something existent, and what he cannot see does not exist for him. All that man perceives, sees, and feels is matter, and that which is the source and cause of all is spirit.

The philosophy of form may be understood by the study of the process by which the unseen life manifests into the seen. As the fine waves of vibrations produce sound, so the gross waves produce light. This is the manner in which the unseen, incomprehensible and imperceptible life becomes gradually known: first becoming audible, and then visible. This is the origin and only source of all life.

The sun, therefore, is the first form seen by the eyes, and it is the origin and source of all forms in the objective world; as such it has been worshipped by the ancients as God, and we can trace the origin of all religions in that mother-religion.

THE MYSTICISM OF SOUND AND MUSIC - THE MYSTICISM OF SOUND - Form

Gayan-016, Alapa-16 - If your fellow-man does not pay you his debts, forbear patiently; someday every farthing will be paid you with interest.

Man does not know in what form he has to pay, nor in what form he does the taking; very often he does not know when he takes or what he gives; but every moment of his life is occupied in give and take, and all the injustice of the world adjusts itself in the end. A clear understanding of this condition will show that it all balances. If there were no balance the world would not exist. This ever-moving world, turning round and round, what holds it, what makes it stable? It is balance. And not only the world, but everything else too: the whole of life in its own way. Being occupied by our worldly life, we are not aware of that balance, but when the inner eye is open and one sees life clearly, one will find that there is a continual balancing process going on, and that we as particles of one mechanism are constantly busy keeping this balance. When once the heart is at rest through the feeling that one has paid, or is paying, one's debts, then one comes to a balanced condition in life. Then the heart, which is likened to the sea, is no longer restless as it is during the storm, but like calm, undisturbed water; and it is that condition which enables man to experience inner life more fully.

The Alchemy of Happiness – The Inner Life

Gayan-017, Alapa-17 - Put thy trust in God for support, and see His hidden hand working through all sources.

It is for them that the Prophet has said, "Tie your camel and trust in God." It was not said to Daniel, "Take your sword and go among the lions." One imagines God, another realizes God; there is a difference between these two persons. The one who imagines can hope, but he cannot be certain. The one who realizes God, he is face to face with his Lord, and it is he who depends upon God with certainty. It is a matter of struggling along on the surface of the water, or courageously diving deep, touching the bottom of the sea.

There is no greater trial for a person than dependence upon God. What patience it needs, besides the amount of faith it requires, to be in the midst of the world of illusion and yet to be conscious of the existence of God! To do this man must be able to turn all what is called life into death, and to realize in what is generally called death -- in that death, the true life. This solves the problem of false and real.

Gatha II Metaphysics - Tawakkul -- Dependence Upon God

ALANKARAS

(Alankara: The fanciful expression of an idea.)

Gayan 018 - Alankara-01 - Indifference! My most intimate friend, I am sorry I have always to act against thee as thy opponent.

The question arises, how can one learn indifference? By learning interest. If in our life we do not learn interest, we cannot learn indifference. A person who is born with no interest in life is only an idiot. The child which does not hold on to the toy in its hands gives no promise of progress. It is natural for the child to hold on to the toy and claim it as its own. That is the first lesson it should learn. It is normal for a child to say the toy belongs to it and to hold on to it. In that way one develops interest, interest in one's well being and in one's progress in life, so that one can accomplish one's purpose in life. All this is natural and normal. It is interest in other people, in their affairs, in those one loves and likes, which develops the character.

By interest in things of the world one helps the world; by interest one contributes one's service to the world. If one had no interest one would not do so, one would not render service to the nation or to the cause of the world.

Evolution goes on step by step, not hurrying. Indifference is attained by developing interest, and by developing discrimination in one's interest. Instead of going backward one should go forward in one's interest; then one will find that a spring will rise naturally in one's heart, when the heart has touched the zenith in the path of interest. Then the fountain of interest will break up gradually, and when this happens, one should follow this trend, so that in the end one may know what interest means, and what indifference means.

The Alchemy of Happiness – Interest and Indifference

Gayan 019 - Alankara-02 - My modesty! Thou art the veil over my vanity.

Modesty is a beauty in itself, and its action is to veil itself; in that veiling it shows the vanity of its nature, and yet that vanity is a beauty itself.

Hay is the finest feeling in human nature, which is called modesty. Modesty is not necessarily meekness, or humility, or selflessness, or pride. Modesty is a beauty in itself, and its action is to veil itself; in that veiling it shows the vanity of its nature, and yet that vanity is a beauty itself. Modesty is the life of the artist, the theme of the poet, and the soul of the musician. In thought, speech, action, in one's manner, in one's movement, modesty stands as the central theme of grace. Without modesty beauty is dead, for modesty is the spirit of beauty. Silence in modesty speaks louder than bold words. The lack of modesty can destroy art, poetry, music, and all that is beautiful.

Gatha Three – Morals – (7) Haya

Gayan 020 - Alankara-03 - My humility! Thou art the very essence of my vanity.

As long as one's little personality stands before one, as long as one cannot get rid of it, as long as one's own person and all that is connected with it interests one, one will always find limitations. That Power is touched only by one way, and that is the way of self-effacement, which in the Bible is called self-denial. People interpret it otherwise. Self-denial, they say, means to deny oneself all the happiness and pleasures of this earth. If it were to deny the happiness and pleasure of this earth, then why was this earth made? Only to deny? If it was made to deny, it was very cruel. For the continual seeking of man is for happiness.

Self-denying is to deny this little personality that creeps into everything, to efface this false ego which prompts one to feel one's little power in this thing or that thing; to deny the idea of one's own being, the being which one knows to be oneself, and to affirm God in that place; to deny self and affirm God. That is the perfect humility. When a person shows politeness by saying, 'I am only a humble little creature', perhaps he is hiding in his words. It is his vanity, and therefore that humility is of no use. When one completely denies oneself, there are no words to speak. What can one say? Praise and blame become the same to one; there is nothing to be said. And how is this to be attained? It is to be attained, not only by prayer or by worship or by believing in God; it is to be attained by forgetting oneself in God. The belief in God is the first step. By the belief in God is attained the losing oneself in God. If one is able to do it, one has attained a power which is beyond human comprehension.

The process of attaining this is called Fana by the Sufis. Fana is not necessarily a destruction in God. Fana results in what may be called a resurrection in God, which is symbolized by the picture of Christ. The Christ on the cross is narrative of Fana; it means, 'I am not.' And the idea of resurrection explains the next stage, which is Baqa, and which means, 'Thou art', and this means rising towards All-might. The divine spirit is to be recognized in that rising towards All-might.... It is by denying one's little self, the false self which covers one's real self, in which the essence of divine Being is to be found.

THE PURPOSE OF LIFE - Chapter IV

Gayan 021 - Alankara-04 - Vanity! Both saint and sinner drink from thy cup.

This is the foundation: a person must develop in his soul, cultivate in his spirit the nobleness of the soul. That is aristocracy. And then he will rise to the democracy, and that democracy is to be kind and good and respectful, tolerant and forgiving and friendly to the saint and sinner both. You go and see the Sufis in the world today: wherever you will go, you will find that spirit with a beautiful manner, with humility, with gentleness, meekness, dignity. Another thing is developed, and that is the democratic feeling. Never to despise anyone, never to hate, never to condemn, never to look down upon anyone, but to see the divine expression in all beings.

That is the balance of life. That is the aristocratic spirit of nobleness and the democratic spirit of tolerance that brings about equality, that brings about the balance we should strike in life.

THE MESSAGE PAPERS - Four Questions July 6, 1926

Gayan 022 - Alankara-05 - Vanity! Thou art the fountain of wine on the earth, where cometh the King of Heaven to drink.

For adepts the struggle in life is not so great with the passions and emotions, which sooner or later by more or less effort can be controlled; but vanity, it is always growing. If one cuts down its stem then one cannot live, for it is the very self, it is the I, the ego, the soul, or God within; it cannot be denied its existence. But struggling with it beautifies it more and more, and makes more and more tolerable that which in its crude form is intolerable.

The Art of Personality - The Art of Personality

Gayan 023 - Alankara-06 - Peacock! Is it not thy vanity that causeth thee to dance?

In the traditions of the Sufis Raqs, the sacred dance of spiritual ecstasy which even now is prevalent among the Sufis of the East, is traced to the time when contemplation of the Creator impressed the wonderful reality of His vision so deeply on the heart of Jelal-ud-Din Rumi that he became entirely absorbed in the whole and single immanence of nature, and took a rhythmic turn which caused the skirt of his garment to form a circle, and the movements of his hands and neck made a circle. It is the memory of this moment of vision which is celebrated in the dance of dervishes.

Even in the lower creation among beasts and birds their joy is always expressed in dance. A bird like the peacock, when conscious of his beauty and the beauty of the forest around him, expresses his joy in dance. Dance arouses passion and emotion in all living creatures.

THE MYSTICISM OF SOUND – Rythmn

Gayan 024 - Alankara-07 - My bare feet! Step gently on life's path, lest the thorns lying on the way should murmur at being trampled upon by you.

No one without courage, strength of will, and patience can follow this path. When a person has to live among people of every different kind, he must make his own character soft as a rose, make it even finer so that no one can be hurt by the thorns. Two thorns cannot harm each other. The thorns can hurt the rose, but the rose cannot tear the thorns. Think what the life of the rose between two thorns must be!

The journey begins with a path of thorns, and the traveller must go barefoot. It is not easy always to be tolerant and patient, to refrain from judging others, and to love one's enemy. It is a dead man who walks on this path, one who has drunk the bowl of poison. The beginning of each path is always difficult and uninteresting, hard for everybody. Ask the violinist about the first days when he practices scales and cannot even form the tones! Often he does not have enough patience to go on till he can play well enough to satisfy himself. The first part of the path is constant strife, struggle with life, but as one approaches the goal the path gets easier; the distance seems greater but the path is smoother and difficulties less.

THE ALCHEMY OF HAPPINESS - The Journey to the Goal (2)

Gayan 025 - Alankara-08 - My ideal! I imagine at moments that we are playing see-saw; when I rise up, thou goest down below my feet; and when I go down, thou risest above my head.

And if we take that spiritual ideal as our recognized aim, that ideal will help us in all our wants and needs and all our troubles, and at the same time it is that ideal that will raise us from the denseness which at times keeps one bound. It does not matter by what way the soul is progressing, whether by devotion, by religion, or by another way, as long as that spiritual ideal is before us we have really that port before us to which all boats go, that peace, constant happiness, that Friend never separated, that Father, always a Father here and in the hereafter, that Mother, the Mother of all humanity, that Ideal of perfect beauty. And keeping that ideal before us, that in our heart that ideal may be reflected, is really the best method of accomplishing the real object of human life.

The Dutch Papers – Philosophy 1 - The Aim of Life (2)

Gayan 026 - Alankara-09 - My self-dependence! Thou makest me poor but at the same time rich.

One sees a constant striving in the life of the adepts to make themselves independent of outside things as much as possible. On the other hand worldly people think it progress if they can become daily more dependent on others. Every step we take is towards dependence; and the more we depend upon others, the more we think we are progressing. In the end we come to such a stage that for what the soul needs, what the mind needs, what the body needs, we depend upon others.

THE ART OF PERSONALITY - EDUCATION - The Education of the Infant

...Very often condition in life shows a picture of captivity, often it seems as if one had to walk between the water and a pit. And to rise above conditions one needs wings, which not everybody has.

The wings are attached to the will, one is independence the other is indifference. Independence needs a great deal of sacrifice in one's life before one can feel independent in life. Indifference against one's nature of love and sympathy is like cutting one's heart asunder before one can practice indifference through life. No doubt once the will is able to spread its wings then one sees the conditions of life far removed, one stands above all conditions that makes man captive.

SOCIAL GATHEKAS – Happiness

GAYAN 027 - ALANKARA-10 - My beloved ideal! When I was looking for thee on the earth, wert thou not laughing at me in heaven?

"The greatness of man lies in the greatness of his ideal.

That which makes us esteem those whom we esteem is their ideal. That which raises man from earth to heaven is his ideal; and that which pulls man down from the heavens to the earth is also his ideal. When he does not live up to his ideal he falls to earth; and when he raises his ideal he goes from earth to heaven. He can rise to any height, according to the stature of his ideal.

One person thinks, 'O, it does not matter; if I have a good dinner, never mind what others have'; another thinks, 'It is no pleasure to me to have had a good dinner, since my family still starve; it gives me much more happiness if I have only a frugal dinner, as long as my family are well satisfied'. This raises him higher than the person who thinks only of his own happiness. A third person thinks, 'it does not matter how I live, so long as I have brought some happiness to the people of my town, or village; that would be worth while'. His ideal is greater still.

The trust that is sent by heaven is the ideal given to man. That is his charge in life, his responsibility in life. To take care of this and prove worthy of this responsibility and position that has been given to us, that is what should prove to be our ideal, our religion, our Dharma. In the Gospel the 'talent' represents the same ideal; at first it is small, but it expands as we go through life."

IN AN EASTERN ROSE GARDEN - The Ideal Life

GAYAN 028 - ALANKARA-11 - My feeling heart! I so often wish thou wert made of stone.

"What closes the doors of the heart is fear, confusion, depression, spite, discouragement, disappointment, and a troubled conscience; and when that is cleared away, the doors of the heart open... The sensation of joy is felt in the center of the breast, also the heaviness caused by depression. Therefore as long as the breast remains choked with anything, the heart remains closed. When the breast is cleared from it [from whatever is choking it], the heart is open. It is the open heart which takes the reflection of all impressions coming from outside. It is the open heart which can receive reflections from the Divine Spirit within. It is the openness of heart, again, which gives power and beauty to express oneself; and if it is closed, a man, however learned, cannot express his learning to others.

The Unity of Religious Ideals – Prophets and Religions – The Sufi's conception of God – The Opening of the Breast of the Prophet

GAYAN 029 - ALANKARA-12 - My limitation! Thou art as a mote in the eye of my soul.

The exact meaning of the inner life is not only to live in the body, but to live in the heart, to live in the soul. Why, then, does not the average man live an inner life when he too has a heart and a soul? It is because he has a heart, and yet is not conscious of it; he has a soul, and knows not what it is. When he lives in the captivity of the body, limited by that body, he can only feel a thing by touching it, he sees only by looking through his eyes, he hears only by hearing with his ears. How much can the ears hear and the eyes see? All this experience obtained by the outer senses is limited. When man lives in this limitation he does not know that another part of his being exists, which is much higher, more wonderful, more living, and more exalted. Once he begins to know this, then the body becomes his tool, for he lives in his heart. And then later he passes on and lives in his soul. He experiences life independently of his body; and that is called the inner life. Once mart has experienced the inner life, the fear of death has expired; because he knows death comes to the body, not to his inner being. When once he begins to realize life in his heart and in his soul, then he looks upon his body as a coat. If the coat is old he puts it away and takes a new one, for his being does not depend upon his coat. The fear of death lasts only so long as man has not realized that his real being does not depend upon his body.

The Inner Life – The Realization of the Inner Life

GAYAN 030 - ALANKARA-13 - Money! Thou art a bliss and a curse at the same time. Thou turnest friends into foes and foes into friends. Thou takest away anxiety in life and at the same time givest it.

Do we only see spiritual persons among those who are sitting in the caves of the Himalayas? Do we not see wonderful personalities in the midst of the world? Very often people say that a person who has struggled along all through his life with business and industry and worldly things has become hardened. But I think that the one who has really gained victory over the earth, who really has made a success which can be called a success, has learned something from it. It is not everyone who becomes successful in earthly affairs; it is one among many. And the one who comes to the top has had his difficulties, has had his problems; his endurance, his patience have been tested. He has gone through a sacrifice. He has understood human nature, standing in the midst of the crowd.

If he has not read one book of philosophy, if he has not meditated one day, still he has arrived at a plane, at an understanding, where he knows something worth knowing. I considered myself most privileged at times when I had conversations with business men, with people who were always busy with the things of the earth and who had really reached the top; and I have simply marveled to think that instead of hardening them it has softened their nature to some extent, it has given them a sense which can come by spiritual understanding, which is a religious sense; it has developed a fairness in them. By having gone through this world of injustice and having seen what one sees in the business world, they have come to a point of honesty where one begins to see life from a different point of view. And besides that, if anyone ever comes forward and says, 'For a philanthropic purpose, for the good of humanity, I give so many millions for education, for the hospitals', it is they who do it. And I would very much wonder if a recluse who has always kept himself away from money, if he had the charge of many millions, would like to part with any. The point is, whether a person is earthly or heavenly, to be true to the purpose of life is the first moral we have to learn. For even an earthly purpose, however material it may seem, will prove in the end to be a stepping-stone even if one had nothing but that ideal before one.

The Unity of Religious Ideals – THE PURPOSE OF LIFE – Chapter VIII

GAYAN 031 - ALANKARA-14 - Waves: We are Upsaras of the ocean. When the wind plays music we dance; earth's treasure is not of our seeking; our reward is Indra's one glance.

The world of the jinns is the world of mind; yet the minds of the jinns are not so developed as the minds of men. The reason for this is that the experience of life on the earth completes the making of mind. In the world of the jinns the mind is only a design, an outline; a design which is not yet embroidered. What is the occupation of the jinns? What does the world of the jinns look like? One may give a thousand explanations, but nothing can explain it fully. For instance, if a person were to ask me what China looks like, I would say, 'Most wonderful, most interesting,' but if he said, 'What is wonderful in China?' I would say, 'Go and take a tour through China in order that you may see it fully.'

We have not adequate words to explain what the jinn is like, or what the world of the jinn is; but what little can be said is that it is a world of music, art, poetry; a world of intelligence, cheer fullness and joy; a world of thought, imagination and sentiment; a world that a poet would long for and a musician would crave to dwell in. The life of the jinn is an ideal life for a thinker; a life which is free from all illness, pure from all bitterness of human nature, free to move about through space without any hindrance. This sphere is a most joyful place, where the sun of intelligence shines, where the trouble of life and death is not so serious, life not so short as on the earth. If there is any paradise it is the world of the jinn. Hindus have called it Indra-loka, and picture Gandharvas and Upsaras* to be there; it is a paradise, of which every prophet has spoken to his followers in the way in which they could understand it.

THE SOUL, WHENCE AND WHITHER? - Towards Manifestation

*Upsaras are heavenly dancers this is a Sanscrit word the Hindi word is Apsara.

GAYAN 032 - ALANKARA-15 - Time! I have never seen thee, but I have heard thy steps.

Every aspect of the life of an individual and of the life of the world has its cycle. In the life of an individual the period from his birth to his death is the first part, and from death to assimilation in the Infinite the second part. The sub-cycles in man's life are from infancy to youth, where one part ends and from youth to old age, which is the close. There are again under-cycles: infancy, childhood, youth, maturity, senility; and there are the cycles of man's rise and fall.

So there is a cycle of the life of the world, and the cycle of the creation of man and his destruction, the cycles of the reign of races and nations, and cycles of time, such as a year, a month, a week, day, and hour.

The nature of each of these cycles has three aspects, the beginning, the culmination and the end, which are named Uruj, Kermal and Zeval; like, for example, new moon, full moon, and waning moon; sunrise, zenith and sunset. These cycles, sub-cycles and under-cycles, and the three aspects of their nature, are divided and distinguished by the nature and course of light. As the light of the sun and moon and of the planets plays the most important part in the life of the world, individually and collectively, so the light of the Spirit of Guidance also divides time into cycles. And each cycle has been under the influence of a certain Master with many controllers under him, working as the spiritual hierarchy which controls the affairs of the whole world, mainly those concerning the inward spiritual condition of the world. The Masters have been numberless since the creation of man; they have appeared with different names and forms; but He alone was disguised in them who is the only Master of eternity.

THE WAY OF ILLUMINATION - Some Aspects of Sufism - The Masters

GAYAN 033 - ALANKARA-16 - Time! In my sorrow thou creepest; in my joy thou runnest; in the hours of my patient waiting thou standest still.

As there is a season for everything, as there is a fixed time for nature to manifest, so there is a season for every happening. Good luck, bad luck, rise, fall, health, illness, success, and failure, all depend upon a certain time. There is a time for every season as well as for every experience; and as there is a time for birth so there is a time for death. Every thought, every action, and every condition has a birth and death, and each has a fixed time. And when one has become convinced of the fact that every happening is brought about by time and is fixed at a certain time, then naturally one develops faith, and then one believes that what is not realized today will be realized tomorrow, some day.

The great drawback we find in humanity today is its lack of patience: if people can accomplish something at once then it is all right, but if not then they think that it cannot be done. Only if anything can be done quickly can it be done; if it cannot be done as quickly as one expects this means that it cannot be done at all. There are thousands of people today who already accept failure before failure becomes apparent, because they have no patience to wait for success to come. Although success may be preparing, yet they are in such haste that they would rather turn the success into a failure than wait for it; the reason is that this mystery, which is the mystery of the mystics--that everything depends upon a certain time--is forgotten by most people.

Time uses conditions to bring about certain results; and very often a seemingly bad condition is preparing a good issue, and a seemingly good condition may be preparing a bad result. Frequently, therefore, a person who depends only upon objective phenomena makes a mistake, is deluded. The mystic sees in both adverse and favorable conditions that which is going to happen. He does this by believing in the action of time and space, and by believing that there is no such thing as coincidence or accident. It is only because we are unaware of where an action has started, of what has brought it about, and of what is preparing, that we call something a coincidence or an accident; in reality there is no such thing. Every happening, whether it comes by our will or by a higher will, is prepared, is directed by wisdom. If it is not directed by our individual will it is directed by a greater wisdom, and it brings about a greater result. The mystic therefore awaits that result which is brought about by time and space through different conditions.

PHILOSOPHY, PSYCHOLOGY, MYSTICISM - MYSTICISM IN LIFE - The Visions of the Mystic

GAYAN 034 - ALANKARA-17 - Time! Thou art the ocean, and every movement of life is thy wave.

It must be understood that every wave of life which is set in motion by the principal cause, works toward a purpose. With its every motion the purpose becomes more definite, and at its every stage of evolution it adjusts itself, making a perfect harmony - although in a limited space this same activity may appear inharmonious. Therefore good and evil, right and wrong, when viewed by the keen sight, correspond with a certain purpose, and thus prove harmonious from the standpoint of the perfect Whole.

THE MYSTICISM OF SOUND AND MUSIC - MUSIC - The Mystery of Sound

GAYAN 035 - ALANKARA-18 - Sky! Thou art a sea whereon the boat of my imagination sails.

Control of the mind consists of control of imaginations, thoughts, emotions and feelings. Emotions are the outcome of thoughts and feelings, the vibrations of which are always ringing in the sphere of the astral plane. The scattered clouds in the sky join and separate, at every moment forming various distinct pictures. In like manner the will- as a magnet - gathers these vibrations in the astral sphere from different directions, forming them accidentally or intentionally into a picture which is either a thought, an imagination, an emotion or a feeling. Just as clouds do not remain unscattered in the sky, so the pictures formed in the astral world are liable quickly to be dispersed, except when the sky is overcast, or when the atmosphere is overwhelmed with depression or joy.

SUFI TEACHINGS - HEALTH AND ORDER OF BODY AND MIND –
Self Control

GAYAN 036 - ALANKARA-19 - My thoughtful self! Reproach no one, hold a grudge against no one, bear malice against no one; be wise, tolerant, considerate, polite and kind to all.

Antipathy turns into malice, and malice culminates in bitterness. To possess it in one's heart is like possessing in one's heart a poison, a poison that clouds wit and produces obscurity. If one keeps one's heart free from malice one has accomplished a great deal, for it is in the clear heart that the light from above is reflected. Often without an intention on one's part malice enters, of which man is unconscious. Often the man who possesses malice is quite innocent, for his heart is reflecting the malice which is projected from another heart. It is therefore that care must be taken to keep one's heart free from the impressions and influences coming from others. The question how can one avoid this is answered thus, that the heart will focus itself to a person or to an influence which is akin to its own quality; that is the nature of the heart.

Therefore even if the impression came from another, for the influence of another the man who reflects it is responsible. To make the heart reflect good qualities one must prepare it, one must train it; for it is the good quality of heart that will keep away undesirable impressions and thoughts, and will only reflect good impressions and desirable influences. As a practice of purifying one's heart is to repeat every morning and every evening, "My thoughtful self! Reproach no one, hold a grudge against no one, bear malice against no one; be wise, tolerate, considerate, polite and kind to all!

Gatha III – Everyday Life - Keep the Heart Free from Poison

GAYAN 037 - ALANKARA-20 - My independence! How many sacrifices I have made for thee, and yet thou art never satisfied.

"Very often conditions in life show a picture of captivity; often it seems as if one had to walk between water and a pit. To rise above conditions one needs wings: two wings attached to the soul, one independence, the other indifference - which not everyone has got. Independence needs a great deal of sacrifice before one can feel independent in life. Indifference is against one's nature of love and sympathy; it is like cutting one's heart asunder before one can practice indifference throughout life. No doubt once the soul is able to spread its wings, one sees the conditions of life as far removed; then one stands above all conditions that make man captive."

SUFI TEACHINGS - THE PRIVILEGE OF BEING HUMAN -
Independence and Indifference

GAYAN 038 - ALANKARA-21 - My simple trust! How often thou has disappointed me, yet I still go on following thee with closed eyes.

For a person to have a simple faith does not mean that he has no sense. Such a person may be the most sensible of all, while one who thinks that he is too clever to trust anybody, who will not be taken in by anyone and is proud of his cleverness, may really be the most foolish. He prides himself on his skepticism, which makes him doubt every person he meets, thinking that he is so clever. But when such cleverness prevents one from having any peace of mind and makes one always restless, going from one belief to another, one would much rather be without the cleverness. Faith is the light that kindles the same substance in another person's heart. By trusting another person one also creates in his heart the same attribute which is within oneself: trust. What peace it brings to have faith and trust!

THE VISION OF GOD AND MAN - Discipleship (2)

GAYAN 039 - ALANKARA-22 - My moods, what are you?--We are the waves rising in your heart.

All the different moods that we are in--inclination to laughter or crying, heaviness, exaltation, or meditation--all result from the breath. It changes in activity so many times during the day and night. As it changes, it expresses a certain element, earth, water, fire, air, or ether, and it makes one feel inclined to do certain things in accordance with the element.

IN AN EASTERN ROSE GARDEN – What the Power of Breath Can Do

GAYAN 040 - ALANKARA-23 - My emotion, where do you come from?-- From the ever flowing spring of your heart.

Question: Could you explain further how the mind is the surface of the heart, and the heart the depth of the mind. Answer: There are five fingers but one hand, there are several organs of the body but one body, and there is a universe full of variety but one Spirit. So there is one heart which feels the various thoughts and imaginations which spring up and then sink into it. The bubbles are to be found on the surface of the sea. The depth of the sea is free from bubbles. The commotion is to be seen on the surface, the depth of the sea is still. The mind is the commotion of that something which is within us, that something which we call heart.

The happiness, the knowledge, the pleasure, the love which is stored in our innermost being is in our profound depth; changing emotions and passions, dreams, ever rising thoughts and imaginations all belong to the surface, as the bubbles belong to the surface of the sea.

The Mysticism of Sound and Music – Cosmic Language – Heart and Mind

GAYAN 041 - ALANKARA-24 - My imagination, what are you?--I am the stream that feeds the fountain of your mind.

As the surface of the heart is known by the imagination and thought, so the depth of the mind, which is the heart, is known by feeling. The difference between thought and imagination is that imagination is an automatic working of the mind. If the mind is fine there is a fine imagination; if the mind is gross there is a gross imagination; if there is a beautiful mentality, the imagination is beautiful. Thought is also imagination, but imagination held, controlled, and directed by will. Therefore when we say: 'He is a thoughtful person', it means that this person does not think, speak, or act on impulse, but behind everything he does there is will-power which controls and directs the action of his mind.

The Mysticism of Sound and Music - Cosmic Language – Mind and Heart

BOULAS

(Boulas: A kindled word.)

GAYAN 042 - BOULA -001 - Heaven and hell are the material manifestation of agreeable and disagreeable thoughts.

In the memory the secret of heaven and hell is to be found. As Omar Khayyam said in his Rubayat: 'Heaven is the vision of fulfilled desire, and hell the shadow of a soul on fire'. What is it? Where is it? It is only in the memory. Therefore memory is not a small thing. It is not something which is hidden in the brain. It is something living, and it is something so vast that a limited mind cannot conceive it. It is something which is a world in itself.

The Mysticism of Sound and Music – Cosmic Language – Memory

At death comes leisure; after death the mind comes to greater life, a life more real than here. Death is an unveiling, the removal of a cover, after which the soul will know many things in regard to its own life and in regard to the whole world which had hitherto been hidden. Therefore the realization of what is said about heaven and hell which we have accumulated in our mind, in the hereafter will be our own. Today our mind is in us; in the hereafter we shall be in our mind. And therefore that mind which is mind just now, in the hereafter will be the world. If it is heaven, it will be heaven; if it is another place, it will be the other place. It is what we have made it. No one is attracted and put there. We have made it for ourselves, for our own convenience…

…Various impressions remain in the mind after death. Because what is individual? Being individual is like being in a mist. When different physical organs cannot any longer hold the spirit then they fail, and the spirit has finished with them. The body departs, the spirit remains. The spirit is as individual as the person was individual in the physical body. After the physical body has gone, the non-physical impressions are more distinct because the limitation of the physical body has fallen away. The physical body is a great limitation. When it has fallen away individuality becomes more distinct, more capable of working than on the physical plane.

Healing and the Mind World – Mental Purification – The Pure Mind

GAYAN 043 - BOULA -002 - All the good deeds of a lifetime may be swept away in the flood caused by a single sin.

The idea of forgiveness is the result of our idealizing God. As we idealize God so He proves to be. Sometimes the sins of a whole life may be wiped off in one instant; sometimes all the virtue and piety of a whole life may be lost by one sin.

A story is told that Moses was going to Mount Sinai and on his way he met a very pious person, who said to him, 'Moses, speak to God of me. All my life I have been pious, I have been virtuous, I have prayed to God, and I have had nothing but troubles and misfortunes.' A little later Moses met a man sitting in the street with a bottle of liquor. He called out, 'Moses! Where are you going?' Moses said, 'To Mount Sinai.' The man called out, 'To Mount Sinai? Then speak to God of me', for he was drunk.

Moses went to Mount Sinai and he told God of the pious person whom he had met. God said, 'For him there is a place in the heavens.' Then he told God of the drunken man whom he had met. God said, 'He shall be sent to the worst possible place in hell.'

Moses went away and first he met the drunken man. He told him, 'God says you shall be sent to the worst possible place in hell.' The man said, 'God spoke of me?' and he was so overjoyed that he could not contain himself but began to dance, just as a poor man might be overjoyed if he heard that a king had spoken of him, even if the king had said nothing good of him. Then he said, 'How happy should I be that He, the Creator and Sovereign of the universe, knows me, the great sinner.' Then Moses told the pious person what God had said. He said, 'Why not? I have spent all my life in the worship of God and in piety, sacrificing all else in life; and therefore I am entitled to have it.'

Both the pious person and the drunkard died, and Moses was curious to know what had become of them. He went to Mount Sinai and asked God. God said, 'The pious person is in hell, and the drunken man is in heaven.' Moses thought, 'Does God break His word?' God said, 'The drunkard's joy on hearing that We had spoken of him has wiped out all his sins. The pious person's virtue was worthless. Why could he not be satisfied if We made the sun shine and sent the rain?'

SPIRITUAL LIBERTY - AQIBAT, LIFE AFTER DEATH – Reincarnation

GAYAN 044 - BOULA -003 - A learned man without will power is like a head without a body.

Man has been able to accomplish tremendous things by will-power. Success and failure are its phenomena. It is only the phenomenon of will which will bring one to success, and when will fails, however qualified and intelligent the person, he fails. Therefore it is not a human power, it is a divine power in man. Its work with the mind is still greater, for no man can hold a thought in his mind for a moment if there is not the strength of his will to hold it. If a person cannot concentrate, cannot keep his thought still for a moment, it means that will-power fails him, for it is will which holds a thought.

The Mysticism of Sound and Music - Cosmic Language – Will

GAYAN 045 - BOULA -004 - All that one holds is conserved; all that one lets go is dispersed.

    … It is not in everybody's power to keep a secret. For the secret is heavier than an elephant to lift, the weak-minded is weighed down by the heavy weight of a secret. The person who has not developed this power feels as it were a congestion of the heart, from which relief can only come when he has given out the secret; till then he is in pain. Also, it must be remembered that the power of the body is nothing in comparison with the power of the mind. And the power of the one who keeps a secret is greater than the power of the giant who lifts a mountain. All that one holds is preserved, all that one lets go is dispersed.

Esoteric Papers – Gatha 2 – Metaphysics – Keeping a Secret

GAYAN 046 - BOULA -005 - A pure conscience gives one the strength of lions, and by a guilty conscience even lions are turned into rabbits.

When it is told in the story of Daniel that he went into the lions' den and made them all lie tamed at his feet, that is again the spiritual power. It shows what power man has; at the same time, not knowing of it, not being conscious of it, not trying to develop it, he debars himself from that great privilege and bliss that God has given; and with his limited powers he works in the world for money. In the end no money remains with him, nor has he ever known power. Power depends greatly upon the consciousness and the attitude of mind. A guilty conscience can turn lions into rabbits. They lose their power once they feel guilty; and so it is with man. When a man is impressed by what others think, if that impression is of disappointment or distress or shame, his power is diminished; but when he is inspired by a thought, a feeling, an action he performs, then he is powerful. It is the power of truth that makes one stronger. Apart from those who know truth, even those who do not know truth, if they think rightly will have some power, the power of sincerity. Very few realize what power sincerity carries.

A false man, however physically strong he is or however great is his willpower, is kept down by his falsehood; it never allows him to rise. It eats into him because it is a rust. Those who have done great things in life, in whatever walk of life it be, have done them by the power of truth, the power of sincerity, of earnestness, of conviction; when that is lacking, power is lacking. What takes away man's power is doubt. As soon as a person thinks, Is it so or not? Will it be or not be? Is it right or not right? then he is powerless. And this is so contagious that every mind catches it. You can go to a doubting person when you have great enthusiasm and hope; and he may so impress you with darkness that you end in the same boat. Doubt takes away courage and hope and optimism.

Healing and the Mind World – Mental Purification – The Power Within Us

GAYAN 047 - BOULA -006 - The only thing that is made through life is one's own nature.

Question: How to understand the sentence from the Gayan: The only thing that is made through life is one's own nature?

Answer: One makes one's nature by one's likes and dislikes, by one's favor and disfavor. When a person has said that he does not like a certain edible thing, he has built a nature in himself. If afterwards he would eat such a thing it would disagree with his nature. It is not because it was not meant to agree with him, but because he has built up the idea that it would not agree. It is the same when one says, "I cannot endure it, I cannot stand it".

One makes one's nature either agreeable or disagreeable. Either one makes one's nature so hard as a rock which will not allow anything to enter; or one makes one's nature so pliable as water, through which all boats and ships can pass without hurting it. Water gives way for all to pass, and it is there just the same.

Man, by his thoughts, makes his nature. When he says, "I cannot agree with this", he will not agree with it; he has made a wall before himself. When he says, "I cannot bear that person", once he has said it, he has created something in himself which makes him sick when that person comes to him. That person becomes his master. The man wants to run away from him; wherever that person comes, he makes him ill. It is not because that person brings him illness: the man has brought that illness upon himself.

Sufi Teachings - Health and Order of Body and Mind – Questions about Vaccination and Inoculation

By the process of Sufism one realizes one's own nature, one's true nature, and thereby one realizes human nature. And by the study of human nature one realizes the nature of life in general. All failures, disappointments, and sorrows are caused by the lack of this realization; all success, happiness, and peace are acquired by the realization of one's own nature.

The Unity of Religious Ideals – The Message and the Messenger – Sufism

GAYAN 048 - BOULA -007 - Be either true or false, for you cannot be both.

If we come face to face with truth, it is one and the same. One may look at it from the Christian, from the Buddhist, or from the Hindu point of view, but in reality it is one point of view. One can either be small or large, either be false or true, either not know or know. As long as a person says, 'When I look at the horizon from the top of the mountain I become dizzy; this immensity of space frightens me,' he should not look at it. But if it does not make one dizzy it is a great joy to look at life from above; and from that position a Christian, Jew, Muslim, and Buddhist will all see the same immensity. It is not limited to those of any one faith or creed. Gradually, as they unfold themselves and give proof of their response to the immensity of the knowledge, they are asked to go forward, face to face with their Lord.

One should remember, however, that there are very few who enjoy reality compared with those who are afraid of it, and who, standing on the top of a high mountain, are afraid of looking at the immensity of space. It is the same sensation. What frightens them is the immensity of things; they seem lost and they hold on to their little self. The difficulty of this is that they not only die in the thought of mortality, but that even while they live it culminates in a kind of disease; and this disease is called self-obsession, obsession by the self. They can think of nothing but themselves, of their fears, doubts, and confusions, of all things pertaining to themselves; and in the end it turns them into their own enemy. First they look upon everybody else as their enemy because they are out of harmony with everybody, and in the end they are a burden to themselves. Such cases are not rare. Whatever religion they have, whatever faith they claim, they do not yet know what religion is. A man who professed to have no religion once said to me very profoundly, 'I am happy, I have no fear!' He was spiritual though he did not know it.

PHILOSOPHY, PSYCHOLOGY, MYSTICISM – MYSTICISM IN LIFE - The Path to God

GAYAN 049 - BOULA -008 - Truth is a divine inheritance found in the depth of every human heart.

A child need not partake the attributes and qualities of his parents, because the soul has no father and no mother; no one can claim to be the parent of a soul. Among very worldly people without a thought of anything but pleasure, a very spiritual child may be born, or from very saintly persons a very devilish child. For those who are walking in the path of truth, there is no heredity. By realizing their divine origin they free themselves from all earthly inheritance. As Christ said: "My Father in Heaven." They realize their origin from the spirit, and by their concentration and meditation, clear all earthly influences from their soul.

The Supplementary Papers – Psychology – Psychology IV – The Law of Heredity

But for those who are walking in the path of truth there is no [earthly] heredity. By realizing their divine origin they free themselves from all earthly inheritance. As Christ said 'My Father in heaven', so they realize their origin from the spirit, and by their concentration and meditation they can create all the merits they wish for and clear away from their soul all influences which they do not like to possess.

Spiritual Liberty – Aqibat - Life after Death – The Law of Heredity

GAYAN 050 - BOULA -009 - It is only out of consideration for others that the kingly soul obeys the law; otherwise, he is above the law.

Therefore those who rise above the ordinary conventionalities of life by their inner development come to another consciousness. For them worldly laws are the taws for the children. Those who begin to see this difference between the laws they set before themselves and the laws that are observed by mankind, at first sometimes condemn and then disregard the common laws. They criticize them, and ask, 'What is it all for?' But those who come to the fuller realization of the inner laws, show respect even for the laws of the children; knowing that they are the laws for the children and not for the grown-up yet they respect them, for they know that it cannot be otherwise. The laws which they know can only manifest to the one whose soul rises to that realization; but before that soul rises it must have some law by which to live in harmony. Therefore advanced souls regard such laws with respect, and observe them when they are in the community. They do not condemn them; they will not criticize them. They realize that harmony is the principal thing in life, and that we cannot be happy through life if we cannot harmonize with all those around us. Whatever be our grade of evolution, whatever be our outlook on life, and whatever be our freedom, we must have regard for the laws of the majority.

The Inner Life – Freedom of Action

GAYAN 051 - BOULA -010 - He who can live up to his ideal is the king of life.

The ideal life is at least to try to live up to one's ideal. But in order to have an ideal one must first awaken to an ideal. Not everyone possesses an ideal; many people do not know of it. It is no exaggeration to say that the wars and disasters we have gone through, the unrest that all feel, and the disagreement among the people which is sometimes seen and sometimes not seen, are all caused by one thing and that is the lack of an ideal. We are progressing commercially, industrially. But in all walks of life progress will be stopped one day or another if the ideal is destroyed. If there is anything which can be said to be the means of saving the world, it is the awakening of idealism. It is the first task that is worth considering.

The Alchemy of Happiness – The Deeper Side of Life

The God of the Sufi is the God of every creed, and the God of all. Names make no difference to him. Allah, God, Gott, Dieu, Brahma, or Bhagwan, all these names and more are the names of his God; and yet to him God is beyond the limitation of name. He sees his God in the sun, in the fire, in the idol which diverse sects worship; and he recognizes Him in all the forms of the universe, yet knowing Him to be beyond all form: God in all, and all in God, He being the Seen and the Unseen, the Only Being. God to the Sufi is not only a religious belief, but also the highest ideal the human mind can conceive.

The Sufi, forgetting the self and aiming at the attainment of the divine ideal, walks constantly all through life in the path of love and light. In God the Sufi sees the perfection of all that is in the reach of man's perception and yet he knows Him to be above human reach. He looks to Him as the lover to his beloved. and takes all things in life as coming from Him, with perfect resignation. The sacred name of God is to him as medicine to the patient. The divine thought is the compass by which he steers the ship to the shores of immortality. The God-ideal is to a Sufi as a lift by which he raises himself to the eternal goal, the attainment of which is the only purpose of his life.

The Way of Illumination – Sufi Thoughts

GAYAN 052 - BOULA -011 - The God who is intelligible to man is made by man himself, but what is beyond his intelligence is the reality.

Islam has in every period held the idea of a formless God; but especially in the period when the Prophet Muhammed came-whose Message, since his coming, was named by the same name, Islam --great stress was put upon the idea of a formless God. It is difficult for man to make God intelligible if he does not give Him any form; and yet a step higher in the realization of God is to make Him intelligible beyond the limit of form. God, therefore, in Islam, was made intelligible by His attributes. As Creator, as Father, as Mother, as Sustainer, as Judge, as Forgiver, as the Source and the Goal of this whole manifestation, One Who is always with His creature, within him, without him, Who notices all his feelings, thoughts, and actions, Who draws the line of man's fate, before Whom man must appear to give his account, is the God of Islam.

Islam believed in One Only God with many attributes, and yet beyond any attributes; invisible, and beyond the comprehension of man; Almighty; Incomparable; no one save He having any power beside Him; the Knower of all things, and pure from all impurities; free from all things, and yet not far from all things; in Him all abiding, and He living in all. The whole essential teaching of Islam (which is called Kakamat) tends to explain clearly the oneness of God; and yet the attributes are suggested, not in order to explain God, but with a view to make God intelligible to the human mind.

These attributes form the external part of God, which is intelligible to man, which is named Sifat; but that which is hidden under attributes, and that which cannot be intelligible to the human mind, that part of the Divine Being is the real Being, and that Being is called Zat. The whole tendency of Islam has been to disentangle man's heart from such thoughts of God as limit and divide Him, and to clear man's heart from duality, which is the nature of this illusory world, and to bring him to that atonement with God which has been the real aim and intention of every religion.

The Unity of Religious Ideals – Prophets and Religions - Muhammed – The God of Islam

GAYAN 053 - BOULA -012 - The closer one approaches reality, the nearer one comes to unity.

Especially, early morning meditations are valuable for consulting with God and receiving help. Gradually, this spiritual communion will become such a power, such a reality, that it will continue day and night. The heart will awaken and the intuition tells one how to act, when to move, to travel, to marry, to make any important change in life, or even to meditate or perform extra spiritual deeds. In this condition, gradually all of life takes on a grand unity.

GITHA II – MEDITATION - Communing with God

GAYAN 054 - BOULA -013 - A lifetime is not sufficient to learn how to live in this world.

To learn the lesson of how to live is more important than any psychic or occult learning. Every day we think we have learnt the lesson, but if we had the world would have become a heaven for us by now. We may seek the higher knowledge or the higher things, but the very smallest thing, the control of all the creatures of the mind, which seems as nothing compared with the higher knowledge, once learnt and acted upon is greater than all. This is a great step; yet how difficult to gain this, how reasonless it seems!

IN AN EASTERN ROSE GARDEN - The Will, Human and Divine

GAYAN 055 - BOULA -014 - Man looks for wonders; if he only saw how very wonderful is the heart of man!

A Hindustani poet describes this wonderfully, 'The land and sea are not too large for the heart of man to accommodate.' In other words, the heart of man is larger than the universe. If there were a thousand universes the heart of man could accommodate them. But man, unaware of his inner being, impressed by outer limitation, remains under the impression of his weakness, limitation, smallness. And that keeps him from using this great power which he can find within himself, this great light with which he can see life more clearly. It is only because he is unaware of himself.

HEALING AND THE MIND WORLD – MENTAL PURIFICATION - Mystic Relaxation (2)

GAYAN 056 - BOULA -015 - Many evils are born of riches, but still more are bred in poverty.

Another thing is that man is mostly selfish, and what interests him is that which concerns his own life. Not knowing the troubles of the lives of others he feels the burden of his own life even more than the burden of the whole world. If only man in his poverty could think that there are others who are poorer than he, in his illness that there are others whose sufferings are perhaps greater than his, in his troubles that there are others whose difficulties are perhaps greater than his! Self-pity is the worst poverty. It overwhelms man and he sees nothing but his own troubles and pains, and it seems to him that he is the most unhappy person in the world, more so than anyone else.

A great thinker of Persia, Saadi, writes in an account of his life, "Once I had no shoes, I had to walk barefoot in the hot sand, and I thought how very miserable I was. Then I met a man who was lame, for whom walking was very difficult. I bowed down at once to heaven and offered thanks that I was much better off than he who had not even feet to walk upon." This shows that it is not a man's situation in life, but his attitude towards life that makes him happy or unhappy. This attitude can even make such a difference between men that one living in a palace could be unhappy and another living in a humble cottage could be very happy. The difference is only in the horizon that one sees: one person looks only at the condition of his life, another looks at the lives of many people; it is a difference of horizon.

Beside this, the impulse that comes from within has its influence on one's affairs: there is an influence always working from within. If it is a discontent and dissatisfaction in life, one finds its effect in one's affairs. For instance, a person impressed by illness can never be cured by a physician or medicines. A person impressed by poverty will never get on in life. A person who thinks, "Everybody is against. me, everybody troubles me, everybody has a poor opinion of me", wherever he goes will always find that it is so. There are many people in the world - in business, in professions who before going to their work bear in their mind as a first thought, "Perhaps I shall not be successful".

Sufi Teachings – The Privilege of Being Human

GAYAN 057 - BOULA -016 - Do not weep with the sad, but console them; if not, by your tears you will but water the plant of their sorrow.

That person is living whose heart is living, and that heart is living which has wakened to sympathy. The heart void of sympathy is worse than rock, for the rock is useful, but the heart void of sympathy produces antipathy. Man is most active physically and mentally, and when his heart is not tuned to sympathy his mental and physical activity takes quite a contrary direction, which leads to inharmony and destruction. No doubt love, affection, or sympathy without wisdom may seem profitless, as for instance, if a person was crying with pain and his sympathetic friend, on hearing his cry, began to weep with him, doubling his pain.

Sympathy can only be useful when man does not make the condition of the person with whom he sympathizes worse, but makes things better. The feeling of sympathy must be within, it need not manifest purely as sympathy but as an action to better the condition of the one with whom one has sympathy. There are many attributes found in the human heart which are called divine, but among them there is no greater and better attribute than sympathy, by which man shows in human form God manifested.

Gatha III - METAPHYSICS- Sympathy

GAYAN 058 - BOULA -017 - The spirit of controversy is fed by argument.

Conciliation is not only the moral of the Sufi: it is the sign of the Sufi. This virtue is not learned and practiced easily, for it needs not only goodwill but wisdom. The talent of the diplomat consists in bringing about such results as are desirable with mutual agreement. Disagreement is easy; among the lower creation one sees it so often; it is agreement that is difficult, for it needs a wider outlook which is the true sign of spirituality. Narrowness of outlook makes man's vision small; the person with a narrow outlook cannot easily agree with another. There is always a meeting ground for two people, however much they differ in thought; but the meeting-ground may be far off, and when that is so a man is not always willing to take the trouble to go so far in order to come to an agreement. Very often this is due to his lack of patience. What generally happens is that each wants the other to meet him at the place where he is standing; there is no desire on either part to move from the spot.

This does not mean that in order to become a real Sufi one should give up one's own ideas in order to agree with someone else; and there is no advantage in always being lenient towards every thought that comes from another, nor in erasing one's own ideas from one's heart; that is not conciliation. The one who is able to listen to another is the one who will make another listen to him. The one who finds it easy to agree with another will have the power of making another agree easily with him. Therefore in doing so one really gains in spite of the apparent loss which might sometimes occur. When a man is able to see both from his own point of view and from that of another, he has complete vision and a clear insight;he so to speak sees with both eyes.

No doubt friction produces light, but light is the agreement of the atoms. Two people having their own ideas and arguing about them can be a stimulus to thought, and then it does not matter so much; but when a person argues for the sake of argument, the argument becomes his game; he has no satisfaction in conciliation. Words provide the means of disagreement and reasons become the fuel for this fire; but wisdom is found where the intelligence is pliable, where it understands all things, even the wrong of the right and the right of the wrong. The soul who arrives at perfect knowledge has risen above right and wrong. He knows them and yet knows not; he can say much and yet what can he say? Then it becomes easy for him to conciliate each and all."

THE ALCHEMY OF HAPPINESS -The Development of Personality

GAYAN 059 - BOULA -018 - Reform has a scope in every period.

The method of world reform which various institutions have adopted today is not the method of the Sufi Movement. Sufis believe that if evil is contagious, goodness must be even more so. The depth of every soul is good; every soul is searching for good, and by the effort of individuals who wish to do good in the world much can be done, even more than a materialistic institution can achieve. No doubt for the general good there are political and commercial problems to be solved; but that must not debar individuals from progress, for it is the individual progress through the spiritual path which alone can bring about the desired condition in the world.

THE UNITY OF RELIGIOUS IDEALS - THE MESSAGE AND THE MESSENGER – Sufism

The Sufi Message which is now being given in the Western world is the child of that mother who has been known for many years as Sufism. The Sufi Message which is being given to the world just now, therefore, connects the two lines of the prophetic mission, the Hindu line and that of Beni Israel, in order that they may become the medium to unite in God and Truth both parts of the world, East and West. It is the same Truth, the same religion, the same ideal, which the wise of all ages have held. If there is anything different, it is only the difference of the form. The Sufi Message given now has adopted the form suitable for the age. It is a Message without claim; and the group of workers in this Message, and those who follow it, are named the Sufi Movement, whose work it is to tread the spiritual path quietly, unassumingly, and to serve God and humanity, in which is the fulfillment of the Message.

THE UNITY OF RELIGIOUS IDEALS - THE SPIRITUAL HIERARCHY - The Prophetic Claim

GAYAN 060 - BOULA -019 - When man touches the ultimate truth he realizes that there is nothing which is not in himself.

The knowledge of truth is the ultimate object of all religions; it is the seeking of all philosophies; it is the spirit of all doctrines. But it is the nature of man that he becomes disappointed with these forms of truth; he wants to find truth outside him when it is really hidden within him in his own heart.....

...How can one attain? In order to attain truth one must make one's own life truthful. This is life in its moral aspect. The more truthful one is in one's every day life the more one practices this moral despite its great difficulty, the more one approaches the only religion which there is. But it is the most difficult to practice this moral in this world of falsehood, where every move one makes is touched by some unreality which impresses one. Every moment of a person's life is touched by falsehood which is likely to impress him...

The love of truth gives one an appreciation of truth, and all the little shadows of truth become reflected in such a person's heart more and more until at length he expresses trueness in his nature. Seeking after truth enables one to learn to appreciate all that comes from truthful hearts. Passing from the state of natural man, through the state of being a lover of truth and a seeker after truth, one begins to express truth....

Did man realize that although his external is human and limited his inner being is divine and unlimited, and if man knew how to dive deep within himself, he would find God. For God is not far away, as people of various religions believe; He is closer to us than anyone else. Such a person will realize that God is the one end of a line, and he himself is the other end. One live has two points; one life has two points. The one is man, and the other is God.

The Dutch Papers – PHILOSOPHY V - The Knowledge of Truth

GAYAN 061 - BOULA -020 - Reason is the illusion of reality.

Reason is a faculty that raises out of itself an answer to every question one asks. There is a store of knowledge of names, and forms, of principles, of feelings; from that store of knowledge an answer rises. It is that which is called reason.

This store of knowledge is different in every individual, and it is therefore that often two people may disagree and at the same time both may have reason for what they say. This shows that reason is not outside of oneself; it is within oneself, and at each stage towards evolution reason changes. The answer that a person may get from within to a certain question in one month may change in the next month. Every object and condition suggests a reason, but the more one penetrates through the object or condition the more one realizes that there is a reason under reason, and one condition may suggest numerous reasons, according to the depths one may touch. When there is a discourse about justice or injustice, right or wrong, one applies one's own reason, and when one cannot understand the reason of another, one's knowledge is incomplete.

The effect that different names and forms produce is an illusion, and so is reason, which is the creation of mind, when it is compared with the ultimate reality. Reality is above reason. When reason follows reality it is helpful, but when reality is covered under reason it is an illusion. The one who penetrates through the numerous covers of reason comes to the depth of knowledge, but the one who clings to the first reason he has touched remains there; for him there is no progress.

Esoteric Papers - Gatha 1- Metaphysics - Number 7 - Reason

GAYAN 062 - BOULA -021 - Death is preferable to asking a favor of a small person.

"The second kind of prayer is asking God to do something. This is for the ordinary person. For him it is better that he should ask of God and bring his need before God, than that he should ask of man. What a humiliation it is to ask, to show his need, before man. The ordinary person cannot depend entirely upon God. He does not altogether believe that God is. He looks to the external sources to supply him. Therefore it is best for him, as a moral, that he should ask of God only, and use his own exertions. By this he learns trust in God, and he learns resignation. If his desire is not granted, if he is left in misery, he learns to think that this is Gods Will."

THE SUPPLEMENTARY PAPERS - RELIGION - RELIGION III – Prayer

GAYAN 063 - BOULA -022 - Lull the devil to sleep rather than awaken him.

No soul is attracted to what we call Satan or the devil. Our soul does not like us to do what is wrong for us. Our soul does not like us to be unkind. Every soul has in it the highest attributes, and has a tendency towards the light and a tendency towards awakening. If it has not there are reasons for it. Either the soul has gathered around it vibrations that are undesirable; or it has not come through the proper channel of manifestation and therefore it is weak; or it clings to its undesirable habits and ideas and will not let them go. The condition of the soul can turn any place into heaven. Not only the earth but even hell could be turned into heaven, if only the soul attained the perfection which is its only goal.

SPIRITUAL LIBERTY - AQIBAT, LIFE AFTER DEATH - The Soul's Experience

GAYAN 064 - BOULA -023 - Movement is life; stillness is death.

Movement is life and stillness is death; for in movement there is the significance of life and in stillness we see the sign of death. One might ask if looking at it from a metaphysical point of view there is a stillness. No, but there is what we call no movement, or at least no movement which is perceptible to us in some form, whether it is visible or audible or in the form of sensation or vibration. The movement which is not perceptible to us we name stillness; the word life we use only in connection with the perceptible existence, the movement of which we perceive. Therefore, with regard to our physical health, movement is the principal thing, regulation of movement, of its rhythm in pulsation and the circulation of the blood. The whole cause of death and decay is to be traced to the lack of movement; all different aspects of diseases are to be traced to congestion. Every decay is caused by congestion, and congestion is caused by lack of movement.

HEALING AND THE MIND WORLD– Health

GAYAN 065 - BOULA -024 - There is no action in this world that can be stamped as sin or virtue; it is its relation to the particular soul that makes it so.

Religion, in the conception of a Sufi, is the path that leads man towards the attainment of his ideal, worldly as well as heavenly. Sin and virtue, right and wrong, good and bad are not the same in the case of every individual; they are according to his grade of evolution and state of life. Therefore the Sufi concerns himself little with the name of the religion or the place of worship. All places are sacred enough for his worship, and all religions convey to him the religion of his soul. 'I saw Thee in the sacred Ka'ba and in the temple of the idol also Thee I saw.'

The Way of Illumination – Sufi Thoughts

GAYAN 066 - BOULA -025 - Reality itself is its own evidence.

Why is God called the Creator? Because the creation itself is the evidence of some wisdom working. No mechanical creation could result in such perfection as is Nature. All the machines of the scientists are built on the model of Nature's mechanism, and every inspiration that the artist has he receives from Nature. Nature is so perfect in itself that in reality it needs no scientific or artistic improvement upon it, except that, to satisfy the limited human fancies, man develops science and art. And yet it is still the creation of God expressed in art and science through man; as in man God is not absent, but more able in some ways to finish His creation, which necessitates His finishing it as man. No better evidence is needed for a sincere inquirer into the Creator-God. If he only concentrates his mind upon Nature, he certainly must sooner or later have an insight into the perfect wisdom which is hidden behind it. The soul that comes into the world is only a divine ray. The impressions it gets on its way while coming to the earth also are from God. No movement is possible without the command of God; therefore, in all creation, in its every aspect, in the end of search and examination God alone proves to be the only Creator.

THE UNITY OF RELIGIOUS IDEALS – THE GOD IDEAL – Creator, Sustainer, Judge, Forgiver

GAYAN 067 - BOULA -026 - It is of no use to try and prove to be what in reality you are not.

If man finds reality in unreality, if that is consoling for him, he may console himself for some few days. But unreality is unreality. Unreality will not prove satisfactory in the end, because satisfaction lies in the knowledge of truth. For the time being, if unreality satisfies one, to think that this is real, one may continue to think in that way. But it must .be said that in the end this will not prove to be real. In order to avoid future disappointment one must find it out soon in one's life if one is to be capable of grasping and then assimilating the ultimate truth.

HEALING AND THE MIND WORLD – The Mind World – Chapter IX

GAYAN 068 - BOULA -027 - Pleasure blocks, but pain clears the way of inspiration.

Man, absorbed from morning till evening in his occupations which engage his every attention to the things of the earth and of self interest, remains intoxicated. Seldom there are moments in his life, brought about by pain or suffering, when he experiences a state of mind which can be called soberness. Hindus call this state of mind sat, which is a state of tranquility. Man then begins to become conscious of some part of his being which he finds to have almost been covered from his eyes. When we look at life from this point of view we find that an individual who claims to be a living being is not necessarily living a full life. It is only a realization of inner life which at every moment unveils the soul, and brings before man another aspect of life in which he finds fullness, a greater satisfaction, and a rest which gives true peace.

Sufi Teachings – The Privilege of Being Human – Truth

GAYAN 069 - BOULA -028 - A biting tongue goes deeper than the point of a bayonet, and cutting words pierce keener than a sword.

By regarding some few things in life as faults, one often covers up little faults, which sometimes are worse than the faults which are pointed out by the world. For instance, when a younger person is insulting to an elderly person, people do not call it a very great fault. Sometimes such a little fault can rise and make a worse effect upon his soul than the faults which are recognized faults in the world. A person by a sharp tongue, by an inquisitive nature, by satiric remarks, by thoughtless words, can commit a fault which can be worse than so-called great sins.

THE SUPPLEMENTARY PAPERS - RELIGION I - Purity of Life

GAYAN 070 - BOULA -029 - The human heart must first be melted, like metal, before it can be molded into a desirable character.

A mureed had been a long time in the service of a spiritual guide, but he could make no progress and was not inspired. He went to the teacher and said, 'I have seen very many mureeds being inspired, but it is my misfortune that I cannot advance at all, and now I must give up hope and leave you.' The teacher advised him to spend the last days of his stay in a house near the Khankah, and every day he sent him very good food and told him to cease the spiritual practices and to lead a comfortable and restful life. On the last day he sent the mureed a basket of fruit by a fair damsel. She set the tray down and immediately went away, though he wished to detain her. Her beauty and charm were so great, and he was now so much disposed to admire and was so much won by them, that he could think of nothing else. Every hour and every minute he longed only to see her again. His longing increased every moment. He forgot to eat, he was full of tears and sighs, finding his heart now warmed and melted by the fire of love. After some time, when the teacher visited the disciple, with one glance he inspired him. 'Even steel can be molded if it be heated in the fire', and so it is with the heart which is melted by the fire of love.

SPIRITUAL LIBERTY – Divine Love

GAYAN 071 - BOULA -030 - The mystic does not wait until the hereafter, but does all he can to progress now.

There is a symbolical picture known in the philosophical world of China that represents a sage with one shoe in his hand and one on his foot. It signifies the hereafter, that the change that death brings is to a wise man only the taking off of one shoe. The body of the philosopher in the picture represents his soul, or his person; the one shoe still on his foot represents his mind, which exists after death; and the withdrawal of the soul from the body is like taking one foot out of the shoe. For the mystic, therefore, the physical body is something he can easily dispense with, and to arrive at this realization is the object of wisdom. When, by philosophical understanding of life, he begins to realize his soul, then he begins to stand, so to speak, on his own feet; he is then himself and the body is to him only a cover.

The teaching of the Prophet is to die before death, which means to realize in one's lifetime what death means. This realization takes away all the fear there is. By the symbol of the shoe is shown also the nothingness of the material existence, or the smallness of the physical being, in comparison with the greatness of the soul, or the spirit. Hafiz says in Persian verse, "Those who realize Thee are kings of life," which means that the true kingdom of life is in the realization of the soul. The idea that one must wait until one's turn will come after many incarnations keeps one far away from the desired goal.

The man who is impatient to arrive at spiritual realization is to be envied. As Omar Khayyam says, "Tomorrow? Why, tomorrow I may be myself with yesterday's seven thousand years." He means by this, "Don't bother about the past, don't trouble about the future, but accomplish all you can just now." Life has taken time enough to develop gradually from mineral to vegetable, from vegetable to animal, and from animal to man, and after becoming man delay is not necessary. It is true that the whole lifetime is not sufficient for one to become what one wishes to be. Still nothing is impossible, since the soul of man is from the spirit of God; and if God can do all things why cannot man do something?

Githa II – SYMBOLOGY – "Die Before Death"

GAYAN 072 - BOULA -031 - Power demands subjection; but if you cannot resist power by conquest, win it by surrender.

One who is really resigned does not show it. Resignation is not an easy thing. How many people in this world try to learn wonderful spiritual things, but this simple thing, resignation, is miraculous; for this virtue is not only beautiful, it is a miracle. There are little things in which we do not see resignation, and where yet it is. Those around us may ask us to do something that does not please us; those around us perhaps say something that we do not wish to take silently, we wish to talk back; then, in everyday life, there are the little pin-pricks from those around us. If we are not resigned, we shall feel excited every moment. To be resigned, therefore, is not weakness, it is a great strength.

When one goes further one finds that one can be resigned even to cold and heat, to places congenial and uncongenial; one finds that all has a meaning, a benefit. Even if one had not formed a habit of being resigned, one could just as well resign oneself, for not having resigned oneself to an experience is the loss of an occasion.

There are two forces working: the individual power and the collective power. In Sufi terms the former is called qadr, the latter qadha. Often the individual power will not surrender, but if it does not do so it is crushed. For instance someone is called to arms in his country, but says he will not join the army. In spite of all the beauty of his ideal he is helpless before the might of the whole nation. Here he must resign to the condition in which there is a conflict between a lesser and a greater power; here resignation is the only solution.

SUFI TEACHINGS - THE PRIVILEGE OF BEING HUMAN - Struggle and Resignation

GAYAN 073 - BOULA -032 - The fountain stream of love rises in the love for an individual, but spreads and falls in universal love.

"Q: What is the process of drowning impressions in the ocean of the consciousness of eternal now?

A: The one who does not know the love of an individual does not know universal love. But if one stands there, one stands there without going forward. The love of an individual in love's path is a doll's play, which is learned for the time to come. So the love of an individual is the first step. But when one progresses then one advances towards the love of a cause, a community, a nation; or even the whole universe. Man, as a human being, is capable of loving one; but his soul, as the light of God, is capable of loving not only the world, but even if there were a thousand worlds. For the heart of man is larger than the whole universe.

Gatha 2 – Everyday Life – Purity of Mind (2)

GAYAN 074 - BOULA -033 - A word can be more precious than all the treasures of the earth.

They say to have learned even one letter or one word from someone, demands respect and consideration for him. So a person who walks on the spiritual path recognizes the goal towards which he is traveling, and realizes that the wealth he will obtain is so great that there is no return he can make which is in proportion to what he has received from his teacher. Therefore the chela (mureed, pupil) in the occult and mystical is more grateful to his master than any person in any other walk in life is to any other. Why is this? It is because he recognizes that there is nothing more precious and worthwhile in life than spiritual wealth and the light of wisdom. Whoever be the one who helped him to receive this light and wisdom, he is surely the archgate of heaven, the final goal into which he desires to enter. It is to this archgate that he makes his first bow. You find this expression in Hafiz and Sa'adi, and in many Sufi poets of Persia, calling their teacher the "arib," the arch, the arch of that gate which is the shrine of God.

THE SUPPLEMENTARY PAPERS - CLASS FOR MUREEDS III - Discipleship

GAYAN 075 - BOULA -034 - He who makes room in his heart for others, will himself find accommodation everywhere.

"The Sufi therefore tries to expand as he progresses; for it is the largeness of the soul which will accommodate all experiences and in the end will become God-conscious and all embracing. The man who shuts himself up from all men, however high spiritually he may be, will not be free in Malakut*, in the higher sphere. He will have a wall around him, keeping away the jinns and even the angels of the angelic heavens; and so his journey will be exclusive. It is therefore that Sufism does not only teach concentration and meditation, which help one to make one-sided progress, but the love of God which is expansion; the opening of the heart of all beings, which is the way of Christ and the sign of the cross."

THE SOUL, WHENCE AND WHITHER? – Manifestation

*NOTE

Malakut: sphere of thought and imagination, World of Symbols, the realm of visions, realm of knowledge.

GAYAN 076 - BOULA -035 - Each human personality is like a piece of music, having an individual tone and a rhythm of its own.

The music of life shows its melody and harmony in our daily experiences. Every spoken word is either a true or a false note, according to the scale of our ideal. The tone of one personality is hard like a horn, while the tone of another is soft like the high notes of a flute.

The gradual progress of all creation from a lower to a higher evolution, its change from one aspect to another, is shown as in music where a melody is transposed from one key into another.

The friendship and enmity among men, their likes and dislikes, are as chords and discords. The harmony of human nature, and the human tendency to attraction and repulsion, are like the effect of the consonant and dissonant intervals in music.

In tenderness of heart the tone turns into a half-tone, and with the breaking of the heart the tone breaks into microtones. The more tender the heart becomes, the fuller the tone becomes; the harder the heart grows, the more dead it sounds.

Each note, each scale, and each strain expires at the appointed time, and at the end of the soul's experience here the finale comes. But the impression remains, as a concert in a dream, before the radiant vision of the consciousness.

THE MYSTICISM OF SOUND – Music

GAYAN 077 - BOULA -036 - One should take oneself to task, instead of putting one's fault on another.

One may try to see from the point of view of another as well as from one's own, and so give freedom of thought to everybody because one demands it oneself; one may try to appreciate what is good in another, and overlook what one considers bad; if somebody behaves selfishly towards one, one may take it naturally, because it is human nature to be selfish, and so one is not disappointed; but if one appears oneself to be selfish, one should take oneself to task and try to improve. There is not anything one should not be ready to tolerate, and there is nobody whom one should not forgive. Never doubt those whom you trust; never hate those whom you love; never cast down those whom you once raise in your estimation. Wish to make friends with everyone you meet; make an effort to gain the friendship of those you find difficult; become indifferent to them only if you cannot succeed in your effort. Never wish to break the friendship once made.

THE WAY OF ILLUMINATION - Some Aspects of Sufism - Life In This World

GAYAN 078 - BOULA -037 - A tender-hearted sinner is better than a saint hardened by piety.

The music of life shows its melody and harmony in our daily experiences. Every spoken word is either a true or a false note, according to the scale of our ideal. The tone of one personality is hard like a horn, while the tone of another is soft like the high notes of a flute.

The gradual progress of all creation from a lower to a higher evolution, its change from one aspect to another, is shown as in music where a melody is transposed from one key into another.

The friendship and enmity among men, their likes and dislikes, are as chords and discords. The harmony of human nature, and the human tendency to attraction and repulsion, are like the effect of the consonant and dissonant intervals in music.

In tenderness of heart the tone turns into a half-tone, and with the breaking of the heart the tone breaks into microtones. The more tender the heart becomes, the fuller the tone becomes; the harder the heart grows, the more dead it sounds.

Each note, each scale, and each strain expires at the appointed time, and at the end of the soul's experience here the finale comes. But the impression remains, as a concert in a dream, before the radiant vision of the consciousness.

THE MYSTICISM OF SOUND – Music

GAYAN 079 - BOULA -038 - The way to overcome error is, first, to admit one's fault; and next, to refrain from repeating it.

Man does not like to admit his wrong attitude to himself; he is afraid of his own faults. But the man who looks his own error in the eye, the man who criticizes himself, has no time to criticize others. It is that man who will prove to be wise. But human nature is generally such that one does something quite different. Everyone seems to be most interested in criticizing another. If one would criticize oneself, there are endless faults, however saintly or wise one may be; there are no end of faults in a human being; and the consciousness of correcting one's faults, of making oneself better, of taking hold of the right attitude, is the only secret of success, and by it one attains to that goal which is the object of every soul.

THE ALCHEMY OF HAPPINESS – The Secret of Life

GAYAN 080 - BOULA -039 - By accusing anyone of his fault, you only make him firmer in it.

Whatever be one's position in connection with another in life, there is one principal thing to be remembered: That by annoyance, by grudging, by complaining, by criticizing, most often one turns things from bad to worse.

Do not think that another person wishes to be corrected by you, be he wise or foolish, older or younger; as soon as one takes the step to correct a person, one, so to speak, does violence to his pride, to his ego, and by doing so one upsets his right thinking. There are ways of doing things. The wiser one is, the more beautifully he accomplishes his purpose in whatever position he may be. If one has to be humble in doing it beautifully, if one has to bend in doing it nicely, instead of making another person bend, it really matters very little. Criticizing a person, accusing a person of his fault is no less than slapping his face, perhaps worse.

In all cases it is consideration which is needed, a respectful attitude towards human nature, whatever be his position in life in connection with you; it is that which gives you a complete mastery. The great kings of the world very often have been pulled down from their thrones by those who for years bowed and bent and trembled at their command, but the Christlike souls who have washed the feet of the disciples are still held in esteem, and will be honored and loved by humanity forever. Their example is the example to follow in life's path, which is full of thorns; and those who have followed their principle, even to the smallest degree, they have arrived safely at their destination.

THE SUPPLEMENTARY PAPERS – MISCELLANEOUS II - One's Attitude Towards Those with Whom One Has to Work

GAYAN 081 - BOULA -040 - The human heart is the shell in which the pearl of sincerity is found.

Does the heart reflect the mind or the mind the heart? In the first place it should be known that the mind is the surface of the heart, and the heart is the depth of the mind. Therefore mind and heart are one and the same thing. If you call it a mirror, then the mind is the surface of the mirror and the heart its depth; in the same mirror all is reflected. 'Mirror' is a very good word, because it applies to both the mind and the heart. If the reflection comes from the surface of the heart, it touches the surface; if it comes from the depth of the heart, it reaches the depth. Just like the voice of the insincere person: it comes from the surface and it reaches the ears. The voice of the sincere person comes from the depth and goes to the depth. What comes from the depth enters the depth, and what comes from the surface remains on the surface.

HEALING AND THE MIND WORLD - THE MIND-WORLD - Chapter II

GAYAN 082 - BOULA -041 - Rocks will open and make a way for the lover.

The sorrow of the lover is continual, in the presence and in the absence of the beloved: in the presence for fear of the absence, and in absence in longing for the presence. According to the mystical view the pain of love is the dynamite that breaks up the heart, even if it be as hard as a rock. When this hardness that covers the light within is broken through, the streams of all bliss come forth as springs from the mountains.

The Moral of Love - LOVE, HUMAN AND DIVINE - SPIRITUAL LIBERTY

GAYAN 083 - BOULA -042 - Man makes his reasons to suit himself.

When we analyze the word reason it opens before us a vast field of thought. In the first place every doer of good and every evil-doer has a reason to support his doing. When two persons quarrel, each says he is in the right, because each has a reason. To a third person perhaps the reason of the one may appear to be more reasonable than that of the other, or perhaps he will say that both have no reason and that he has reason on his side. All disputes, arguments and discussions seem to be based upon reason, and yet reason, before one has analyzed it, is nothing but an illusion and keeps one continually in perplexity. The cause of all inharmony, all disagreement is the perplexity which is caused by not understanding one another's reason....

...Besides, reason is the servant of the mind. The mind feels like praising a person - reason at once brings a thousand things in praise of him, in his favor. The mind has a desire to hate a person - at once reason brings perhaps twenty arguments in favor of hating him. So we see that a loving friend can find a thousand things that are good and beautiful in his friend, and an adversary will find a thousand faults in the best person in the world - and he has reasons....

...Reasoning is a ladder. By this ladder one can rise, and by this ladder one may fall. For if one does not go upward by reasoning, then it will help one to go downward too, because, if for every step one takes upward there is a reason, there is also a reason for every step downward.

The Mysticism of Sound and Music – Cosmic Language - Reason

GAYAN 084 - BOULA -043 - Singleness of mind ensures success.

"Any study of psychology shows that success and happiness in life are found in singleness of mind. To focus itself the mind takes a single direction; and singleness of vision cannot fail to develop singleness of purpose. Many are the paths that lead to success; the difficulty lies in keeping strictly to the chosen path, or in other words in retaining singleness of mind. There is one means only by which man can attain to a realization of the religious ideal of the Godhead, and that is through sincerity and single-mindedness in the conduct of everyday life."

THE ART OF PERSONALITY - LIFE'S CREATIVE FORCES: RASA SHASTRA - Monogamy

GAYAN 085 - BOULA -044 - Love of form, progressing, culminates in love of the formless.

"When someone says, 'I love the formless', he professes something which is inaccurate. He cannot love the formless without first having given his love a form. If he has not recognized the formless in form he has not arrived at the love of the formless, and when the beginning is not right the end cannot be right. When one has recognized the formless in form and has loved the formless in a form so that one has experienced what self-abnegation means, when one has lost oneself, then the next step is the love of the formless. And what is this love? How does it manifest? It manifests in the love of all, making a man a fountain of love, pouring out over humanity the love that gushes from his heart, and not only to mankind; it may even reach all living beings.

PHILOSOPHY, PSYCHOLOGY, MYSTICISM – MYSTICISM IN LIFE – Love

GAYAN 086 - BOULA -045 - When man rises above the sense of duty, then duty becomes his pleasure.

In the language of the Hindus duty is called Dharma, which means religion. The more one studies the nature and character of what we call duty, the more one begins to see that it is in the spirit of duty that the soul of religion is to be found. If duty was not so sacred as to play such an important part in one's life, a form of religion would be nothing to a thoughtful soul. It was, therefore, wise on the part of the ancient people who called religion duty, or duty religion. For religion is not in performing a ceremony or a ritual; the true religion is the feeling or the sense of duty. Duty is not necessarily the purpose of life, but it is as the lighthouse in the port, which shows one, 'Here is the landing place, here you arrive, here is your destination.' It may not be the final destination, but still in duty one finds a road which leads one to the purpose of life.

It seems that, though the knowledge of duty is acquired after a child has come into the world, yet the child has also brought with him into the world the sense of duty. And according to the sense of duty which the child shows, he gives promise of a good future. A person may be most learned, capable, qualified, powerful, influential, and yet if he has no sense of duty, you cannot rely upon him. As soon as you find out that there is a living sense of duty in a person, you at once feel confidence; you feel you can depend upon that person. And this feeling that you get is greater than any other impression a person could make upon you; in this is all virtue and strength and power and blessing. You value a friend whom you can trust; you value a relation in whom you can have confidence. Therefore, all the qualifications that man possesses seem to be on the surface, but beneath them there is one spirit which keeps them alive and makes them really valuable, and that spirit is the sense of duty. Those who have won the confidence of the whole nation, and there have been few in the history of the world who have won the trust of a multitude, those have proved to be really great; and it was accomplished by developing the sense of duty.

THE WAY OF ILLUMINATION– THE PURPOSE OF LIFE – Chapter VII

GAYAN 087 - BOULA -046 - The external life is but the shadow of the inner reality.

"The life one recognizes is only the mortal aspect of life. Very few have ever seen or been conscious of the immortal aspect at all. Once one has realized life, that which one has hitherto called life is found to be only a glimpse or shadow of the real life that is beyond comprehension. To understand it one will have to raise one's light high from under the cover that is hiding it like a bushel. This cover is man's mind and body; it is a cover that keeps the light active on the world of things and beings. 'Do not keep your light under a bushel' means that we are not to keep the consciousness absorbed in the study of the external world, and in its pleasures and enjoyments. Man is always apt to say that the religious thinker is a dreamer, lost in vague ideals, having no proof of what he believes, and far from what he himself would call the reality. He never thinks that what he calls real has in its turn become unreal to the one to whom the silent life has become reality. Can you call this life real which is subject to such changes every moment? Every activity and the object of everyone's life--riches, power, love, friendship, childhood, youth, health, pleasure, displeasure, happiness, and poverty--all change sooner or later. Can anybody think that such things are reality? What can one call all this that is subject to change, whose source is unseen and whose end is unseen, and which is subject to death and destruction, after which it is seen no more? Is that reality? Or are not the realities perhaps really behind the scene, from whence everything came and to which everything goes?"

IN AN EASTERN ROSE GARDEN – Silent Life

GAYAN 088 - BOULA -047 - The secret of all success is strength of conviction.

"What I am speaking about now is the psychological attitude we ought to have. Always hope for the best, and we certainly shall have the best. What we can do is to make ourselves strong enough to go through life on earth; and it is only by this strength of conviction that by whatever path we journey, we shall arrive at the spiritual goal; and whatever be our life, professional, industrial, commercial, it does not matter, we shall live religion, Nature's religion, turning our life into a religion, making of our life a religion. And so even with every earthly success, we shall be taking steps towards spiritual attainment."

THE PURPOSE OF LIFE - Chapter VIII

GAYAN 089 - BOULA -048 - Those who try to make virtues out of their faults grope further and further into darkness.

Crime is natural. If crime were not natural, from where would it come? All men are subject to fault; their very virtues develop into faults. The great teacher has therefore taught patience, which means to be patient, and not to expect patience. He has taught respect, which means to show respect, not to demand it. He has taught unselfishness, which means to be unselfish without expecting a reward. The great teacher has found his religion in his study of life, and has shown the interdependence of human lives; and that what a man gives, that he receives. He has taught man to lift his light upon high, so that he may live in light; in that light which is never extinguished in man although usually kept under a covering cloud or a bushel of selfishness and greed, so that its owner lives in a darkened room.

THE ART OF PERSONALITY - LIFE'S CREATIVE FORCES: RASA SHASTRA – Prostitution

GAYAN 090 - BOULA -049 - When envy develops into jealousy, the heart changes from sourness into bitterness.

Where does jealousy come from? Where does envy, aching of the heart come from? It all comes from lack of generosity. A man may not have one single coin to his name, and yet he can be generous, he can be noble, if only he has a large heart of friendly feeling. Life in the world offers every opportunity to a man, whatever be his position in life, to show if he has any spirit of generosity.

THE ART OF PERSONALITY - CHARACTER AND PERSONALITY - Character-Building

GAYAN 091 - BOULA -050 - A worldly loss often turns into a spiritual gain.

To the view of a mystic a gain is not a gain nor is a loss a loss; for that which appears to be a loss at one time may appear at another to be a gain. The more deeply we think about it, the more we see that in every gain there is a loss, and in every loss there is a gain. That which seemed to be a gain yesterday may prove to be a loss tomorrow, and that which is a loss at one time proves to yield a gain at another. Consequently the mystic realizes the joy of the gain and the sorrow of the loss in their right aspect; he discerns what it is that turns a gain to a loss, or converts a loss to a gain. The more deeply we consider the subject, the more do we discern that there are certain gains which are only transient, because material, and that to attain them we may have sacrificed a greater gain. Of course if we do not see that greater gain, we do not mind the loss. We can only see what we have lost or what we have gained after we have discovered whether the gain we have sacrificed really was a greater one or not.

IN AN EASTERN ROSE GARDEN - Gain and Loss

GAYAN 092 - BOULA -051 - Patient endurance is a sign of progress.

It is a great difficulty that the people in this land of America are losing this quality of patience more and more every day, because Providence has blessed them so much. They have conveniences, they have comforts, they are the spoilt children of Providence, and when it comes to having patience, it is very hard for them. Individuals have to practice this spirit, for we do not know what may come to follow. We live in this world of uncertainty, and we do not know in what condition we may be placed to-morrow; if we have no strength of resistance we may easily break down. Therefore it is most necessary for the human race to develop patience in all conditions of life, in all walks of life, in all positions in life. Whether we are rich or poor, high or low, this is the one quality that must be developed. It is patience that gives endurance, it is patience that is all-powerful, and by lack of patience one loses so much. Very often the answer to one's prayer is within one's reach, the hand of Providence not very far off- but one has lost one's patience and so lost the opportunity.

Sufi Teaching – Health and Order of Body and Mind – Physical Control

GAYAN 093 - BOULA -052 - The ideal is the means, but its breaking is the goal.

It is the ideal which prompts man to sacrifice, and the most important thing he can sacrifice is his own life. A man without ideal has no depth, he is shallow. However pleased he may be with his everyday life, he can never enjoy that happiness which is independent of outer circumstances. The pleasure which is experienced through pain is the pleasure experienced by the idealist. But what of the pleasure that has not come out of pain? It is tasteless. Life's gain, which people think so much of, what is it after all? A loss caused by an ideal is a greater gain than any other gain in this world.

The true ideal is always hidden behind a man-made ideal which covers it. For instance the fragrance is hidden in the petals of the rose, and when one wants to extract the spirit from them one has to crush them; but thereby the same rose that could have lasted for only a few days has been turned into spirit, into essence, which can last a whole lifetime. That is what is meant by the saying from the Gayan: 'The ideal is a means, but its breaking is the goal.' The ideal can also be pictured as an egg:its breaking is the fulfillment, as with the egg when the chick comes forth. It is necessary for the ideal to break; if it is not broken then the ideal is not used.

The ideal recedes when one approaches it, but the keener one's sight becomes, the greater becomes the beauty of the ideal. In this way one is not removed further from the ideal; one is brought closer to it.

THE ALCHEMY OF HAPPINESS – Ideal

GAYAN 094 - BOULA -053 - Many feel, a few think, and fewer still there are who can express their thoughts.

The great poets who gave us beautiful teachings in moral, in truth, where did they get them from? This life here is the school in which they learned, this life is the stage on which they saw and gathered. They are the worshippers of beauty in nature and in art. In all conditions of life they meditate upon beauty and find good points in all those they see. They gather all that is beautiful, from the good and the wicked both. Just like the bee takes the best from every flower and makes honey from it, so they gather all that is beautiful and express it through their imagination in the form of music, poetry and art, as well as in their thoughts and deeds in everyday life.

SUFI TEACHINGS - HEALTH AND ORDER OF BODY AND MIND - The Control of the Mind

GAYAN 095 - BOULA -054 - The value of sacrifice is in willingness.

He who wants anything becomes smaller than the thing he wants; he who gives away anything is greater than the thing he gives. Therefore to a mystic each act of renunciation becomes a step towards perfection.

Forced renunciation, whether forced by morality, religion, law, convention, or formality, is not necessarily renunciation. The real spirit of renunciation is willingness; and willing renunciation comes when one has risen above the thing one renounces. The value of each thing in life, wealth, power, position, possession, is according to the evolution of man. There is a time in his life when toys are his treasures, and there is a time when he puts them aside; there is a time in his life when copper coins are everything to him, and there is another time when he can give away gold coins; there is a time in his life when he values a cottage, and there is a time when he gives up a palace.

Things have no value; their value is as man makes it; and at every step in his evolution he changes their value. Certainly there is no gain in leaving home, friends, and all affairs of life, and going to the forest and living the life of an ascetic; and yet who has the right to blame those who do so? How can the worldly man judge and understand the point of view of the one who renounces? Perhaps that which seems of the greatest value to the worldly man is nothing to the one who has renounced.

The Sufi makes no restrictions and has no principles of renunciation, nor does he teach renunciation. He believes that to sacrifice anything in life which one does not wish to sacrifice is of no use, but that renunciation is a natural thing, and grows in one with one's evolution. A child which cries for its toy at one stage of its childhood, comes to an age when it is quite willing to give away the toy it once cried for.

Moral Culture - The Law of Renunciation - Life in God

GAYAN 096 - BOULA -055 - Nothing can take away joy from the man who has right understanding.

...the lack of joy is the result of error. Nothing can take away joy from the man who has right understanding. Through all conditions of life he will retain it, but the one who lacks understanding, nothing in the world or Heaven there is which can bring him a lasting joy. This shows that, in reality, joy does not come from the external life, though always it seems so. Joy has only one source and that is the heart of man, which is the globe over his soul's light. And the absence of joy does not mean that the soul has lost its light.

Sangatha III - METAPHYSICS

GAYAN 097 - BOULA -056 - Do not fear God, but regard carefully His pleasure and displeasure.

The saintly souls, who consider it as their religion to seek the pleasure of God and to be resigned to His will, are really blessed, for their manner is pleasing to everyone, for they are conscientious lest they may hurt the feeling of anyone, and if by some mistake they happen to hurt someone's feelings, they feel they have hurt God Whose pleasure they must constantly seek, for the happiness of their life is only in seeking the pleasure of God. They watch every person and every situation and condition, and their heart becomes so trained by constantly observing life keenly, as a lover of music whose ears become trained in time, who distinguishes between the correct and the false note. So they begin to see every desire that springs in their heart, if it is in accordance with the Will of God. Sometimes they know the moment the desire was sprung; sometimes they know when they have gone halfway in the path of its pursuit; and sometimes they know at the end of strife. But even then, at the end of it, their willingness to resign to the Will of God becomes their consolation, even in the face of disappointment. The secret of seeking the Will of God is in cultivating the faculty of sensing harmony, for harmony is beauty, and beauty is harmony. The lover of beauty in his further progress becomes the seeker of harmony, and by trying always to maintain harmony man will tune his heart to the Will of God.

The Unity of Religious Ideals – The God Ideal – The Will Human and Divine

GAYAN 098 - BOULA -057 - Optimism is the result of love.

Optimism represents the spontaneous flow of love. Also optimism represents trust in love. This shows that it is love trusting love which is optimism. Pessimism comes from disappointment from a bad impression which is there of some hindrance in the path. Optimism gives a hopeful attitude in life, while by pessimism one sees darkness in one's path. No doubt sometimes pessimism shows conscientiousness, cleverness also, and pessimism also shows experience. But in point of fact can we be conscientious enough if we only though what difficulties one had before one in one's life. It is trust which solves the problem.

Social Gatheka #3 - Optimism and Pessimism

GAYAN 099 - BOULA -058 - He who is a riddle to another is a puzzle to himself.

The Knower manifested as man in order that He might become known to Himself, and now, what may man do in order to help the Knower to fulfill this purpose? Seek continually an answer to every question that arises in his heart. Of course, there are different types of minds. There is one mind that will puzzle and puzzle over a question, and trouble himself for something which is nothing, and will go out by the same door by which he has come in. That person will trouble himself and will wreck his own spirit, and will never find satisfaction. There is no question which has not its answer somewhere. The answer is nothing but an echo of the question, a full echo. And therefore one must rise above this confused state of mind which prevents one from getting the answer from within or from without to every question that arises in one's heart. In order to become spiritual, one need not perform miracles. The moment one's heart is able to answer every question that rises in one's heart, one is already on the path. Besides, the thing that must be first known, one puts off to the last, and that which must be known at the last moment, one wants to know first. It is this which causes confusion in the lives of many souls.

THE PURPOSE OF LIFE – Chapter XII

GAYAN 100 - BOULA -059 - When the miser shows any generosity he celebrates it with trumpets.

"There is such a great difference between the quiet person and a noisy person. One is like a restless child, the other like a grown-up person. One constructs, the other destroys. A quiet way of working must be practiced in everything. By making too much ado about nothing one creates commotion, disturbance in the atmosphere; useless activity without any result. One also finds noise in the tendency to exaggeration, when someone wants to make a mountain out of a molehill. Modesty, humility, gentleness, meekness, all such virtues are manifest in the person who works quietly through life."

THE ART OF PERSONALITY - CHARACTER AND PERSONALITY - Character-Building

GAYAN 101 - BOULA -060 - A sincere man has a fragrance about him which is perceived by a sincere heart.

"Love for God is the expansion of the heart, and all actions that come from the lover of God are virtues; they cannot be otherwise. There is a different outlook on life when the love of God has filled a man's heart. The lover of God will not hate anyone; for he knows that by doing so he will hate the Creator by hating His creation. He cannot be insincere, he cannot be unfaithful; for he will think that to be faithful and sincere to mankind is to be faithful and sincere to God. You can always trust the lover of God, however unpractical or however lacking in cleverness he may appear to be, for simply to hold strongly in mind the thought of God purifies the soul of all bitterness, and gives man a virtue that he could obtain nowhere else and by no other means."

The Art of Personality – Moral Culture - The Law of Beneficence - Our Dealings with God

Gayan #102 – Boula #61 - If you are not able to control your thought you cannot hold it.

"...After this comes control of the thoughts, which is the second step, control of the body coming first. Thousands of people have found that they can sit in the postures for hours, but cannot keep their mind still. This has to be learned by degrees. A person cannot control his mind by willing to think of nothing; that will never be possible. First let the mind hold whatever thought interests it, any thought of love, of goodwill - whatever interests it. Check its tendency to jump from one thing to another. When you catch the mind jumping from one thing to another, bring it back and hold it. You must say: I am greater than my mind, my will is greater than my mind, and I will make my mind obey my will."

SUFI TEACHINGS - HEALTH AND ORDER OF BODY AND MIND –
Self Control

"The mind is just like a restive horse. Bring a wild horse and yoke it to a carriage; it is such a strange experience for it that it will kick and jump and run and try to destroy the carriage. So it is a weight for the mind to carry when you make it take one thought and hold it for a while. It is then that the mind becomes restless, because it is not accustomed to discipline. There is a thought that the mind will hold by itself: a thought of disappointment, or pain, or grief, of sorrow or failure. The mind will hold it so fast that you cannot take it away from its grip; the mind holds it by itself. But when you ask the mind to hold a particular thought, then the mind will not hold it; it says: 'I am not your servant, sir!'

When once the mind is disciplined by concentration, by the power of will then the mind becomes your servant. Once the mind has become your servant, then what more can you wish? Then your world is your own, you are the king of your kingdom. No doubt, one might say: 'Why should we not let the mind be free also, as we are free?' But we and the mind are not two beings. It is like saying: 'Let the horse be free and the rider be free'. Then the horse wants to go to the south and the rider wants to go to the north. How can they go together?"

THE MYSTICISM OF SOUND AND MUSIC - COSMIC LANGUAGE -
Will

GAYAN 103 - BOULA -062 - The answer is in the question; a question has no existence without an answer.

There is a stage of evolution in man's life where his every question is answered by the life around him. If there is a living being before him or if there is nature around him, if he is wakeful or if he is asleep, the answer to his question comes as an echo of the very question. As certain things become an accommodation for the air in order to turn it into sound, so for every thought of a sage everything becomes an accommodation in order to help it to resound, and in this resonance there is an answer. In point of fact the answer is in the question itself; a question has no existence without answer. It is man's limited vision that makes him see the question only, without the answer.

(Vol.14) THE SMILING FOREHEAD – Insight

Gayan #104 - Boula #63 - All that detains man on his journey to the desired goal is temptation.

"In regard to the Sufi's attitude towards right and wrong--that these are man-made--one may ask how then it can matter what a person does. The answer is, it matters to those to whom it matters, and it does not matter to those to whom it does not matter. In this respect, if the Sufi has to say anything to his follower, it is this:refrain from doing that which hinders you from accomplishing the purpose in your inner and your external life. Do not act against your ideal, for it will never be satisfactory to you; you will not be pleased with yourself and this inharmony in your inner and your external self will prevent peace, which is your life's craving, without which life becomes unhappy. 'Right' is the straight path which the soul is inclined to take in life, but when one walks astray, leaving the straight path in life owing either to negligence or ignorance, or by reason of weakness, or by the attraction of some temptation on the way, one can say that is wrong."

THE WAY OF ILLUMINATION – The Sufi

GAYAN 105 - BOULA -064 - - Fatalism is one side of the truth, not all.

"It seems more reasonable when a person says that the illness is brought about by his own actions. But it is not always true, it is not true in every case. Very often the most innocent and the best souls, who have nothing but good wishes and kind thoughts, will be found among sufferers.

Thinking that it is the debt of the past life gives one the idea of fatalism, that there is a certain suffering through which one must pass, that there is no other way, and that therefore one must patiently endure something which is most disagreeable. I have seen a young man suffering from an illness, who most contentedly told me, on my giving him advice to do something for his health, 'I believe that this is a debt of the past that I have to pay. I might just as well pay it.' From a business point of view it is very just, but from a spiritual person's point of view it can be looked at differently. What man does not wish for himself is not for him, is not his portion. For in every soul there is the power of the Almighty, there is a spark of divine light, there is the spirit of the Creator; and therefore all that man wishes to have is his birthright. Naturally a soul does not wish to have an illness unless he is unbalanced. If the soul knew the power of his natural inclination"

HEALING AND THE MIND WORLD - HEALTH

GAYAN 106 - BOULA - 065 - Keep your goodness apart, that it may not touch your vanity.

...On the other hand, if he (the mureed) has some powers he hides them in his humility, and if his inspiration is developing, he should bow his head down, that his fellow men may not see it. Always consider that this is the one thing that you will meet on this path, and the one enemy you will avoid: vanity. You must be on your guard against it from which ever side it comes. It comes so swiftly and so subtly that it is difficult to recognize. When you are on your guard you will see that even your humble words and your meek actions will prove to be vain. This is the thing which throws man from the highest stage. Even prophets have to fight and to fight it. Know the danger of this path, and do not waste your time in falling into it. The one thing to rely upon is God's favor. Build neither on your study nor on your meditation, although they both help you. You are dependent not even on your murshid but on God alone. Seek Him, trust Him. In Him lies your life's purpose, and in Him is hidden the rest of your soul.

The Dutch Papers – Class for Mureeds – Mureedship

GAYAN 107 - BOULA -066 - When man denies what he owes you, then it is put on the account of God.

"There comes a stage in the moral evolution of man when he perceives and understands the moral of beneficence, and he learns to return good for evil. At this stage in his progress he hears a chord that connects and runs through him and through all. He finds himself as it were a dome, in which good and evil find re-echoing tones. Evil done to him echoes within him in a desire to do evil in return; and good done to him echoes within him in a desire to return good. Therefore, in order that his own actions may in their turn call out nothing but good, he desires always to do good, and to return both good for good, and good for evil.

But there is a higher stage to which he may progress. And then it seems to him that this connecting chord swells into a great sea, and he realizes that the interdependence of lives is such, because the spirit is one, and because it is the spirit that unites and the spirit that gives life."

Excepts THE ART OF PERSONALITY – LIFE'S CREATIVE FORCES: RASA SHASTRA – Prostitution

GAYAN 108 - BOULA - 067 - A refined manner with sincerity makes a living art.

The art of personality is like the art of music: it needs ear training and voice culture. To a person who knows life's music the art of personality comes naturally; and it is not only inartistic but also unmusical when a soul shows lack of this art in the personality. When a man looks at every soul as a note of music and learns to recognize what note it is, flat or sharp, high or low, and to what pitch it belongs, then he becomes the knower of souls, and he knows how to deal with everybody. In his own actions, in his speech, he shows the art;he harmonizes with the rhythm of the atmosphere, with the tone of the person he meets, with the theme of the moment. To become refined is to become musical; it is the musical soul who is artistic in his personality. Spoken in different tones, the same word changes its meaning. A word spoken at the proper moment and withheld at the moment when it should not be expressed, completes the music of life.

It is the continual inclination to produce beauty which helps one to develop art in the personality. It is amusing how readily man is inclined to learn outer refinement, and how slow many souls are to develop that art inwardly. It must be remembered that the outer manner is meaningless if it is not prompted by the inner impulse towards beauty. How God takes pleasure in man can be learned from the story of Indra, the king of Paradise, at whose court Gandharvas sing and Upsaras dance. When interpreted in plain words this means that God is the essence of beauty; it is His love of beauty which has caused Him to express His own beauty in manifestation, for it is His desire fulfilled in the objective world.

It is amusing sometimes to watch how good manners annoy someone who is proud of his bad manners. He will call it shallow, because his pride is hurt at the sight of something which he has not got. The one whose hand does not reach to the fruit says, when he fails, that the grapes are sour. And for some it is too free to become refined, just as many will not like good music but are quite satisfied with popular music. And many even become tired of a good manner, for it seems foreign to their nature. As it is not a merit to become unmusical, so it is not wise to turn against refinement. One must only try and develop beauty, trusting that the beauty in the depth of one's soul, and its expression, in whatever form, is the sign of the soul's unfoldment.

The Art of Personality - The Art of Personality part X

GAYAN 109 - BOULA -068 - - The longing for vengeance is like a craving for poison.

Man unites with others in the family tie, which is the first step in his evolution, and yet families in the past have fought with each other, and have taken vengeance upon one another for generations, each considering his cause to be the only true and righteous one. Today man shows his evolution in uniting with his neighbors and fellow-citizens, and even developing within himself the spirit of patriotism for his nation. He is greater in this respect than those in the past; and yet men so united nationally have caused the catastrophe of the modern wars, which will be regarded by the coming generations in the same light in which we now regard the family feuds of the past.

THE WAY OF ILLUMINATION - Sufi Thoughts

GAYAN 110 - BOULA -069 - The truly great souls become streams of love.

Although there can be no trace of the personality of God to be found on the surface, yet one can see that there is a source from which all personality comes, and a goal to which all must return. And if there is one source, what a great Personality that one Source must be! It cannot be learnt by great intellect, or not even by the study of metaphysics or comparative religion, but only understood by a pure and innocent heart full of love.

The great personalities who have descended on earth from time to time to awaken in man that love which is his divine inheritance found an echo in innocent souls rather than in great intellects. Man often confuses wisdom with cleverness and cleverness with wisdom. But these two are different; man can be wise and can be clever, and man can be clever and not wise; and by cleverness a person will strive and strive, and will not reach God. It is a stream--the stream of love--which leads towards God.

THE UNITY OF RELIGIOUS IDEALS - THE GOD IDEAL - God is Love

GAYAN 111 - BOULA -070 - God is the central theme of the true poet, and the portrait which the prophets paint.

The most important philosophical point in religion is that besides all the moral principles and ethics that religion teaches, there is the central theme which can be traced as the nature of life, of spirit, and that is to make the perfect Being intelligible to the limited mind of man. To do this the ideal of God is preached. The central theme of every religion the messengers have brought was the God-ideal, and every one of them has tried his best to make a picture of that ideal, in order that the people of that time could easily grasp it and benefit by it, to fulfill the purpose of spiritual perfection.

It is true that the different pictures that the great prophets of the world have drawn very often differ from one another. But one finds that in order to make one clear photograph there have to be many different processes; a plate has to be made and has to be developed, and then the picture is transferred to paper; then it is touched up, and all these different processes go to make a photograph complete.

And so it has been with those who have tried to make a picture of the Deity, a picture which cannot be made fully, because it is beyond man's power to do so. They have done their best; artists have painted that picture. When three artists paint the portrait of one person, the three pictures are different. They only differ because they are different artists; and so it is with the prophets, though all have one and the same motive: to make that picture intelligible to the limited mind of man, who only knows what he knows about himself and about his fellow-man. Thus the best picture he can make of God is that of a man. In the ancient religions of the East, God was first pictured in the form of man; then in the pictures of later days man was pictured as God. After that came a reformation by which man and God were separated in order to break with the confusion caused by these two opposite ideas, that God was man and man was God.

THE UNITY OF RELIGIOUS IDEALS – THE MESSAGE AND THE MESSENGER

GAYAN 112 - BOULA -071 - He whose love has always been reciprocated does not know the real feeling of love.

"And now we come to the next step. This is the law of beneficence. And this law means being unconcerned with how another person responds to us in answer to what we do to him in love and sympathy. What concerns one is what can one do for the other person. It does not matter if a favor is not appreciated. Even if the favor were absolutely ignored, still the satisfaction of the beneficent man comes from what he has done, not from what the one who has received it has expressed. When this sense is born in man, from that day he begins to live in the world. For his pleasure does not depend upon what he receives from others but depends upon what he does for others. His happiness is not dependent on anything; his happiness is independent; he becomes the creator of his happiness; his happiness is in giving, not in taking."

The Alchemy of Happiness – The Law of Action

GAYAN 113 - BOULA -072 - True belief is independent of reason.

And then again there is a fourth belief. That belief is a belief of conviction, which stands above reason. The conviction in man is not discovered for some time in life; but there comes a time when it is discovered; and that is a blessed day. Then there arises an idea, an idea which no reason can break, a feeling which is not a passing feeling but is a conviction. However high the idea may be, one seems to be an eyewitness of that idea; one is as strong, as confident, as a person who has seen with his own eyes. One can be convinced of ideas so subtle that they cannot even be expressed in words, and one is more convinced of them than if one had seen them with one's own eyes. It is this belief which is called by the Sufis and Persian mystics Iman, which means conviction.

I remember the blessing my spiritual teacher, my murshid, used to give me every time I parted from him. And that blessing was, 'May your Iman be strengthened'. At that time I had not thought about the word Iman; on the contrary I thought as a young man, is my faith so weak that my teacher requires it to be stronger? I would have preferred it if he had said, may you become illuminated, or may your powers be great, or may your influence spread, or may you rise higher and higher, or become perfect. But this simple thing, may your faith be strengthened, what did it mean? I did not criticize but I pondered and pondered upon the subject. And in the end I came to realize that no blessing is more valuable and important than this. For every attached to a conviction. Where there is no conviction there is nothing. The secret of healing, the mystery of evolving, the power of all attainments, and the way to spiritual realization, all come from the strengthening of that belief which is a conviction, so that nothing can ever change it.

THE ALCHEMY OF HAPPINESS - Stages on the Path of Self-realization

GAYAN 114 - BOULA -073 - Wisdom is like the horizon: the nearer you approach it, the further it recedes.

Wisdom is that which is learned from within; intellect is that which is acquired from without. The source of wisdom is above, the source of intellect is below, and therefore it is not the same method, it is not the same process which one adopts in order to attain wisdom, as that which one adopts to acquire intellect.

THE MYSTICISM OF SOUND AND MUSIC - The Power of the Word

GAYAN 115 - BOULA -074 - When the soul is attuned to God, every action becomes music.

Through right meditation, one becomes attuned to God and so to all creation, including humanity. There are many grades and steps in spiritual devotion, wherein one becomes attuned to his teacher, to the world teacher, to the Prophets of God, and to Allah himself. Even after one reaches the last stages it is only a beginning, for then man ceases to be and God lives truly in and through him. This is called Baq by the Sufis. Of this condition, Christ has said, "Many are called but few are chosen," and Krishna taught that very few realized his being and of these only a few sustained that realization.

The true work of the Sufi is not only to attain to God-consciousness but to make this realization absorb more and more of life. In that condition, one never loses sight of Allah for an instant, day or night, asleep or awake. This may truly be called the purpose of life, the fulfillment of the inner life.

But progress does not cease there. In that state, called Fana-fi-Allah, when the soul absorbed in God, one loses the false sense of being and finds the true reality. Then one finally experiences what is termed Baqa-i-Fan , where the false ego is annihilated and merged into the true personality, which is really God expressing Himself in some wondrous ways. This is the same also as Nirvana, where the true reality of life is experienced and expressed. This means that the true life is in God, the only Being, and through God-realization man finds his true self.

Githa I – The Path of Attainment – Patience

GAYAN 116 - BOULA -075 - It is the spirit of hopelessness that blocks the path of man and prevents his advancement.

Hopelessness can be overcome by faith. In the first place by faith in God, at the same time knowing that the soul draws its power from the divine source. Every thought, every impulse, every wish, every desire comes from there, and in its accomplishment there is the law of perfection. And in that way a person feels hopeful. But when one thinks, 'what shall I do? What am I to do? How am I to do it? I have not got the means; I have not got the resources; I have not got the inspiration to do it'; when one is pessimistic about things, one destroys the roots of one's desires, because, by denying one casts away that which could otherwise have been attained. For in recognizing the divine Father in God, one becomes conscious of one's divine heritage, and that there is no lack in the divine Spirit, and therefore there is no lack in life. It is only a matter of time. If one builds one's hope in God, there is an assured fulfillment of it.

The Sufi Message of Hazrat Inayat Khan The Purpose of Life - Chapter 10

GAYAN 117 - BOULA -076 - The unselfish man profits by life more than the selfish, whose profit in the end proves to be a loss.

But remember, we can never claim to be unselfish; however unselfish we may be, we are selfish just the same. But we can be wisely selfish, and if we are to be selfish, it is just as well to be wisely selfish. It is the same thing as what we call unselfishness, and it is profitable to be that instead of being foolishly selfish; because the former gains and the latter loses.

From Healing and the Mind World – Mental Purification – The Distinction Between the Subtle and the Gross

GAYAN 118 - BOULA -077 - Sincerity is like a bud in the heart of man, that blossoms with the maturity of the soul.

...a real seeker, one who is not false to himself, will always meet with the truth, with the real, because it is his own real faith, his own sincerity in earnest seeking that will become his torch. The real teacher is within, that lover of reality is one's own sincere self, and if one is really seeking truth sooner or later one will certainly find a true teacher. And supposing one came into contact with a false teacher, what then? Then the real One will turn the false teacher also into a real teacher, because reality is greater than falsehood.

THE PATH OF INITIATION AND DISCIPLESHIP - The Path of Initiation

GAYAN 119 - BOULA -078 - Success is in store for the faithful, for faith ensures success.

To a mystic, faith is the unique power that works through the whole of creation. He does not mean by faith a belief in a certain religion or dogma or ceremony or book or teacher; he means trust, a trust even in the absence of reason.

… So many things take away that natural and powerful quality which was at first present, that faith which is the secret of the whole creation, the secret of all success that can ever be attained in life. This faith is broken by life's discouraging experiences. When confidence in others is lost, then confidence in self is lost also; and the more it is lost, the more failures one meets. A doubting person considers himself to be wise and one of simple faith to be a fool. Whoever he sees he suspects; whatever he hears he questions whether it be right or wrong…

… If we could only develop the quality which is called faith, about which so much is said in the scriptures, in the Bible, in the Qur'an, we should find what power it would carry. It is the secret of all success.

IN AN EASTERN ROSE GARDEN – Faith

GAYAN 120 - BOULA -079 - No one will experience in life what is not meant for him.

And now you will ask me what explanation have I to give about that belief which has always existed and believed by the wise and foolish, that there exists some such a thing which is called "predestination." And I will explain it. That there was an artist and he planned in his mind, he made in his mind, planned that he wants to produce it on a canvas. And no sooner he took the colors and brush in his hand and began to paint his picture, every line he made and every color he put, it suggested to him something, and that altered altogether his plan; the very plan with which he began then became an obscurity to his mind, and what was produced before him was quite a different thing than he had thought before.

What does it show? This shows the three stages of the picture. The first stage of the picture is that plan which, before bringing on the canvas, the artist had designed, the artist had planned; and the other aspect is that action of producing that picture which went as changes, right and wrong and right and wrong, and so on it went; and the third aspect is the completion of that plan, the completion of that picture which stood quite different from the plan first conceived. Therefore, what may be called "predestination" is that plan which is made beforehand, and what may be called "Karma" as they say in the Hindustanic tongues, is that process through which the picture is made; and the completion of that picture is what may be called "mastery."

It does not always happen that the picture is altogether different from what it was planned, and yet it often happens. And however much different the picture may be from the plan yet the foundation remains there as first planned. And therefore, how much different the life may be from that mark of predestination which was before, and yet the life is built, the life is erected upon the same plan which has been first made. No doubt the astrologers and the fortune-tellers, the future-tellers, the prophets will not always say the thing that is really coming, they may make a mistake, and yet the predestination is there; the mistake is in their reading, not in the predestination.

And still that saying of old that the feet of the infant tell what he is going to be will always prove true. It is the lack of seeing, that men cannot see, but the one who can see, can see from infancy what the child is going to be. And that old saying that the fate of the child is written on his forehead, it is the same in reality; every part and particle of the infant is expressive of what he is going to be. The one who can read the eyes and the ears and the features and the forms as letters, he can read an infant - a human being - as a letter.

THE SUPPLEMENTARY PAPERS – PSYCHOLOGY - PSYCHOLOGY III
- Is Man the Master of His Destiny?

GAYAN 121 - BOULA -080 - It is not possible to be praised only and not to incur blame at any time. Praise and blame go hand in hand.

...Praise cannot exist without blame, for nothing has existence without its opposite, just as pleasure cannot exist without pain. No one can be great and not small; no one can be loved and not hated. There is no one who is hated by all and not loved by someone; there is always someone to love him.

If one would realize that the world of God, His splendor and magnificence, are to be seen in the wise and the foolish, in the good and the bad, then one would think tolerantly and reverently of all mankind...

THE UNITY OF RELIGIOUS IDEALS - THE MESSAGE AND THE MESSENGER - part iii

GAYAN 122 - BOULA -081 - To be in uncongenial surroundings is worse than being in one's grave.

No doubt man has it in his power to improve his life's conditions greatly if only he does not lose patience before a desirable condition is brought about, if his courage has not been exhausted, and if his hope has endured.

And now the question is how can one become at one with the rhythm of life, in other words with the conditions of life? One's condition of life and one's own desire are generally two conflicting things. If desire gives in to the condition, then the condition gets the upper hand; and if the condition is mastered, then no doubt desire has the upper hand. But the condition is not always master when there is a conflict, a struggle; only one needs caution in fighting a condition in life. If harmony can be established peacefully it is better to avoid battling, though it is a fact that those who complain most about life and those who are most disappointed and troubled with life are the ones who struggle most with life's conditions. Therefore in achieving atone-ment with the conditions of life one need not always use a weapon; one should first try to harmonize with a particular condition of life. The great heroes who have really fought through life and gained life's victory in the real sense of the word, have not been those who have fought against conditions; they made peace with the conditions of life. The secret of the lives of the great Sufis, in whatever part of the world they have been, was that they met conditions, whether favorable or unfavorable, with the aim of becoming at one with the rhythm of life.

A desire is sometimes our friend and sometimes our own enemy. Sometimes in unfavorable conditions desire becomes agitated and loses its patience, and wishes to break the condition; and instead of breaking the conditions it breaks itself. The great souls have extended their hand first to their worst enemy, because the one who makes his enemy his friend will make a friend of his own self. A condition as bitter as poison will be turned into nectar if we can get into rhythm with that condition, if we can understand it, if we will endure that condition with patience, with courage, with hope. When there is a favorable condition we are very often afraid that it may pass, but when there is an adverse condition we do not generally think that it will pass; we think that it will last for ever. This comes from fear, from agitation, from the desire to get out of this condition, and thus we lose even hope, the only source that keeps us alive. When we see the nature of life, and how from morning till evening everything changes, why should we not keep the hope that an unfavorable condition will change and turn into a favorable condition?

THE ALCHEMY OF HAPPINESS– What is Wanted in Life?

GAYAN 123 - BOULA -082 - Science is born of the seed of intuition, conceived in reason.

Many people think that science is based upon the knowledge of facts proved by reason and logic, and very few know that at the beginning there was always intuition. All scientific discoveries spring from intuition; after that reason has its place, and logic helps. The scientists analyze and make their discoveries intelligible to others, but in the beginning these come from intuition. If the great inventors of America such as Edison and others had been great mechanics only it would not have been sufficient; behind this, however, there was intuition.

The Alchemy of Happiness – Communicating with Life

GAYAN 124 - BOULA -083 - Truth alone is success, and real success is truth.

The work of the Sufi Movement is not to collect all the rainwater in its own tanks, but to work and make a way for the stream of the message to flow, supplying water too the fields of the world. The work of the Sufi mission is sowing; reaping we shall leave to humanity to do for the fields do not belong to our particular movement; and all the fields belong to God. We who are employed on this farm of the world, to do the work, we must do, and leave the rest to God. Success we do not trouble about, and those who strive for it, let them seek in some other directions. Truth alone is our success, for lasting success is truth.

SOCIAL AND RELIGIOUS GATHEKAS – Social Gatheka #8 – What the World Needs Today

GAYAN 125 - BOULA -084 - The key to all happiness is the love of God.

It is only those who are blessed by perceiving the origin and source of all things who awaken to the fact that the real inclination of every life is to attain to something which can not be touched or comprehended or understood. The hidden blessing of this knowledge is the first step to perfection. Once awake to this fact, man sees there is something in life that will make him really happy and give him his heart's desire. He can say, 'Though there are many things in life which I need for the moment and for which I shall certainly work, yet there is only that one thing, around which life centers, that will satisfy me: the spiritual attainment, the religious attainment, or, as one may even call it, the attainment of God'. Such a one has found the key to all happiness, and has found that all the things he needs will be reached because he has the key to all. 'Seek, and ye shall find: knock, and it shall be opened unto you. Seek first the kingdom of God, and all these things shall be added unto you.' This kingdom of God is the silent life; the life inseparable, eternal, self-sufficient, and all-powerful. This is the life of the wise, whatever be the name given to it; this is the life which the wise contemplate. It is the face of this life that they long to see; it is the ocean of this life that they long to swim in; as it is written, 'In Him we live and have our being'.

IN AN EASTERN ROSE GARDEN – The Silent Life

GAYAN 126 - BOULA -085 - As the shadow is apparent, yet non-existent, so is evil.

I remember a Persian verse made by my murshid which relates to the self: 'When I feel that now I can make peace with my self, it finds time to prepare another attack.' That is our condition. We think that our little faults, since they are small, are of no consequence; or we do not even think of them at all. But every little fault is a flag for the little self, for its own dominion. In this way battling makes man the sovereign of the kingdom of God. Very few can realize the great power in battling with and conquering the self.

But what does man generally do? He says, 'My poor self, it has to withstand the conflicts of this world; should I also battle with this self?' So he surrenders his kingdom to his little self, depriving himself of the divine power that is in the heart of man. There is in man a false self and a real self. The real self contains the eternal; the false self contains the mortal. The real self has wisdom; the false self ignorance. The real self can rise to perfection; the false self ends in limitation. The real self has all good, the false self is productive of all evil. One can see both in oneself: God and the other one. By conquering the other one, one realizes God. This other power has been called Satan; but is it a power? In reality it is not. It is and it is not. It is a shadow. We see shadow and yet it is nothing. We should realize that this false self has no existence of its own. As soon as the soul has risen above the false self, it begins to realize its nobility.

[Vol. 6] THE ALCHEMY OF HAPPINESS - The Struggle of Life (2)

GAYAN 127 - BOULA -086 - By accusing another of his fault you only root him more firmly in it.

Whatever be one's position in connection with another in life, there is one principal thing to be remembered: That by annoyance, by grudging, by complaining, by criticizing, most often one turns things from bad to worse.

Do not think that another person wishes to be corrected by you, be he wise or foolish, older or younger; as soon as one takes the step to correct a person, one, so to speak, does violence to his pride, to his ego, and by doing so one upsets his right thinking. There are ways of doing things. The wiser one is, the more beautifully he accomplishes his purpose in whatever position he may be. If one has to be humble in doing it beautifully, if one has to bend in doing it nicely, instead of making another person bend, it really matters very little. Criticizing a person, accusing a person of his fault is no less than slapping his face, perhaps worse.

In all cases it is consideration which is needed, a respectful attitude towards human nature, whatever be his position in life in connection with you; it is that which gives you a complete mastery. The great kings of the world very often have been pulled down from their thrones by those who for years bowed and bent and trembled at their command, but the Christlike souls who have washed the feet of the disciples are still held in esteem, and will be honored and loved by humanity forever. Their example is the example to follow in life's path, which is full of thorns; and those who have followed their principle, even to the smallest degree, they have arrived safely at their destination.

THE SUPPLEMENTARY PAPERS OF HAZRAT INAYAT KHAN (AKA THE DUTCH PAPERS) - MISCELLANEOUS II - One's Attitude Towards Those with Whom One Has to Work

GAYAN 128 - BOULA -087 - Death is a tax the soul has to pay for having had a name and a form.

Man may most justly be called the seed of God. God the Infinite, most conscious within Himself, embraces His nature full of variety, in this way He is one and He is all. The whole manifestation is just like a tree sprung from the divine root. Nature is like its stem, and all the aspects of nature are like the branches, the leaves, the fruit, and the flowers, and from this tree again the same seed is produced - the human soul - which was the first cause of the tree. This seed is man, his spirit, and as God constitutes the whole universe within Himself, being single, so man constitutes within himself the whole universe, as His miniature. Therefore neither can God be anything other than what He is, nor can man, for the very reason that He is one and at the same time He is all. This applies to both. Neither can man be reincarnated nor can God.

...In our dreams all the inhabitants of our mind resurrect, forming a world within ourselves. We see things and beings, a friend, a foe, an animal, a bird, and they come from nowhere, but are created out of our own selves. This shows that the mind Or an individual constitutes a world in itself, which is created and destroyed by the conscious or unconscious action of the will, which has two aspects, intention and accident. We experience ourselves in this world of mind even while awake, but the contrast between the world within and without makes the world without concrete and the world within non-concrete. Someone may ask: "If all that we see in the dream are we ourselves, then why do we see, even in the dream, ourselves as an identity, separate from all other things before us in the dream?" The answer is: "Because the soul is deluded by our external form, and this picture it recognizes as I, and all other images and forms manifesting before it in the dream stand in contrast to this I; therefore the soul recognizes them as others than I."

THE SUPPLEMENTARY (Dutch) PAPERS - MYSTICISM IV - Man, the Seed of God

GAYAN 129 - BOULA -088 - Before trying to know the justice of God, one must oneself become just.

In order to judge, our vision must become as wide as the universe; then we might have a little glimpse of the Justice which is perfect in itself. But when we try to judge every action by limiting God and by attaching the responsibility of every action to God, we confuse our faith, and by our own fault we begin to disbelieve. The error is in man's nature; from childhood we think all we do and say is just and fair, and so when man thinks of God he has his own conception, and by that he tries to judge God and His justice; if he is forgiving, he tries to overlook God's apparent injustice, and to find goodness in God and to see the limitation of man. This is better, but in the end man will realize that every movement is controlled and directed from One Source, and that Source is the Perfection of Love, Justice, and Wisdom, a Source where nothing lacks. But it is so difficult for man to have a perfect conception of the God-Ideal, and he cannot begin in a first lesson to conceive of God as perfect. So the wise must be tolerant of all the forms in which souls picture their God.

THE UNITY OF RELIGIOUS IDEALS - THE GOD IDEAL - The Kingship of God

GAYAN 130 - BOULA -089 - To whom the soul truly belongs, to Him in the end it returns.

Just as the body which is made of clay is drawn to the earth, so the soul which belongs to the spirit is drawn to the spirit. 'But', one may say, 'we can see the body drawn to the earth, we can see all things of the earth drawn to the earth, but we do not see the law of gravitation working in the soul.' Actually we do see it, but we deny it, because we do not look at it in that way. For there is a dissatisfaction, a discontent, in every soul. A man may be in a palace or in a cottage, but no matter what condition he lives in there is an innate yearning and longing which even he himself does not recognize. One thinks today that one longs for money, tomorrow for a position, for fame or name; one goes from one thing to another. It just goes on, and when in the end one has reached one's object one wants something else. It is the law of gravitation, that yearning towards the Spirit, the Sun, which is at the back of it. That is why in ancient times people worshipped the sun god as a symbol of the sun within us, the sun which cannot be seen by our eyes, but which is the source and goal of all beings, from which we have come and to which we are drawn. As it is said in the Qur'an, 'From God we all come and to Him we have to return'. That means: there is a spirit, the spirit of all things, the essence of life from which we come and towards which we are drawn.

THE ALCHEMY OF HAPPINESS - Man, the Master of His Destiny (2)

GAYAN 131 - BOULA -090 - In order to realize the divine perfection man must lose his imperfect self.

The whole aim of the Sufi is, by the thought of God, to cover his imperfect self even from his own eyes, and that moment when God is before him and not his own self is the moment of perfect bliss to him. My Murshid, Abu Hashim Madani, once said that there is only one virtue and one sin for a soul on this path: virtue when he is conscious of God, and sin when he is not. No explanation can fully describe the truth of this except the experience of the contemplative to whom, when he is conscious of God, it is as if a window facing heaven were open, and to whom, when he is conscious of the self, the experience is the opposite; for all the tragedy of life is caused by being conscious of the self. All pain and depression is caused by this, and anything that can take away the thought of the self helps to a certain extent to relieve man from pain, but God- consciousness gives perfect relief.

SUFI TEACHINGS - THE PRIVILEGE OF BEING HUMAN - Selflessness - Inkisar

GAYAN 132 - BOULA -091 - When the cry of the disciple has reached a certain pitch, the teacher comes to answer it.

One day I was walking in a city and met a dervish with a wonderful personality. He was dressed in a patched robe, but his speech, his voice, his thought, his movements, his atmosphere, were all most winning. At that time I was very young in the pursuit of philosophy. Youth is a time when pride has full play. So as we were walking along, and he called me 'Murshid', I was very glad. He addressed me as Murshid every time he spoke to me! Presently we met another person, who seemed to be without any education, without any knowledge of philosophy or religion or anything out of the way, but he called him 'Murshid' too. My pride was hurt, especially when next he came across a policeman whom he also called 'Murshid'. So then I asked my teacher what could be the meaning of all this, and he said, 'Your dervish showed you the first step towards recognizing God: to recognize all beings as your teacher. A foolish person can teach you, a wise person, a learned person, a student, a pious or a wicked person, even a little child; everyone can teach you something. Therefore have this attitude towards everybody, then it may be said that you recognize God.'

There is a Hindu saying, 'When the chela is ready, the guru appears', which means that when you are ready to discern it, you will find your teacher beside you.

THE VISION OF GOD AND MAN - The Divine Presence

GAYAN 133 - BOULA -092 - The best way of living is to live a natural life.

No doubt very often man does not live a natural life. That is, his business or profession or responsibility holds him. Some work or some thought for the needs of the body, for bread and butter or any other everyday need holds him and absorbs the whole of his thoughts, so that he becomes useless for the discovery of the beauty and joy and happiness of life. Hence, as we see around us today, life is becoming so difficult and so full of anxiety and trouble and responsibility. From morning till evening man is just loaded with his responsibilities, toil day and night.

Art and Music IV – The Divinity of Art

GAYAN 134 - BOULA -093 - Do not take the example of another as an excuse for your wrongdoing.

Christ's teaching that man should be kind and charitable, and that of all other teachers who showed humanity the right path, seems to differ from what one sees from the practical point of view which is called common sense; yet according to uncommon sense, in other words super-sense, it is perfectly practical. If you wish to be charitable, think of the comfort of another; if you wish to be happy, think of the happiness of your fellow-men; if you wish to be treated well, treat others well; if you wish that people should be just and fair to you, first be so yourself to set an example.

THE ART OF PERSONALITY - The Law of Beneficence - Our Dealings with Our Fellow-men

GAYAN 135 - BOULA -094 - People who are difficult to deal with are difficult with themselves.

There is a great deal of pessimism in all parts of the world, and the more civilized the country, the greater the pessimism and the greater the strife. It is not that the support of the Unknown has been taken away from man, but life is so difficult today that, far from his depending upon the unknown, it is difficult for even the idea of the unknown to reach him.

When we think of the hundreds and thousands of men at this time not knowing from one day to the next what they should do, anxious about how they can get on in life, we see that there is no progress. A progress that can make a person worried and anxious so that he cannot depend upon life, how can we call it progress? Progress means ease, relief, peace, happiness, less strife, less struggle; that is progress. Progress does not mean greater struggle, greater uneasiness, greater anxiety, and greater worry.

IN AN EASTERN ROSE GARDEN - Dependence

GAYAN 136 - BOULA -095 - All situations of life are tests to bring out the real and the false.

Many in this world seem to be confused about false and true, but there comes a moment when one can see the difference between false and true without any difficulty, because false cannot stand longer than a moment all the tests that come from all sides. It is the real gold that stands all tests - so it is with true holiness. Holiness is enduring, knowing, forgiving, understanding, and yet it stands beyond all things, above all things. It is unbreakable, unshakable; it is beauty, it is power, and it is divinity when it reaches its perfection.

SUFI TEACHINGS - THE PRIVILEGE OF BEING HUMAN - HOLINESS

GAYAN 137 - BOULA -096 - The true seeker will never stop half-way; either he finds or he loses himself entirely.

What one values in life is worth striving for, whether material or spiritual gain. Those who weigh the object that they wish to attain with the difficulty or the cost that is required for its attainment neither know the full value of the object nor do they know the way of attainment. The first principle that one must learn in the path is to esteem the object of attainment more than the cost one has to pay for it.

Even if the object be not of the value of its cost, still the law of attainment is to attain a desired object at every cost. The great ones who have achieved great things in life have achieved in this way. Nothing in the world could take them away from what they wished to achieve. Even a life's cost they considered too small a price for the object of attainment. When this spirit directs the spiritual path, man arrives at having God-communion, for the true pursuer will never go halfway. Either he gains, or he loses himself.

Githa II - THE PATH OF ATTAINMENT - Attaining Perfection

GAYAN 138 - BOULA -097 - It is sympathy rather than good food that will satisfy your guest.

The heart may be likened to soil. Soil may be fertile or a barren desert, but the soil which is fertile is that which bears fruit. It is that which is chosen by living beings to dwell in, although many are lost in the soil of the desert, and lead in it a life of grief and loneliness. Man has both in him, for he is the final manifestation. He may let his heart be a desert, where everyone abides hungry and thirsty, or he may make it a fertile and fruitful land, where food is provided for hungry souls, the children of the earth, strong or weak, rich or poor, who always hunger for love and sympathy.

SPIRITUAL LIBERTY – METAPHYSICS - The Destiny of the Soul - The Radiance of the Soul (2)

GAYAN 139 - BOULA -098 - The hereafter is the continuation of the same life in another sphere.

It would not be an exaggeration if one called the mind a world; it is the world that man makes and in which he will make his life in the hereafter, as a spider weaves his web to live in. Once a person thinks of this problem he begins to see the value of the spiritual path. The soul learns on the path in which it is trained not to be owned by the mind, but to own it; not to become a slave of the mind, but to master it.

THE SOUL, WHENCE AND WHITHER? -M anifestation

GAYAN 140 - BOULA -099 - The man who is not courageous enough to take risks will accomplish nothing in life.

The one who treads the path must be willing to risk the difficulties of the path; to be sincere, faithful, truthful, undoubting, not pessimistic or skeptical, otherwise with all his efforts he will not reach his aim. He must come whole-heartedly, or else he should not come at all. Half-heartedness is of no value.

THE PATH OF INITIATION - SUFI MYSTICISM - Repose

GAYAN 141 - BOULA -100 - Not only man but even God is displeased by self-assertion.

Inkisar, in the terms of the Sufis, means selflessness. The psychology of human nature is such that man feels inclined to hit every head that is raised. Not only man, but all living creatures have that tendency. To protect themselves from that, many intelligent creatures in the lower creation make holes in the earth, to live there, hiding themselves from the beasts and birds of prey. No sooner do they raise they heads from their holes than they are caught by their enemies, who thirst for their blood. As humankind is evolved, man does not immediately hit the raised head, but he cannot keep from being agitated at the sight of it.

Understanding this mystery of human nature and studying the secret of the whole life, the Sufi has traced that spirit in its essence, belonging to the Source of all things. He calls that spirit Kabir, or Kibriyy, the Ego, or Egoistic. It has taught the Sufi a moral, that not only man but even God is displeased by self-assertion. And the manner that he adopts in order not to arouse that agitating spirit he calls Inkisar, meaning selflessness.

In theory it is a small thing, in practice it is a great art. It is an art which wants a great deal of study of human nature, it requires careful observation and constant practice. This art teaches to take precautions before every activity in speech or in actions so as to cause least disturbance to human feeling. It is the thorough study of human susceptibility and practice of delicate manner which teaches man Inkisar. The further he progresses the more his sense becomes keen; therefore he finds more and more mistakes in his own life as he goes forward in this path. This subject is so delicate that one does not only commit a fault by showing pride or conceit but even in expressing modesty or humility. Inkisar wants a great delicacy of sense. One must be able to see the lights and shades produced by every action and word one does or says. And once a person has mastered this art he has mastered the same art which Christ promised to the fishermen, saying "Come hither, I will make you Fishers of Men."

The Sufi gives more importance to this subject than a yogi, for the way of the yogi is asceticism. The way of the Sufi is the development of humanity in nature. But according to the prophetic point of view the only way of pleasing God is Inkisar, which is greater than so-called goodness. A good person proud of his goodness turns his pearls into pebbles. A bad person, full of remorse for his faults, may turn his pebbles into jewels. Selflessness is not only pleasing to man but it is pleasing to God.

ESOTERIC PAPERS - GATHA III - MORALS - Inkisar (Selflessness)

GAYAN 142 - BOULA -101 - Those who live in the presence of God look to Him for guidance at every move they make.

There used to be courtiers in the ancient times in India who at every moment would know the state of mind and the attitude of the king, even to such an extent that very often everything was arranged as the king liked without him having uttered one word about it. There were nine courtiers attached to the court of Akbar; every one of them knew the state of mind of the Emperor at every moment. The Sufi, whose duty in the world is to live in the presence of God and who recognizes His presence in all His creatures, His personality especially in man, he fulfils his duty of a courtier with every man. A person who lives as dead as a stone among his surroundings does not know whom he has pleased, whom he has displeased, who expects of him thought, consideration, who asks of him sympathy or service, who needs him in his trouble or difficulty.

GATHA III – INSIGHT - Number 3 - The Expression and the Idea

GAYAN 143 - BOULA -102 - It is not by self-realization that man realizes God; it is by God-realization that man realizes self.

Often one wonders what the word holy means. Sometimes people understand by it spiritual, pious, good, pure, religious. But none of these words can fully explain the meaning of the word holy. Holy is the next degree to pious. God-realizing is pious, self-realizing is holy. The first step to self-realization is God-realization; it is not by self-realization that man realizes God, it is by God-realization that man realizes self.

Sufi Teachings - THE PRIVILEGE OF BEING HUMAN - Holiness

GAYAN 144 - BOULA -103 - If you wish to follow the path of saints, first learn forgiveness.

In order to learn forgiveness man must learn tolerance first. And there are people whom man cannot forgive. It is not that he must not forgive, but it is difficult, beyond his power to forgive, and in that case the first thing he can do is to forget. The first step towards forgiveness is to forget. It is true that the finer the man is the more he is subject to be hurt by the smallest disturbance that can produce irritation and inharmony in the atmosphere. A person who gives and takes hurts is capable of living an easy and comfortable life in the world. Life is difficult for the fine person, for he cannot give back what he receives in the way of hurt, and he can feel it more than the average person.

Many seek protection from all hurting influences by building some wall around themselves. But the canopy over the earth is so high that a wall cannot be built high enough, and the only thing one can do is to live in the midst of all inharmonious influences, to strengthen his will-power and to bear all things, yet keeping the fineness of character and a nobleness of manner together with an ever-living heart.

To become cold with the coldness of the world is weakness, and to become broken by the hardness of the world is feebleness, but to live in the world and yet to keep above the world is like walking on the water. There are two essential duties for the man of wisdom and love; that is to keep the love in our nature ever increasing and expanding and to strengthen the will so that the heart may not be easily broken. Balance is ideal in life; man must be fine and yet strong, man must be loving and yet powerful.

GATHA II – Morals - Forgiveness

GAYAN 145 - BOULA -104 - Be sparing of your words if you wish them to be powerful.

Sparing of words is the secret of sages. Most troubles and pains in life can be avoided by the economy of words. Silence is taught in every school of inner cult, especially in Sufism; which, plainly speaking, is quietism. Besides, when a person says one word, to express his ideas, instead of ten words, that one word becomes equal to a hundred words in power. The yes or no of a serious and silent person has more weight and has a greater influence then a hundred words of a talkative person.

Sangatha I

GAYAN 146 - BOULA -105 - As the flower is the forerunner of the fruit, so man's childhood is the promise of his life.

The beginning of a person's life is of greater importance than the latter part, because it is in childhood that the road is made for him to go forward in life. And who makes the road? It is the guardian of the child who makes the road for it. If that road is not made and the guardian is asleep, then the child has great difficulty when it is grown-up. School education and college education will come afterwards; but the education of the greatest importance in the life of a soul comes in its infancy.

THE ART OF PERSONALITY – EDUCATION " The Education of the Infant"

GAYAN 147 - BOULA -106 - The gardener uses roses in the flower-bed and thorns in making the hedge.

The finer an ego becomes the less it jars upon others. In the different degrees of evolution of man one sees this gradual development of the ego. There are people who seem to have no thorns; and yet they have a thorn which makes itself felt in the presence of another, it is their ego. Others are like the rose with its softness, beauty and fragrance. No doubt not everyone is a rose, but everyone desires the rose and not the thorn. The best training is to try to turn this thorny ego into a rose. It is very hard. And the finer and the more evolved the ego the harder life becomes for man. The higher and the more refined you are the greater trials you will have to go through in life; the more sensitive you become the more you will have to suffer. The thorn cannot hurt another thorn, but the slightest thing can hurt a rose. It is not surprising if an ego that has become a flower does not wish to live among thorns, but that is its destiny, and in spite of all sufferings it is preferable to be a rose rather than a thorn.

GATHA I - MORALS - "What is the Ego?"

GAYAN 148 - BOULA -107 - Love which manifests as tolerance, as forgiveness, that love it is which heals the wounds of the heart.

The work of the Sufi, therefore, is to stop and think before being annoyed and see what is the matter with a person, to find out what is at the back of it, to find out where is the sore, where is the wound which is hidden. Then his work is to wash that wound with the water of life and then try to heal it. What it needs is cooling, not irritating, which is mostly done by the ignorant. Annoyed with the wounded, they give back a little more irritation. No, it is cooling which is required; a word of love, of affection, a word of consoling can cool its irritation. Love which manifests as tolerance, as forgiveness, that love it is which heals even the wounds of the heart. Only patience is required and a continual work with faith and confidence in the divine power of love.

Esoteric Papers - Sangatha 1 - TASAWWUF - METAPHYSICS

To become cold with the coldness of the world is weakness, and to become broken by the hardness of the world is feebleness, but to live in the world and yet to keep above the world is like walking on the water. There are two essential duties for the man of wisdom and love; that is to keep the love in our nature ever increasing and expanding and to strengthen the will so that the heart may not be easily broken. Balance is ideal in life; man must be fine [refined] and yet strong, man must be loving and yet powerful.

Hazrat Inayat Khan Esoteric Papers - Gatha 2 – Morals – Forgiveness

GAYAN 149 - BOULA -108 - The greatest love in life is often that which is covered under indifference.

As our self-identification migrates towards higher states of being we become more loving though outwardly we may appear less passionate because much of our life then is lived inwardly rather than through our body.

The soul of the spiritually-inclined man is constantly thirsty, looking for something, seeking for something; and when it thinks it has found it, the thing turns out to be different; and so life becomes a continual struggle and disappointment. And the result is that instead of taking interest in all things, a kind of indifference is produced; and yet in the real character of this soul there is no indifference, there is only love.

Although life seems to make this soul indifferent, it cannot really become indifferent; and it is this state working through this life that gives a man a certain feeling, to which only a Hindu word is applicable, no other language having a word which can render this particular meaning so adequately. The Hindus call it Vairagya from which the term Vairagi has come. Vairagi means a person who has become indifferent; and yet indifference is not the word for it. It describes a person who has lost the value in his eyes of all that attracts the human being. It is no more attractive to him;it no more enslaves him. He may still be interested in all things of this life, but is not bound to them. The first feeling of the Vairagi is to turn away from everything. He shows the nature of the deer, which runs away at the flutter of a leaf; for he becomes sensitive and convinced of the disappointing results that come from the limitation and changeableness of life in the world.

Hurt within, he becomes sensitive, and the first thing that occurs to his mind is to fly [away], to hide somewhere, to go into a cave in the mountains, or into the forest where he will meet no one. No affair of this world, no relation, no friendship, no wealth, no rank, position or comfort, nothing holds him. And yet that does not mean that he in any way lacks what is called love or kindness, for if ever he lives in this world it is only out of love. He is not interested in the world and it is only love that keeps him here, the love which does not express itself any more in the way of attachment, but only in the way of kindness, forgiveness, generosity, service, consideration, sympathy, helpfulness, in any way that it can; never expecting a return from the world, but ever doing all that it can, pitying the conditions, knowing the limitations of life and its continual changeability.

The Inner Life – The Angel-Man

GAYAN 150 - BOULA -109 - Indifference and independence are the two wings which enable the soul to fly.

Selflessness does not only beautify one's personality, giving grace to one's word and manner, but it also gives a dignity and a power, together with a spirit of independence which is the real sign of a sage. It is selfishness which often produces humiliation in one's spirit, taking away the intoxication which enriches the soul.

Independence and indifference, which are as the two wings which enable the soul to fly, spring from the spirit of selflessness. The moment the spirit of selflessness has begun to sparkle in the heart of man, he shows in his word and action a nobility which nothing earthly - neither power nor riches can give.

There are many ideas which intoxicate man, many feelings there are which act upon the soul as wine, but there is no stronger wine than the wine of selflessness. It is a might and it is a pride that no worldly rank can give. To become something is a limitation, whatever one may become.

Sufi Teachings - THE PRIVILEGE OF BEING HUMAN - Selflessness - Inkisar

GAYAN 151 - BOULA -110 - To offend a low person is like throwing a stone in the mud and getting splashed.

For God is love. What do we expect from love? Grace. The grace of God is the love of God, love of God manifesting in innumerable blessings, blessings which are known and unknown to us. Human beings live on earth in their shells, mostly unaware of all the privileges of life, and therefore ungrateful to the Giver of them. In order to see the grace of God one must open one's eyes, raising one's head from the little world that one makes around oneself, and thus see above and below, right and left, before and behind, the grace of God reaching one from everywhere in abundance. If one tries to thank, one might thank for thousands of years and it would never be enough. But if one looks in one's own little shell one does not find the grace of God; what one finds is miseries, troubles, difficulties, injustice, hard-heartedness, coldness of the world, all ugliness from everywhere.

Because when a person looks down he sees mud, but when he looks up there are beautiful stars and planets. It only depends which way one looks, upwards or downwards. What is this mortal world? What is this physical existence? What is this life of changes? If it were not for belief, what use is it all? Something which is changing, something which is not reliable, something which is liable to destruction. Therefore it is not only for the sake of truth, but for life itself that one must find belief in oneself, develop it, nurture it, allow it to grow every moment of one's life, that it may culminate in faith. It is that faith which is the mystery of life, the secret of salvation.

HEALING AND THE MIND WORLD – HEALTH

GAYAN 152 - BOULA -111 - The self-made man is greater than the man who depends upon another to make him.

By independence is meant self-sufficiency: that what they can get from their own self they must not look for outside. That is the principal motive of those who are striving for self-attainment, because it is the means of overcoming the sorrows and troubles and woes of this life. One sees a constant striving in the life of the adepts to make themselves independent of outside things as much as possible. On the other hand worldly people think it progress if they can become daily more dependent on others. Every step we take is towards dependence; and the more we depend upon others, the more we think we are progressing. In the end we come to such a stage that for what the soul needs, what the mind needs, what the body needs, we depend upon others. And, not knowing this, we teach the child to put something else instead of its little hand in its mouth. In reality, it is natural for an infant to put its hand in its mouth; and that is the purest and the cleanest toy that it can have to play with.

THE ART OF PERSONALITY - EDUCATION - The Education of the Infant

GAYAN 153 - BOULA -112 - False politeness is like imitation jewelry, and false kisses are like imitation flowers.

...It is not simple to be thoughtful, it is not easy to be considerate. It requires a great deal of delicacy, skill; one must know the art of approaching another. And the other point of view of the Sufi is still more difficult, and that is to maintain sincerity, to maintain faithfulness, to maintain truth. False flattery, polished politeness, made-up refinement, these things are against the Sufi's ideal.

Esoteric papers - SANGATHA I

GAYAN 154 - BOULA -113 - The unsociable person is a burden to society.

He who perceives this realizes, 'What I have taken from another, I have lost; what I have given to another, I have gained. Whatever good I have done to another is my gain, and whatever good another has done to me is my loss.' The kindness, the service, the love and sympathy that another has given are all lost when the giver is gone; it could only be there so long as he was there. But deeds of goodness, of kindness, of consideration done to another, will remain with him who does them both here and hereafter.

[Vol. 7] IN AN EASTERN ROSE GARDEN - The Desire of Nations

GAYAN 155 - BOULA -114 - Divinity is human perfection and humanity is divine limitation.

There are those who see divinity in Christ. They say, 'Christ was God, Christ is divine.' And there are others who say, 'Christ was a man, one like all of us.' When we come to look at this question, we see that the man who says, 'Christ is divine' is not wrong. If there is any divinity shown it is in man. And the one who says, 'Christ was a man' is not wrong either. In the garb of man Christ manifested. Those who do not want Christ to be a man, drag down the greatness and sacredness of the human being by their argument, by saying that man is made of sin, and by separating Christ from humanity. But there is nothing wrong in calling Christ God or divine. It is in man that divine perfection is to be seen. It is in man that divinity is manifested. There are Christ's own words, 'I am Alpha and Omega'. Many close their eyes to this, but the one who said, 'I am Alpha and Omega' existed also before the coming of Jesus, and the one who says, 'first and last', must exist also after Jesus.

In the words of Christ there is the idea of perfection. He identified himself with that spirit of which he was conscious. Christ was not conscious of his human part, but of his perfect being when he said, 'I am Alpha and Omega'. He did not identify himself here with his being known as Jesus. He identified himself with that spirit of perfection which lived before Jesus and will continue to live to the end of the world, for eternity. If this is so then what does it matter if some say, 'Buddha inspired us', and millions are inspired by Buddha? It is only a difference of name. It is all Alpha and Omega. If others say Moses, or Mohammed, or Krishna, what difference does it make? Where did the inspiration come from? Was it not from one and the same spirit? Was it not the same Alpha and Omega of which Jesus Christ was conscious? Whoever gives the message to the world, whatever illuminated human beings have raised thousands and millions of people in the world, they cannot but be that same Christ whom the one calls by this name and the other by another name. Yet human ignorance always causes wars and disasters on account of different religions, different communities, because of the importance they give to their own conception, their own corrupted conception which differs from another. Even now on the one hand there is materialism and on the other there is bigotry. What is necessary today is to find the first and last religion, to come to the message of Christ, to divine wisdom, so that we may recognize wisdom in all its different forms, in whatever form it has been given to humanity. It does not matter if it is Buddhism, Islam, Judaism, Zoroastrianism, Hinduism. It is one wisdom, that call of the Spirit which awakens man to rise above limitation and to reach perfection.

THE ALCHEMY OF HAPPINESS - From Limitation to Perfection (1)

GAYAN 156 - BOULA -115 - The wise show their admiration by respect.

He is really respectful who gives respect, but he who looks for respect from another is greedy, he will always be disappointed. Even to give respect in order to get respect in return is a kind of business. Those who reach a spiritual realization will only give respect generously, without thinking for one moment of getting it in return. When one sincerely gives respect to anyone, not for show but from the feeling of one's heart, a happiness rises from it, which is the product only of the respectful attitude and which nothing else can give. There are many to whom one is indebted for their help, kindness, protection, support, for their service or assistance, and there is nothing material in the world, neither gold nor silver, which can express the gratitude so fully as a real respect can. Remember, therefore, that for something that you cannot pay back in silver or gold you can only make return in one way, and that is by humbly offering respect.

Gatha III – Morals – Adab (Respect) 1

GAYAN 157 - BOULA -116 - Many admit the truth to themselves, but few confess it to others.

The truth is that the soul of the mystic is a dancing soul. It has realized that inner law, it has fathomed that mystery for which souls long and in the joy of that mystery the whole life of the mystic becomes a mystery. You may see the mystic twenty times a day, and twenty times he will have a different expression. Every time his mood is different; and yet his outward mood may not at all be his inner mood. The mystic is an example of God's mystery in the form of man.

The fifth form in which a person who lives the inner life appears is a strange form, a form which very few people can understand. He puts on the mask of innocence outwardly to such an extent that those who do not understand may easily consider him unbalanced, peculiar, or strange. He does not mind about it, for the reason that it is only his shield. If he were to admit before humanity the power that he has, thousands of people would go after him, and he would not have one moment to live his inner life. The enormous power that he possesses governs inwardly lands and countries, controlling them and keeping them safe from disasters such as floods and plagues, and also wars; keeping harmony in the country or in the place in which he lives; and all this is done by his silence, by his constant realization of the inner life. To a person who lacks deep insight he will seem a strange being. In the language of the East he is called Madzub. That same idea was known to the ancient Greeks and traces of it are still in existence in some places, but mostly in the East. There are souls to be found today in the East, living in this garb of a selfrealized man who shows no trace outwardly of philosophy or mysticism or religion, or any particular morals; and yet his presence is a battery of power, his glance most inspiring, there is a commanding expression in his looks; and if he ever speaks, his word is the promise of God. What he says is truth; but he rarely speaks a word, it is difficult to get a word out of him; but once he has spoken, what he says is done.

There is no end to the variety of the outward appearance of spiritual souls in life; but at the same time there is no better way of living in this world and yet living the inner life than being oneself, outwardly and inwardly. Whatever be one's profession, work, or part in the outer life, to perform it sincerely and truthfully, to fulfil one's mission in the outer life thoroughly; at the same time keeping the inner realization that the outer life, whatever be one's occupation, should reflect the inner realization of truth.

THE WAY OF ILLUMINATION - THE INNER LIFE - The Five Different Kinds of Spiritual Souls

GAYAN 158 - BOULA -117 - It is the twist of thought that is the curl of the Beloved.

In the Sufi literature, which is known to the world as the Persian literature, there is much talk about the "curls of the Beloved," and many have often wondered what it means. The curl is a symbol of something which is curved and round. The curve denotes the twist in the thought of wisdom. Very often a straight word of truth hits upon the head harder than a hammer. That shows that truth alone is not sufficient, the truth must be made into wisdom. And what is wisdom? Wisdom is the twisted truth. As raw food cannot be digested, and therefore it is cooked, although raw food is more natural than cooked food, so the straight truth is more natural, but is not digestible, it needs to be made into wisdom.

And why is it called the Beloved's curl? Because truth is of God, the Divine Beloved, and truth is God, and that twist given to His Own Being, which is truth, amplifies the divine beauty, as the curl is considered to be the sign of beauty. Then what is not straight is a puzzle. So wisdom is a puzzle to the ordinary mind. Besides, the curl hangs low down; so the heavenly beauty which is wisdom is manifested on earth. In other words, if someone wishes to see the beauty of the heavenly Beloved he may see it in wisdom.

Wisdom is traced not only in the human being, but even in the beasts and birds, in their affection, in their instinct. Very often it is most difficult for man to imitate fully the work which birds do in weaving their nests. Even the insects do wonderful work in preparing a little abode for themselves which is beyond man's art and skill. Besides this, if one studies nature, after keen observation and some contemplation upon it one will find that there is perfect wisdom behind it. Once man has thought on the subject, he can never, however materialistic he may be, deny the existence of God. Man's individuality is proved by his wisdom and distinguished by comparison. The wisdom of God, being perfect, is unintelligible to man. The glass of water cannot imagine how much water there is in the sea. If man would realize his limitation he would never dare question the existence of God.

The symbol of the curl also signifies something which is there, attractive, and yet a puzzle, a riddle. One loves it, admires it, and yet one cannot fathom its length and breadth. It is that which is wisdom. Its surface is human, but its depth is divine. It could be hell or heaven, and the knowledge of it can enable man always to keep in touch with his heaven, instead of waiting for it till the hereafter.

Gatha II – Symbology - The Curl of the Beloved

GAYAN 159 - BOULA -118 - Do not accept that which you cannot return, for the balance of life is in reciprocity.

The first degree is the law of reciprocity. It is in this degree that one learns the meaning of justice. The law of reciprocity is to give and to take sympathy, and all that sympathy can give and take. It is according to this law that the religion and the laws of the state and of the community are made. The idea of this law is that you may not take from me more than you could give me: I will not give you more than I could take from you. It is fair business: you love me, I can love you; you hate me, I can hate you. And according to this law if a person has not learned the just measure of give and take, he has not practised justice. He may be innocent, he may be loving, but he has no common sense, he is not practical.

The danger in this law is that a person may value most what he himself does and may diminish the value of what is done by another. But the one who gives more than he takes is progressing towards the next grade.

It is easy for us to say that this is a very hard and fast law. But at the same time it is the most difficult thing to live in this world and to avoid it. One must ask a practical man, a man with common sense, if it is possible to live in this world and not to observe this law of give and take. If the people of the world did no better than keep this law properly there would be much less trouble in this world. It is no use thinking that people will become saints or sages or great beings; if they became just it would already be something."

THE ALCHEMY OF HAPPINESS- The Law of Action

GAYAN 160 - BOULA -119 - Those whom their individuality fails seek refuge in community.

Sufis in all ages, mystics of India, Persia, and Egypt have considered the awakening of the heart quality to be the principal thing in life. For all the virtues that the priest can teach and prescribe, the virtues that one is told to practice in life, come naturally when the heart opens. Then one need not learn virtue, virtue becomes one's own. All virtues as taught by people-how long do they last? If there is any virtue it must come by itself. spirituality is natural. And if animals and birds can feel spiritual exaltation, why not we? But we do not live a natural life. We have tried in our civilization, in our life, to be as far removed from nature and natural life as possible, breathing an artificial atmosphere to withstand climatic influences, eating food that we have prepared and improvised, turning it into something quite different from what nature had made and given us.

Besides that, the deeper we go into the life of the community, the more we find that we are not on the track as we ought to be. We seem to have lost our individuality. We have called it progress—a progress towards a certain condition. And there we begin to feel that we are in a maze. Now has come the time-and more and more so every day-that thoughtful people, wise people who are just and honest realize, "We are not progressing, we are in a maze and we are looking for the door. "

(Vol. 14) THE SMILING FOREHEAD - Spirituality, the Tuning of the Heart

GAYAN 161 - BOULA -120 - Taking the path of disharmony is like entering the mouth of the dragon.

...It is for this reason that to some extent life becomes easy for a mystic to deal with. For he knows every heart, every nature, whereas those who are untouched by the mystic's secret suffer from their difficulties both at home and outside. They dread the presence of people they do not understand; they want to run away from them, and if they cannot escape they feel as if they' are in the mouth of a dragon; and perhaps they are placed in a situation which cannot easily be changed. The consequence is that they heap confusion upon confusion. And how very often one sees that when two people do not understand one another, a third comes and helps them to do so, and the light thrown upon them causes greater harmony! The mystic says: whether it be agreeable or disagreeable, if you are in a certain situation, make the best of it; try to understand how to deal with such a situation. Therefore a life without such understanding is like a dark room which contains everything you wish: it is all there, but there is no light.

THE PATH OF INITIATION - SUFI MYSTICISM - The Nature and Work of A Mystic

GAYAN 162 - BOULA -121 - **Satan comes in most beautiful garbs to hide from man's eyes his highest ideal.**

The chief point in the teachings of holy Zarathustra is the path of goodness; and he separates goodness from badness, calling God the All-good and Satan the All-bad. According to this point of view of the Master, God was, as He is always, the Ideal of worship; and nothing but good can be praised, and none but the good worshiped, and all which is bad naturally leads man astray and veils from his eyes all good. The spirit of evil was personified by the Master, as it had already been personified by the ancients, as Satan.

As the point of view makes all the difference in every teaching, so it made a difference in this teaching of Zoroaster. So that many, instead of taking the true spirit of this idea, have drawn a line between good and bad, and produced, so to speak, two gods: God, the All-good, and Satan, the Lord of Evil; which helped morally to a certain extent, but deprived many, who could not catch the real spirit of the Master, of the realization of God, the Only Being. The good God is named by Zoroaster Ahura Mazda, the first word meaning literally 'indestructible', the next word meaning 'supreme God'.

The Unity of Religious Ideals – Prophets and Religions - Zarathustra – The Teachings of Holy Zarathustra

GAYAN 163 - BOULA -122 - Life is an opportunity, and it is a great pity if man realizes this when it is too late.

How few in this world know what an effect it makes on one's personality, talking ill of another; what influence it has on one's soul! Man's self within is not only like a dome where everything he says has an echo, but that echo is creative and productive of what has been said. Every good and bad thing in one's life one develops by taking interest in it. Every fault one has, as long as it is small, one does not notice it; and so one develops the fault till it results in a disappointment. Life is so precious, and it becomes more and more valuable as one becomes more prudent; and every moment of life can be used for a much greater purpose. Life is an opportunity and the more one realizes this, the more one will make the best of this opportunity which life offers.

CHARACTER AND PERSONALITY - Character-Building – Chapter IX

GAYAN 164 - BOULA -123 - Behind us all is one spirit and one life; how then can we be happy if our neighbor is sad?

In the history of the world this lesson has been taught not once, but a thousand times. As long as a nation works for the interest of God and humanity it will always be prosperous, but as soon as it uses religion in order to exalt the national ideal, then it falls down like a house of cards. We can see this in the history of Hinduism, in the history of Islam, in the history of the European religious sects. If there is the wish to rise, the ideal must be high; if there is the desire to fall, let the ideal be low. It is the love of the earth that will attract man to the earth; but it is the love of heaven that will attract him to heaven. It is as the Bible says, 'Where your treasure is, there will your heart be also'. When the whole of man's ideal in life is his degree of education, his success in trade, all towards exalting the self, the individuality, then he is descending and not ascending. He is selfish as an individual, he becomes selfish as a nation, then as a race, and at last there is warfare; the racial ideal expresses its selfishness in great wars. Even people of the same nation will fight one another.

The same thing develops further when it appears between classes and parties, between labor and capital, the higher against the lower. All of them have a wrong ideal; selfishness is allowed to rule instead of the higher ideal.

And even that is not the end. The next thing which develops is disharmony of sex. Families become inharmonious because of the selfish ideal; the husband wants his own way; the wife wants her own way. The husband thinks, 'As long as I am happy, that is all that is necessary'. In whatever direction you may journey in life you will meet this tendency. Selfishness may begin with the thought, 'As long as my country is benefited, that benefits me'; and then it will narrow down to, 'If my family is benefited, if we become wealthy and have desirable things, that is sufficient for the present!' And then it narrows down again, 'For my father, or mother, or wife or children,' until it ends in, 'Nothing matters as long as I am happy myself'. Man has now become cold, ignorant, and blind to the law that life depends on the happiness of those with whom we live. The whole of life is one. In all these different names and manifestations life is one. The true thought is, 'If my wife is not happy, if my children, my neighbors, my servants are not happy, how can I ever be happy?' An insult given to someone will one day return.

IN AN EASTERN ROSE GARDEN– The Desire of Nations

GAYAN 165 - BOULA -124 - The human heart is the home of the soul, and upon this home the comfort and power of the soul depend.

The nature of the memory is to hold an impression, agreeable or disagreeable, and therefore a person holds a thought in mind, whether it is beneficial to him or not, without knowing the result which will come from it. It is like a child who holds a rattle in his hand and hits his head with the rattle and cries with the pain, and yet does not throw the rattle away. There are many who keep in their mind a thought of illness or a thought of unkindness done to them by someone and suffer from it, yet now knowing what it is that makes them suffer so, nor understanding the reason of their suffering.

They go on suffering and yet hold on in memory the very source of suffering. Memory must be one's obedient servant; when it is a master then life becomes difficult. A person who cannot throw away from his memory what he does not desire to keep in mind is like a person who has a safe, but the key of that safe he has lost. He can put in money, but he cannot take it out. All faculties in man become invaluable when a person is able to use them at will, but when the faculties use the person, then he is no longer master of himself.

Concentration is taught by the mystics in order to exercise the will, making it capable of making use of all faculties. A person with will-power can remember what he wishes to remember and can forget what he wishes to forget. All things that deprive one of one's freedom in life are undesirable. The mind must be free from all bad impressions of life, which take away the rest and peace of life. By concentration one is able to hold a certain thought one desires and to keep away all other thoughts, and when one is able to keep away all the thoughts one does not wish to think about, it becomes easy to throw away the impressions of years, if one wishes to forget them. Bad impressions, however old and intimate, are like rubbish accumulated, which should be removed in order to make the house clean. The human heart is the home of the soul, and upon this home the comfort and peace of the soul depends.

ESOTERIC PAPERS - GATHA II -EVERYDAY LIFE – Purification

GAYAN 166 - BOULA -125 - Resignation is of no value except after a deed is done and cannot be undone.

There are two forces working: the individual power and the collective power. In Sufi terms the former is called qadr, the latter qadha. Often the individual power will not surrender, but if it does not do so it is crushed. For instance someone is called to arms in his country, but says he will not join the army. In spite of all the beauty of his ideal he is helpless before the might of the whole nation. Here he must resign to the condition in which there is a conflict between a lesser and a greater power; here resignation is the only solution.

No doubt everything must be understood rightly. Resignation preached foolishly is of no benefit. There was a mureed who learned from a Murshid the lesson of resignation, and thinking on this subject the simple mureed was walking in the middle of a road, when a mad elephant came from the other side. As he was walking in the thought of resignation he stayed in the middle of the road. A wise man told him to go out of the way, but he would not do so, because he was resigned to the elephant, until he was pushed away by its strength. They brought him to his Murshid who asked him how he came to be hurt so much. He answered that he was practicing resignation. The Murshid said, "Was there not somebody who told you to go away?" "Yes", he answered, "but I would not listen". "But", said the Murshid, "why did you not resign yourself to that person?" Often beautiful principles can be practiced to the greatest disadvantage. Nevertheless, resignation has proved to be the path of saints, because it develops patience in man. And what is patience? It is all the treasure there is. Nothing is more valuable, nothing is a greater bliss than patience.

SUFI TEACHINGS - THE PRIVILEGE OF BEING HUMAN - Struggle and Resignation

GAYAN 167 - BOULA -126 - Love is the Divine Mother's arms; and when those arms are outspread, every soul falls into them.

Once four little girls were disputing. One said, 'My mother is better than yours.' The second girl said, 'My mother is better than your mother.' So they were arguing and being quite disagreeable to one another. But someone who was passing by said to them, 'It is not your mother or their mother, it is the mother who is always the best. It is the mother quality, her love and affection for her children.' This is the point of view of the mystic in regard to the divine ideal.

The moral principle of the mystic is the love principle. He says, "The greater your love, the greater your moral. If we are forced to be virtuous according to a certain principle, a certain regulation, certain laws or rules, that is not real virtue. It must come from the depths of our heart; our own heart must teach us the true moral.' Thus the mystic leaves morality to the deepening of the heart quality. The mystic says that the more loving someone's heart is, the greater is his morality.

PATH OF INITIATION - SUFI MYSTICISM – Mysticism

GAYAN 168 - BOULA -127 - The greatest tragedy of the world is the lack of general evolution.

The whole tragedy of humanity today is that lack of the inner voice, and the cause of this is that the soul seems to be buried under matter. A person with a living heart goes with a torchlight to find somewhere someone who can understand what he says. What with the condition the world is in, it is hard to find. When one person among thousands come to some understanding, more realization of life, the first thing he feels is like running away from the whole crowd and never coming back to it again. For the ignorant, perhaps life here is a joy, but for a person of understanding, a person of wisdom, it is the greatest tragedy to live.

THE SUPPLEMENTARY (Dutch) PAPERS of - CLASS FOR MUREEDS VI - The Inner Voice

Man's greatest privilege is to become a suitable instrument of God, and until he knows this he has not realized his true purpose in life. The whole tragedy in the life of man is his ignorance of this fact. From the moment a man realizes this he lives the real life, the life of harmony between God and man. When Jesus Christ said, "Seek ye first the kingdom of God", this teaching was an answer to the cry of humanity: some crying, "I have no wealth", others crying, "I have no rest", others crying, "My situation in life is difficult", "My friends are troubling me", or, "I want a position, wealth". The answer to them all is, "Seek ye first the kingdom of God, and all these things shall be added unto you".

Sufi Teachings - The Privilege of Being Human – The Privilege of Being Human

GAYAN 169 - BOULA -128 - There is nothing that is accidental; all situations in life work towards some definite end.

All that we call accident is only our conception; because we did not know it beforehand we call it accident. …there is a plan; it is all planned out and known beforehand to the spirit and to those who know. There are sages who know of their death a year before. There is no such thing as accident. When a person does not know, it means he does not see; but it is there [symbolical evidence].

HEALING AND THE MIND WORLD – MENTAL PURIFICATION – Insight (2)

GAYAN 170 - BOULA -129 - Forgiveness belongs to God; it becomes the privilege of mortal man only when asked by another.

However great a fault may be, if this person only comes and says, I am very sorry; I will never do it again; pray forgive," the friendship at once comes back. On the other hand, however trivial and slight the fault may have been, if pride prevents the man from asking forgiveness and pardon, perhaps he will lose that friendship for the rest of his life. His pride prevents him from asking pardon. The fault may have been very small, and he may say, "I do not care about it," and yet the friendship is broken. How many there are who would be ready to forgive if only the person came and said, "I am sorry." But everybody will not do it; they will not admit they have been in fault.

To ask forgiveness of another produces a proper sense of justice in one's mind. He perceives the need for asking God to pardon his faults. When he asks for forgiveness, that forgiveness develops in his nature too, and he becomes ready to forgive others. Christ says in His prayer, "Forgive us as we forgive others." The virtue, the secret, is in that. By asking forgiveness of God, you give up the desire to demand forgiveness from your fellow man, and you desire to give forgiveness to him. We see this with the Arabs and Bedouins in Mecca and the desert. They are so ready to fight one another and kill each other. They may be fighting, and actually have their knives drawn to kill one another, and yet if a third person comes and says, "Forgive, for the sake of God and the Prophet," as soon as they hear these words they both throw away their knives and shake hands, and the handshake is the seal of friendship. Though the Bedouin has no education, yet he has such a devotion to God and His Prophet that no sooner does he hear these words than he at once offers his hand, and from that day there is no spite nor evil thought in his heart.

If we only had that! With all our education and learning, with all the claims of civilization that we make, we are not as good as these. We retain the bitterness in our hearts. We never reflect what a poison it is. The very person who would shudder at the idea of having something in his body that is decayed and offensive--something that should not be there, but should be taken off or cut out or removed--will tolerate that poison of bitterness in his mind: he will not take it out; he will foster it. Had he not lacked the sense of forgiveness and had he not neglected to cultivate the habit of asking forgiveness, he would have become ready to forgive and forget.

[Vol. 9] THE UNITY OF RELIGIOUS IDEALS - RELIGION - The Effect of Prayer

GAYAN 171 - BOULA -130 - Before you can know the truth you must learn to live a true life.

Right living in my sense is not only virtuous living. Right living has a still deeper meaning, for what I call a right life is the first step to that which may be called true life. The third step is truth itself. The mystics say that there are three steps to the goal: right life, true life and truth. A person who loves to live a right life and who tries to do it, even if he is not a contemplative or meditative or religious person, must certainly arrive at that high stage, at that goal which is the ideal goal; for within man there is truth, and the seeking of man is truth. Therefore right living helps him to realize truth.

If I were to interpret the words of Christ, "Strait is the gate and narrow is the way", I would say that there is a path in life, a path of going strait, and that path is like walking upon a wire. In the circus they make a show of it. It is exactly the picture: at every step one takes there is fear of falling either to one side or to the other. Jugglers in India even make a better picture of it. They take two very light bamboos and tie a rope on the top of them. The juggler stands on the rope in a brass tray and his task is to go from one point to the other. While he is travelling thus, his colleagues from below beat drums and sing horrible songs in order to distract his mind. He has to keep his concentration and secure his balance in spite of all the music calling him from below. That is the picture of right living.

Question: But once one is failing... ?

Answer: Truth is merciful. One cannot fall but on truth; if one falls, one will only fall in the arms of truth. A seeker after truth has no loss. If apparently he loses something, it is not a loss in the end.

Question: What does it mean "to fall in the arms of truth"?

Answer: If a fall is caused in a certain struggle one has fallen in the arms of that particular struggle. If it is in the struggle for love, then it is in the arms of love that one falls. If it is in the struggle for righteousness, one falls in the arms of righteousness. Just as they say that. in a holy war a person gives his life for a holy purpose, and is therefore in the arms of that holy object, so, if a person has fallen in the struggle for truth, he has fallen in the arms of truth.

SUFI TEACHINGS - THE PRIVILEGE OF BEING HUMAN - Man is likened to the Light

GAYAN 172 - BOULA -131 - Life itself becomes a scripture to the kindled soul.

People often fight and argue and discuss. Over what? Over a reason. When two persons dispute, each has a reason. Each thinks his reason the right one. They may dispute for years and yet will arrive nowhere because the reason of each is different. Therefore to think more is to see behind the reason. And the moment we have begun to see behind the reason, we will look at life quite differently. Then we find that behind what we blame the other for there is perhaps something to praise; and where there is something to praise there is perhaps a reason for blame. We shall begin to see what is beyond all appearances and that will give us the proof that the whole of life is a kind of unfoldment. The deeper we look into life the more it unfolds itself, allowing us to see more keenly. Life is revealing. It is not only human beings who speak; if only the ears can hear even plants and trees and all nature speak, in the sense that nature reveals itself, reveals its secret. In this way we communicate with the whole of life. Then we are never alone, then life becomes worth living.

THE ALCHEMY OF HAPPINESS - The Deeper Side of Life

GAYAN 173 - BOULA -132 - Every moment of your life is more valuable than anything else in the world.

Life is interesting in every phase; on the journey towards manifestation as well as on the soul's return towards the goal. Every moment of life has its particular experience, one better than the other, one more valuable than another. In short, life may be said to be full of interest. Sorrow is interesting as well as joy; there is beauty in every phase, if only one can learn to appreciate it.

[Vol. 1] THE SOUL, WHENCE AND WHITHER? - Towards the Goal

GAYAN 174 - BOULA -133 - He is an unbeliever who cannot believe in himself.

He does not believe in himself; and as he does not believe in himself, he does not believe in God. His belief in God is mostly superficial. Numberless souls believe in God, and yet they know not if He really exists. They only believe because others believe in God. They have no proof, and they live their whole life without a proof of the belief in God. And there is no way of getting proof of God's existence, except by becoming acquainted with oneself; by experiencing the phenomena which are within one; and the greatest phenomenon that one can experience, which is one's heart. Could anything, therefore, be more interesting in life, more precious to give life to, than the thought that you could be an instrument for knowing all that is in the person who is before you, his nature, his character, his condition, his past, his present, his future, his weakness, and his strong points? Nothing in the world could be more interesting and more precious than arriving at this stage, than experiencing this; more precious than wealth, or power, or position, or anything in the world. And this is something which is attained without cost, even without the hard work which man does for his livelihood. When we think of this we feel that man thirsts for water, standing near the stream. What man thirsts after is within himself; and what keeps him from it, is the lack of belief in himself, in truth, in God.

HEALING AND THE MIND WORLD - THE MIND-WORLD - Chapter VII

GAYAN 175 - BOULA -134 - Love is a weapon that can break all obstacles on one's path in life.

The great teachers of humanity become streams of love. It is the first sign of the sage or holy man that he himself becomes love. His voice, his feeling, his presence, everything makes one realize that there is something open in him which we do not find in everybody; this something is his deep love.

The development of love is often hindered by different obstacles in life. The first obstacle is ourselves. We begin our life with selfishness, and all that we want is for self and if there is a tendency to love, it is for one's own happiness, and one's own joy. When the question comes, 'How much do you love me, and how much do I love you?' it has come to be a trading in love. 'I love you, but you do not love me' is as much as to say, 'I have bid so much, and I expect a return of love'. This is trading in love, and trade cannot lead anywhere, because it makes one think of the self, and love is beyond that. To love is to give; it is not to take at all. The true lover never speaks of what he has done for his beloved, for he loves for love's sake, not for the sake of a return. If a person begins to love and makes it a love fed by the love of his beloved, then he seeks an impossible thing. If a person keeps waiting for the love of the beloved, he is bound to find that nature cannot grant that desire, unless both are traders in love. Then each takes the best of the other; each may think he loves, but neither truly loves.

Love teaches the lover patience, forbearance, gentleness, because he thinks, 'My beloved will be displeased; I will be as gentle as possible in my action and in my movements'. These thoughts are a correction to the lover. With every such thought that passes in the life of the lover he corrects himself. Hope is the only thing in life which keeps us alive, because it feeds on love. Patience is fed by love. We can never have patience with anybody without love. How valuable is patience! As it is said in the Qur'an, 'Allah loves the patient'.

IN AN EASTERN ROSE GARDEN - Love, Human and Divine

GAYAN 176 - BOULA -135 - Self-pity is the cause of all the grievances of life.

Self-pity is the worst poverty. When a person says, 'I am...' with pity, before he has said anything more he has diminished himself to half of what he is; and what is said further, diminishes him totally; nothing more of him is left afterwards. There is so much in the world that we can pity and which it would be right for us to take pity upon, but if we have no time free from our own self we cannot give our mind to others in the world. Life is one long journey, and the further behind we have left our self, the further we have progressed towards the goal. Verily when the false self is lost the true self is discovered.

THE ART OF PERSONALITY - CHARACTER AND PERSONALITY -
Character-Building

GAYAN 177 - BOULA -136 - What is given in love is beyond price.

In all things there is God, but the object is the instrument, and the person is life itself. Into the object the person puts life. When a certain thing is being made, it is at that time that a life is put into it, which goes on and on as a breath in a body. This also gives us a hint that, when we take flowers to a patient and we have a healing thought with them, the flowers convey the thought of healing. As the patient looks at the flowers he will receive from them the healing which was put there. Any eatable or sweet, anything that we take to a friend with a thought of love - its use must create a harmonious, happy result for him. Therefore every little thing given and taken in love, with a harmonious and good thought, has a greater value than the object itself; for it is not the object, it is what is behind it. Does this not teach us that it is not always doing or preparing things in our everyday life that counts, but that it is giving these things a life with a harmonious, constructive thought, so that our work may become a thousand times greater in effect and real value?

This also teaches us that while doing a small thing we should be accomplishing something very great if we did it with this attitude, with this idea at the back of it: that we are not only making a thing, but we are making it living. Does this not open before us a vast field of work that we could do easily without much cost or effort? In its result that work could be of a much greater importance than anyone could think or imagine. Is it not at the same time a great blessing to be able to do a thing of great importance without any outward pretence?

THE MYSTICISM OF SOUND AND MUSIC - COSMIC LANGUAGE -
The Magnetism of Beings and Objects

GAYAN 178 - BOULA -137 - It is our perception of time which passes, not time itself; for time is God, and God is eternal.

It is indeed an error on the part of man to limit God in the idea of a Personal Being, and is wrong in the person who believes in the Absolute God to efface the Being of God from his conception of it. As they say: "To explain God is to dethrone God." To say that God is abstract is like saying: "God is space, God is time." Can you love space? Can you love time? There is nothing there to love. A beautiful flower would attract you more than space. And nice music will attract you more than time. Therefore the believer in the abstract God has only his belief, but he is not benefited by it. He may just as well believe in no God as in an abstract God. Yet he is not wrong. He is uselessly right.

THE UNITY OF RELIGIOUS IDEALS - RELIGION - The Sufi's Religion

GAYAN 179 - BOULA -138 – Man learns his first lesson of love by loving a human being; but in reality love is due to God alone.

The fourth aspect of prayer is the call of the lover to the beloved. No doubt this is a higher form; and to be able to pray in this manner man must rise above the ordinary level of life. As it is difficult for a human being to love man, whom he sees, so it is more difficult to love God, Whom one has never seen. Loving one's fellow man, yes; but not everyone is capable of loving the Formless, the God-Ideal, and to evolve by the lesson of love. For in this love there is no disappointment, and only the love of God can fulfill the desire of the human soul, and all other forms of love are only as steps that lead to the love of God. But who can explain the love of God to one who has never felt it? Because God is the perfect ideal, His love is the perfect love. There is the love of the mate, of parents, of friends, of children, but in the love of God all is found combined. Therefore its joy is perfect. The love of God is living and everlasting and the love of the true Beloved.

THE UNITY OF RELIGIOUS IDEALS - RELIGION – Prayer

GAYAN 180 - BOULA -139 – When man closes his lips, God begins to speak.

No study can teach more than what silence can, no meditation is greater than silence itself. When the shell closes its lips pearls are formed. It is the heart of man which is the shell of the real pearls. By closing the lips, all the beauty which is seen and heard is received in it, and there a pearl is formed which becomes as a Philosopher's Stone. It is man who is blessed with the power of self-control, not the animals, and when man shows in his character something which is beyond the power of the lower creation he proves himself to be human. It is self-discipline which leads to mastery. When the self is in one's power the whole life is in one's possession. That person becomes the conqueror of life who learns to control his tongue.

SANGATHA I

GAYAN 181 - BOULA -140 – That person becomes conqueror of life who learns to control his tongue.

Sparing of words is the secret of sages. Most troubles and pains in life can be avoided by the economy of words. Silence is taught in every school of inner cult, especially in Sufism; which, plainly speaking, is quietism. Besides, when a person says one word, to express his ideas, instead of ten words, that one word becomes equal to a hundred words in power. The yes or no of a serious and silent person has more weight and has a greater influence then a hundred words of a talkative person.

No study can teach more than what silence can, no meditation is greater than silence itself. When the shell closes its lips pearls are formed. It is the heart of man which is the shell of the real pearls. By closing the lips, all the beauty which is seen and heard is received in it, and there a pearl is formed which becomes as a Philosopher's Stone. It is man who is blessed with the power of self-control, not the animals, and when man shows in his character something which is beyond the power of the lower creation he proves himself to be human. It is self-discipline which leads to mastery. When the self is in one's power the whole life is in one's possession. That person becomes the conqueror of life who learns to control his tongue.

ESOTERIC PAPERS - SANGATHA I

GAYAN 182 - BOULA -141 – Optimism comes from God, and pessimism is born of the human mind.

"…The psychological effect of optimism is such that it helps to bring success. For it is by the optimistic spirit that God has created the world. Therefore optimism comes from God and pessimism is born out of the heart of man.

What little experience of life man has, he learns; 'this will not succeed, that will not go, this will not come right'. For the one who is optimistic, if it does not come right in the end, it does not matter, he will take his chance. And what is life? Life is an opportunity, and to the optimistic person this opportunity is a promise, and for the pessimistic person this opportunity is lost. It is not that the Creator makes man lose it, but it is himself who fails to seize the opportunity. Many in this world prolong their illness by giving way to pessimistic thought. Mostly you will find that those who have suffered for many years from a certain illness, that illness becomes so real that its absence becomes unnatural.

SOCIAL GATHEKAS - Optimism and Pessimism

GAYAN 183 - BOULA -142 – The mystic begins by marveling at life, and to him it is a phenomenon at every moment.

There is only one thing in the world which shows the sign of heaven, which gives the proof of God, and that is pure unselfish love. For all the noble qualities which are hidden in the soul will spring forth and blossom when love helps them and nurtures them. Man may have a great deal of good in him and he may be very intelligent, but as long as his heart is closed he cannot show that nobleness, that goodness which is hidden in his heart; and the psychology of the heart is such that once one begins to know it one realizes that life is a continual phenomenon. Then every moment of life becomes a miracle; a searchlight is thrown upon human nature and all things become so clear that one does not ask for any greater phenomenon or miracle; it is a miracle in itself. What one calls telepathy, thought-reading, or clairvoyance, and all such things, come by themselves when the heart is open.

THE PATH OF INITIATION - SUFI POETRY - Farid-ud-din-Attar

GAYAN 184 - BOULA -143 – You need not look for a saint or a master: a wise man is sufficient to guide you on your path.

No doubt there comes a time in a man's life when even if he were initiated a thousand times by nature he still seeks for a guide walking on earth. Many will say, 'Why is God not sufficient? Why must there be someone between God and man? Why must it be a man who is just as limited as we are? Why can we not reach the spirit of God directly?' But in a man who is your enemy and who has tortured you throughout your life, in another who is your greatest friend, and in your teacher who inspires and guides you, in all these is to be seen the hand of God. They have all three guided you on the path of inspiration; they are all three needed in order that you may go further in life. The one who has disappointed you, who has harmed you, is also your initiator, for he has taught you something, he has put you on the road, even if not in the right way. And he who is your friend is your initiator too, for he gives you the evidence of truth, the sign of reality; only love can give you a proof that there is something living, something real. And then there is the inspiring teacher, be he a humble man, an illiterate person, or a meditative soul, a great teacher or a humble one, he is what you think him to be, as everyone is to us what we think them to be.

THE PATH OF INITIATION - THE PATH OF INITIATION AND DISCIPLESHIP - Three Aspects of Initiation

GAYAN 185 - BOULA -144 – The man who cannot learn his lesson from his first fault is certainly on the wrong track.

It seems as if the whole life is tending towards freedom, towards the unfoldment of something which is choked up by coming on earth. This freedom can be gained by true purity of life. Of course it is not for everybody to understand what action, what thought brings remorse or causes discomfort. Another thing, the life of the individual is not in his control. Every rising wave of passion or of emotion or of anger or of wrath or of affection carries away his reason, blinds him for the moment, so that he can easily give in to mistakes, and in a moment's impulse can give way to an unworthy thought or action. Then comes remorse. But still, a man who wishes to learn, who wishes to improve himself, a man who wishes to go on further in his progress, at the thought of his faults and mistakes will go on, because every fault will be a lesson, and a good lesson. Then he does not need to read in a book or learn from a teacher, because his life becomes his teacher.

However one should not for one's personal experience wish for the lesson. If one was wise, one could learn the lesson from others, but at the same time one should not regard one's fault as one's nature. It is not one's nature. A fault means what is against one's nature. If it was in one's nature, it could not be a fault. The very reason that it is against one's nature makes it a fault. How can nature be a fault? When one says, "I cannot help being angry and I cannot help saying what I want to say when I feel bitter," one does not know that one could if one wished to. I mean to say, that he does not wish to, when he says, "I cannot help." It is lack of strength in a man when he says, "can't." There is nothing which he can't. The human soul is the expression of the Almighty and therefore the human mind has in his will the power of the Almighty, if only he could use that power against all things which stands in his way as hindrances on his journey to the goal.

THE SUPPLEMENTARY PAPERS - RELIGION I - Purity of Life

GAYAN 186 - BOULA -145 – There is a pair of opposites in all things; in each thing there exists the spirit of the opposite.

The next step in mental purification is to be able to see the right of the wrong and the wrong of the right, and the evil of the good and the good of the evil. It is a difficult task, but once one has accomplished this, one rises above good and evil.

One must be able to see the pain in pleasure and the pleasure in pain; the gain in the loss and the loss in the gain. What generally happens is that one is blunted to one thing and that one's eyes are open to another thing; that one does not see the loss or that one does not see the gain; if one recognizes the right, one does not recognize the wrong. Mental purification means that impressions such as good and bad, wrong and right, gain and loss, and pleasure and pain, these opposites which block the mind, must be cleared out by seeing the opposite of these things. Then one can see the enemy in the friend and the friend in the enemy. When one can recognize poison in nectar and nectar in the poison, that is the time when death and life become one too. Opposites no more remain opposites before one. That is called mental purification. And those who come to this stage are the living sages.

Healing and the Mind World – Mental Purification - Unlearning

GAYAN 187 - BOULA -146 – A clean body reflects the purity of the soul, and is the secret of health.

Beasts and birds all have a tendency to be clean and pure, and for man it is necessary that he should develop this tendency. It helps, not only on the spiritual path, but also in the development of mind. To the artist in his art, to the scientist in his science, in all aspects of life it gives happiness. When man neglects it, that does not mean that he does not like it, it is only out of negligence that he overlooks things that are of the first importance. One's body is of all things in the world the closest to oneself, and its influence has a great effect, and an immediate effect, upon one's mind and soul. A great many illnesses are caused by the lack of consideration of the necessary cleanliness of the body, which is a science and an art in itself. On the soul and mind one's own body makes the first impression, all other things come afterwards. Yes, there are souls who have arrived at such a plane of spirituality that the condition of the body does not matter to them. But they are not to be followed as examples. It is the normal path which is safe and is for all. The question, "Would this not give one too much the thought of self?" may be answered thus: The thought of oneself exists when the light of God is absent; in the presence of every beautiful thing man forgets himself.

ESOTERIC PAPERS - GATHA I - EVERYDAY LIFE - Natural Self

GAYAN 188 - BOULA -147 – It is the purity of the soul itself that gives the tendency towards cleanliness of body.

The body is an instrument, the most sacred instrument, an instrument which God Himself has made for His divine purpose. If it is kept in tune and the strings are not allowed to become loose, then this instrument becomes the means of that harmony for which God created man:

How must this instrument be kept in tune? In the first place strings of gut and wires of steel both require cleaning. The lungs and veins in the body also require cleaning; it is that which keeps them ready for their work. And how should we clean them? By carefulness in diet, by sobriety, and by breathing properly and correctly; because it is not only water and earth that are used for cleansing, the best means of cleansing is the air and the property that is in the air, the property that we breathe in; and if we knew how by the help of breathing to keep these channels clean, then we should know how to secure health. It is this which maintains the tone, the proper note of each person, without being disturbed. When a person is vibrating his own note which is according to his particular evolution, then he is himself, then he is tuned to the pitch for which he is made, the pitch in which he ought to be and in which he naturally feels comfortable.

HEALING AND THE MIND WORLD - HEALTH

GAYAN 189 - BOULA -148 – A pure life and a clean conscience are as bread and wine for the soul.

The finer the person the finer his conscience, and grossness makes the conscience gross. It is therefore that one person is more conscientious about his doings than the other person, one person repents more for his mistakes and failures than another person. But the most interesting thing in the law of life which one might watch is that the scheme of nature is so made that a conscientious person is taken to task more seriously by the scheme of nature for his evil-doing than an ordinary person who never thinks what he says or does. It might seem as if even God did not take notice of his wrong-doing. According to the metaphysical point of view in thee soul of the conscientious God is more awake; in the soul of the other person God slumbers, He does not take serious notice of things. If one were to watch one's own conscience one would no longer have a thirst for phenomena, for there is no greater phenomenon than what is going on within oneself and the action and reaction of every experience in life which materializes and manifests to one's view in various ways and forms. A clear conscience gives the strength of a lion, but the guilty conscience might turn a lion into a rabbit. But who is it in the conscience who judges? In the spheres of conscience the soul of man and the spirit of God both meet and become one. Therefore to a soul wide-awakened Judgment Day does not come after death, for him every day is Judgment Day.

ESOTERIC PAPERS - GATHA III - METAPHYSICS - Conscience

GAYAN 190 - BOULA -149 – Righteousness comes from the very essence of the soul.

Spirituality comes from the softening of the heart, which becomes frozen by the coldness of the surrounding life. The influence of worldly life upon the mind generally has a freezing effect; for selfishness coming from all sides naturally makes a man cool and selfish. Therefore it is the constant softening of the heart of the youth that is necessary. There are two ways of softening the heart; one is by helping the youth to open himself to the beauty which is shining in all its various forms. The other is to give him a tendency to righteousness, which is the very essence of the soul. These things cannot be taught, but they can be awakened in the heart of the youth if the parents or the guardians only know how. The child must not be forced by principles, but love of virtue should be created in his heart, for in the inner nature of every soul there is love of virtue. Spirituality in the real sense of the word is the discovering of the spirit, which is attained by rising above self or by diving into self.

THE ART OF PERSONALITY - EDUCATION - The Training of Youth

GAYAN 191 - BOULA -150 – Reserve gives dignity to the personality; to be serious and yet gracious is the way of the wise.

The secret of all attainment is centered in reserve. Spiritual or material, when a person has told his plans to others, he has let out the energy that he should have kept as a reservoir of power for the accomplishment of his object. A thing unspoken is alive in the mind, and when spoken, it is as dead. The more valuable your object, the more it must be guarded, as all precious things need strong guarding. When a person tells others of his plan, each one looks at it from his point of view. Some understand, some do not understand; some have a sympathetic point of view, and some take an unfavorable attitude toward it. And every person's attitude has something to do with your life and with your affairs, and if you have whole-heartedly engaged yourself in the accomplishment of a plan, many outside influences can hinder it.

GITHA I - THE PATH OF ATTAINMENT - Reserve

GAYAN 192 - BOULA -151 – When even our self does not belong to us, what else in the world can we call our own?

All that we collect and gather in the external world for our happiness and comfort is limited. Not even a thousandth part of this world that we possess can we really call our own kingdom, our world. But our mind can create and can collect numberless thoughts and impressions, which all make up its real world. All our possessions, all that we collect in life, all these things which we shall have to leave one day are transitory; but that which we have created in our thought, in our mind, that lives.

IN AN EASTERN ROSE GARDEN - Mental Creation

GAYAN 193 - BOULA -152 – All things in life are materials for wisdom to work with.

The same is with all things in life. Every moment in our lives is an opportunity which brings a benefit and blessing. And the one who knows how to be benefited by it, and how to be blessed by it, receives the benefit and the blessing. Everyone seems living and awake, but few souls really are living and awake. There are opportunities of benefit and blessing on every plane of one's life--on the physical plane, on the mental plane, on the spiritual plane--and every opportunity is invaluable. But often one realizes the truth when it is too late. There is no greater and better opportunity than the moment that can give a spiritual illumination, a moment when one can receive the blessing of God. It is a priceless moment. Who knows it and understands it and tries to be benefited by it is blessed.

The Sufi´s Conception of God – The Ten Virgins

GAYAN 194 - BOULA -153 – Overlook the greatest fault of another, but do not partake of it in the smallest degree.

Man is born with such a critical tendency and has so much developed this tendency that he easily seeks what is bad in everything. The Sufi takes the contrary way; he seeks for what is good in everyone and everything. The way of morality is to think that if someone has done us some good it is very great, and if we have done good to someone to think that it is very little and that we might have done more. If a person has done something bad to us we should forget it as soon as possible, and if we have done something bad we should think that a great fault. If we see something that seems bad to us we should overlook it, disregard it, forgive it. This is the only way of happiness and peace.

THE PRIVILEGE OF BEING HUMAN – Moral Culture

GAYAN 195 - BOULA -154 – There is no source of happiness other than the heart of man.

In point of fact, whatever one makes of oneself, one becomes that. The source of happiness or unhappiness is all in man himself. When he is unaware of this, he is not able to arrange his life, but as he becomes more acquainted with this secret he gains mastery, and the process by which this mastery is attained is the only fulfillment of the purpose of this life.

THE PATH OF INITIATION - SUFI POETRY - Farid-ud-din-Attar

GAYAN 196 - BOULA -155 – Not until sobriety comes after the intoxication of life does man begin to wonder.

The first thing that a seeker after truth must realize, is the purpose of life. No sooner does a soul begin to feel sober from the intoxication of life, than the first thing it asks itself is, 'What is the purpose of my life?' Each soul has its own purpose, but in the end all purposes resolve into one purpose, and it is that purpose which is sought by the mystlc. For all souls, by the right and the wrong path, either sooner or later, will arrive at that purpose, a purpose which must be accomplished, a purpose for which the whole creation has been intended; but the difference between the seeking soul and the soul who blindly works towards that purpose is like that between the material and the maker of it. The clay works towards the purpose of forming a vessel and so does the potter; but it is the potter's joy and privilege to feel the happiness of the accomplishment of the purpose, not the clay's; and so it is with the beings who are unconsciously striving towards that purpose and the souls who are consciously striving towards it, both in the end corning towards the same accomplishment; the difference is in the consciousness.

THE PURPOSE OF LIFE - Chapter I

GAYAN 197 - BOULA -156 – A life with a foolish companion is worse than death.

Question: How can we overcome the disagreeable vibrations of people of our immediate surroundings with whom we daily have to live. Answer: By being positive. It is true that one cannot always be positive. At such times one may retire from one's associates. But as you evolve so your contact becomes more powerful than the influence of the other person. Therefore the other person receives more benefit from you, while the harm you receive is less. If by receiving a little harm you are able to do more good to the other person, it is just as well. It is only a matter of self-discipline, and love can conquer all things. In every person, however wicked, there is a good string somewhere; you must know where to find it. If one always thought about it, one could always touch the best point of the other person and overlook the other points. Nevertheless, it is a struggle!

Question: How can we protect ourselves from association with a wicked person. Answer: In order to answer this we must go into the law of harmony. A person harmonizes with his like, and he harmonizes with his opposite. A wise person may harmonize with a thoughtful person, and he may harmonize with a foolish person. The half wise is a greater trouble for him than the foolish one, because the half wisdom makes a barrier. The foolish person is open, so a harmony can be established at once. The wisdom of another wise person makes him closer, and there is a kind of response between the two; so there is harmony.

It is not surprising that one often finds two persons becoming most harmonious or great friends in whose evolution there is so vast a difference that one cannot understand how it can be possible. But, as said before, association must have an effect. However thoughtful and wise a person may be, there can come a cloud upon his thought and wisdom through association. Perhaps that cloud may be dispersed after a time, but it can cover the light of the sun. The cloud is much smaller compared to the sun, but often it can cover the whole sun from our sight. The influence of a wicked person may cover the light of a good and wise person, and this may remain until the clouds have dispersed.

THE MYSTICISM OF SOUND AND MUSIC - COSMIC LANGUAGE -
Impressions

GAYAN 198 - BOULA -157 – The pain of life is the price paid for the quickening of the heart.

What is sensitiveness? Sensitiveness is life itself. And as life has both its good and evil sides, so has sensitiveness. If one expects to have all life's experiences, these will have to come through sensitiveness. However, sensitiveness must be kept in order if one wants to know, understand, and appreciate all that is beautiful, and not to attract all the depression, sorrows, sadness, and woes of the earth. Once a person has become so sensitive as to be offended with everybody, feeling that everybody is against him, trying to wrong him, he is abusing his sensitiveness. He must be wise as well as sensitive. He must realize before being sensitive that in this world he is among children, among drunken men. And he should take everything, wherever it comes from, as he would take the actions of children and drunken people; then sensitiveness can be beneficial....

...What is most advisable in life is to be sensitive enough to feel life and its beauty and to appreciate it, but at the same time to consider that one's soul is divine, and that all else is foreign to it; that all things that belong to the earth are foreign to one's soul. They should not touch one's soul. When objects come before the eyes they come into the vision of the eyes; when they are gone the eyes are clear. Therefore one's mind should retain nothing but beauty, all that is beautiful. For one can search for God in His beauty; all else should be forgotten. And by practicing this every day, forgetting all that is disagreeable, that is ugly, and remembering only what is beautiful and gives happiness, one will attract to oneself all the happiness that is in store.

THE ALCHEMY OF HAPPINESS - Life, a Continual Battle (2)

GAYAN 199 - BOULA -158 – Endurance makes things precious and men great.

Those who love their enemies and yet lack patience are like a burning lantern with little oil. It cannot keep alight, and in the end the flame fades away. The oil in the path of love is patience, and besides this it is unselfishness and self-sacrifice from beginning to end.

Some say, 'I have loved dearly once, but I was disappointed.' It is as if a man were to say, 'I dug in the earth, but when the mud came I was disappointed.' It is true that mud came, but with patience he would have reached the water one day. Only patience can endure. Only endurance produces greatness.

Imitation gold can be as beautiful as real gold, the imitation diamond as bright as a real diamond. The difference is that the one fails in the test of endurance, and the other stands up to it. Yet man should not be compared with objects. Man has something divine in him, and he can prove this by his endurance in the path of love.

THE PATH OF INITIATION - SUFI MYSTICISM - The Mystical Heart

GAYAN 200 - BOULA -159 – The fulfillment of every activity is in its balance.

A man who is one-sided, however great his power of clairvoyance or clairaudience, whatever be his knowledge, yet is limited; he cannot go very far, for it requires two wheels for the vehicle to run. There must be a balance, the balance of the head and the heart, the balance of power and wisdom, the balance of activity and repose. It is the balance which enables man to stand the strain of this journey and permits him to go forward, making his path easy. Never imagine for one moment that those who show lack of balance can ever proceed further on the spiritual journey, however greatly in appearance they may seem to be spiritually inclined. It is only the balanced ones who are capable of experiencing the external life as fully as the inner life; to enjoy thought as much as feeling; to rest as well as to act. The center of life is rhythm, and rhythm causes balance.

THE INNER LIFE - The Preparation for the Journey

GAYAN 201 - BOULA -159 – The heart of man is a temple; when its door is closed to man, it is also closed to God.

God cannot be found in temples, for God is Love; and love does not live in temples, but in the heart of man, which is the temple of God. The true religion would be to recognize it so and to tolerate, to forgive and to love each other. No doubt there are difficulties; we are not angels and we cannot expect to act like them. Many have no clear vision before them as they are indulging in the life of intoxication. Perhaps the time will come when everything we depend upon will be taken from us; the best would be to consider life from a philosophical point of view. Then we really should be able to smile at life; today this thing is most necessary.

THE SUPPLEMENTARY PAPERS - BROTHERHOOD I - Universal Brotherhood of Humanity

GAYAN 202 - BOULA -159 – Faithfulness has a fragrance which is perceptible in the atmosphere of the faithful.

The fruit must be of a certain degree of ripeness before its taste becomes sweet. So the soul must be of a certain development before it will handle wisdom with wisdom. The developed soul shows his fragrance in his atmosphere, color, the expression of his countenance, and sweetness of his personality, as a flower spreads its fragrance around, and as a fruit when ripe changes its color and becomes sweet.

THE WAY OF ILLUMINATION - The Sufi

GAYAN 203 - BOULA -159 – Spirituality is the tuning of the heart; one can obtain it neither by study, nor by piety.

Seen metaphysically, the artistic spirit of God is satisfied by fulfilling its artistic tendency through the art of the human being. Therefore those who consider art from a higher point of view recognize the artistic impulse not only as a human impulse, not only as brain work, but as a true artistic impulse, as an inspiration in itself. But in order to prepare the mind for the artistic impulse, what is necessary? Does one need some kind of learning, or some kind of study? Is there some preliminary study to be make first? No. It requires a tuning, a bringing of ourselves to an object to whose beauty the human heart can respond, to a beauty which the heart can appreciate. When the heart can concentrate upon beauty, then it works itself up to a certain pitch, for inspiration is not a thing which one can pull upon to obtain as by pulling a rope. Inspiration is a thing which comes only when the heart is tuned to that object, when it is in a position to receive it. Therefore inspired artists have been divinely gifted, and the spirit of art is one, though the arts are so many. When the heart is tuned to the proper pitch, it is not only capable of producing or appreciating one kind of art and beauty, but all kinds.

THE SUPPLEMENTARY PAPERS – Art and Music IV - The Divinity of Art

GAYAN 204 - BOULA -159 – A person's morality must be judged from his attitude rather than from his actions.

No doubt the sense of right and wrong is different in every mind. The right of one may be wrong to another, and for another the wrong of one may be right. The law of action is too complex to be put in words. For every step advanced gives a certain amount of freedom of action, and as one goes along further and further in the path of truth his freedom is greater and greater at every step. And yet no individual lives a life between the four walls of his individual self, every person is related and connected with a thousand ties with the others, known and unknown even to himself. Therefore the souls do not need regard for themselves only, but for the whole being, since every soul is a part in the whole scheme of nature. And conscience is the test which can voice that inner harmony in everything one thinks, says or does, thus keeping the soul tuned to its proper note.

ESOTERIC PAPERS - GATHA III - METAPHYSICS – Conscience

CS-0205 – Bola-164 - Right and wrong depend upon attitude and situation, not upon the action.

What determines that something should be called right or wrong? Four things: the motive behind the action, the result of the action, the time, and the place. Wrong action with the right motive may be right; and a right action with wrong motive may be wrong. We are always ready to judge an action, and we hardly think of the motive. That is why we readily accuse a person for his wrong, and excuse ourselves readily for our wrong, because we know our motive best. We would perhaps excuse another person as we excuse ourselves if we tried to know the motive behind his action too.

A thought, a word, or an action in the wrong place turns into a wrong one, even if it was right in itself. A thought or word or action at a wrong time may be wrong although it may seem right. And when we analyze this more and more we shall say as a Hindu poet has said, 'There is no use in feeling bad about the wrong deed of another person. We should content ourselves with the thought that he could not do better.' To look at everything, trying to see what is behind it, to see it in its right light, requires divine illumination, a spiritual outlook on life. And this outlook is attained by the increase of compassion. The more compassion one has in one's heart, the more the world will begin to look different.

There is another side to this question. Things seem to us according to how we look at them. To a wrong person everything looks wrong, and to a right person everything looks right; for a right person turns wrong into right, and a wrong person turns right into wrong. The sin of the virtuous is a virtue, and the virtue of a sinner is a sin. Things depend very much upon our interpretation, as there is no seal on any action, word, or thought which determines it to be wrong or right.

THE ALCHEMY OF HAPPINESS - The Law of Action

CS-0206 – Bola-165 - In the belief of every person there is some good for him; and to break that belief is like breaking his God.

Sufis are inclined to recognize four stages of belief:

Iman-e Muhmil, when someone believes in a thing which others believe in, but no matter how strong his belief may be, when those in his surroundings change their belief, he will likewise change his.

Iman-e Kamil, the next stage of belief, is the belief of the idealist who has faith in his scripture and savior. He believes because it is written in the scripture, or taught by the savior. His belief, of course, will not change with the weather, but still it may waver, if by any means reason were awakened in his soul. At least it would be dimmed just as the light of a candle would become dimmed by the rising sun. When the sun of the intelligence rises, it would break through and scatter the clouds of emotion and devotion made by this belief.

Haq al-Iman, the third stage of belief, when man believes because his reason allows him to believe; such a man is journeying through life with a torch in his hand. His belief is based on reason, and cannot be broken except by a still greater reason, for it is the diamond that alone can cut the diamond, and reason alone can break reason.

'Ain al-Iman, the fourth stage of belief, is a belief of conviction; not only reason, but every part of one's being is convinced and assured of the truth of things, and nothing on earth can change it. If a person were to say to him, 'Do not cross over this place, there is water here,' he will say, 'No, it is land, I can see for myself.' It is just like seeing with the eyes all that one believes. This belief is the belief of the seer whose knowledge is his eyewitness, and therefore his belief will last for ever and ever. Of course, as a soul evolves from stage to stage, it must break the former belief in order to establish the later, and this breaking of the belief is called by Sufis Tark, which means abandonment; the abandoning of the worldly ideal, the abandonment of the heavenly ideal, the abandoning of the divine ideal, and even the abandoning of abandonment. This brings the seer to the shores of the ultimate truth.

THE WAY OF ILLUMINATION - The Sufi

CS-0207 – Bola-166 - Reason is a flower with a thousand petals, one covered by another.

There is a story told about Moses who was passing with Khidr through a country. Khidr was the Murshid of Moses when Moses was being prepared for prophetship. Moses's first lesson of discipline was to keep quiet under all circumstances. While they were walking through the beauty of nature both teacher and pupil were quiet. The teacher was exalted in seeing the beauty of nature, and the pupil also felt it. So they arrived on the bank of a river, where Moses saw a little child drowning, and the mother crying aloud for she could not help. Here Moses could not keep his lips closed. He had to break that discipline and say: 'Master, save him! The child is drowning!' Khidr said: 'Quiet!', and Moses was quiet. But the heart of Moses was restless, he did not know what to think: 'Can the Master be so thoughtless, so inconsiderate, so cruel, or is the Master powerless?' He could not understand which was which. He did not dare to think such a thought, and yet it made him feel very uncomfortable.

As they went further they saw a boat sinking. Moses said: 'Master, that boat is sinking, it is going down!' The Master again ordered him to be quiet; so then Moses was quiet, but he was still more uncomfortable. When they arrived home he said: 'Master, I thought that you would have saved that little innocent child from drowning, and that you would have saved the boat which was going down in the water - but you did nothing. I cannot understand, but I should like to have an explanation'. The Master said: 'What you saw, I also saw. We both saw. So there was no use in your telling me, because I saw. You did not need to tell me what was happening, for I knew. If I had thought that it was better to interfere, I could have done it. Why did you take the trouble to tell me, and spoil your vow of silence?'

He continued: 'The child who was drowning was meant to bring about a conflict between two nations, and thousands and thousands of lives were going to be destroyed in that conflict. When he was drowned this averted the other danger which was to come'. Moses looked at him with great surprise. Then Khidr said: 'The boat that was sinking was the boat of pirates. It was sailing in order to wreck a large ship full of pilgrims, and then to take what was left in the ship and bring it home. Do you think that you and I can be judge of it? The Judge is behind. He knows what He is doing, He knows his work. When you were told to be quiet, your work was to keep your lips closed and to see everything, as I was doing, silently, in reverence'.

THE MYSTICISM OF SOUND AND MUSIC - COSMIC LANGUAGE - Reason

GAYAN 208 - BOULA -167 – He who does not recognize God now, will sooner or later recognize Him.

Question: Shall I see God after my death?

Answer: You may see Mr. Asquith a thousand times in the park, driving in a motorcar, but if you do not know him and cannot recognize him, if you are asked, "Have you seen Mr. Asquith?" you will say, "No." God's faces are everywhere. There is nothing on the earth, in the sky, in the sea, where He is not seen; but if we do not recognize Him we do not know that we see Him. A great Indian poet, Amir, says, "O eyes, that are longing to see the Beloved, why do you complain of His absence?" This means, the Beloved is before you, He has not run away, but your eyes must recognize Him. The Qur'an says, "Who is blind in life is blind after death." This is the time to see God. This physical existence was made that man might recognize God. This life is the most important time, and the only chance of seeing God.

THE SUPPLEMENTARY PAPERS - RELIGION - RELIGION II - The Ideal of God

GAYAN 209 - BOULA -168 – Fighting against nature is rising above nature.

Then we come to the question of how we can maintain our will. The nature of the life we live is to rob us of our will. Not only the struggle we have to undergo in life, but also our own self, our thoughts, our desires, our wishes, our motives, weaken our will. The person who knows how our inner being is connected with the perfect Will, will find that what makes the will smaller, narrower, more limited, is our experience throughout life. Our joys rob us of our will as do our sorrows; our pleasures rob us of our will as do our pains; and the only way of maintaining the power of will is by studying the existence of will and by analyzing among all the things in ourselves what will is.

It might seem that motive increases will-power, but no doubt in the end we will find that it robs us of will-power. Motive is a shadow upon the intelligence, although the higher the motive, the higher the soul, and the greater the motive, the greater the man. When the motive is beneath the ideal, then this is the fall of man; and when his motive is his ideal it is his rise. According to the width of motive man's vision is wide, and according to the power of motive man's strength is great.

HEALING AND THE MIND WORLD - MENTAL PURIFICATION - The Will

GAYAN 210 - BOULA -169 – Success is achieved when free will and circumstances work hand in hand.

The quality in the mind which makes it still at times and active at other times, which makes it reflect what it sees at one time and makes it avoid every reflection at another so that no outer reflection can touch it, this quality develops by concentration, contemplation, and meditation. The mind is trained by the master-trainer by diving deep, by soaring high, by expanding widely, and by centralizing the mind on one idea. And once the mind is mastered a person becomes a master of life. Every soul from the time it is born is like a machine, subject to all influences, influences of weather and of all that works through the five senses. For instance, no one can pass through a street without seeing the placards and advertisements. A man's eyes are compelled by what is before him. He has no intention of looking, but everything outside commands the eyes. So a man is constantly under the influence of all things of the outside world that govern him unknowingly. A person says, 'I am a free man; I do what I like.' But he never does. He does what he does not like many times. His ears are always subject to hear anything that falls on them, whether it is harmonious or inharmonious, and what he sees he cannot resist. And so a man is always under the influence of life.

Then there are the planetary influences and the living influences of those around him; and yet a man says, 'I have free will; I am a free man.' If he knew to what little extent he is free he would be frightened. But then there is one consolation, and that is that in man there is a spark somewhere hidden in his heart which alone can be called a source of free will. If this spark is tended a person has greater vitality, greater energy, greater power. All he thinks will come true, all he says will make an impression, all he does will have effect. What does a mystic do? He blows this spark in order to bring it to a flame till it comes to a blaze. This gives him the inspiration, the power which enables him to live in this world the life of free will. It is this spark which may be called the divine heritage of man, in which he sees the divine power of God, the soul of man; and to become spiritual means that by blowing upon this spark one produces light from it and sees the whole of life in this light. And by bringing the inner light to a blaze one is more able to think, to feel, and to act.

HEALING AND THE MIND WORLD - MENTAL PURIFICATION - The Control of the Mind

GAYAN 211 - BOULA -170 – A sincere feeling of respect needs no words; even silence can speak of one's respectful attitude.

A respectful attitude is the first and principal thing in the development of personality, not only respect toward someone whom one considers superior but respect for everyone one meets in life, in proportion to what is due to him. It is through conceit that man gives less honor where more honor is due, and it is by ignorance that man gives more respect than what is due. Respecting someone does not only require a desire to respect but an art of respecting. One ignorant of this art may express respect wrongly. It is self-respect which makes one inclined to respect another.

The one who has no respect for himself cares little if he respects another or if respect is at all necessary in life. To respect means to honor. It is not only bowing and bending, or external action, which expresses respect. A disrespectful person may bow his head before another and strike him on the face by his word. True respect is from the attitude which comes from the sincere feeling of respect. The outward expression of respect has no value without inner feeling. Inspired by a respectful attitude, man expresses his feeling in thought, speech, or action, which is the true expression of respect. A sincere feeling of respect needs no words, even the silence can speak of one's respectful attitude.

There are three different expressions of respect. One is when the position or rank of a person commands one to respect, whether one be willing or unwilling, and under the situation one cannot help having respect, which is nothing but an outer expression of respect. The second expression of respect is when a person wishes to please another by his respectful manner, to let him feel how respectful he is and what a good manner he has. By this expression one has two objects in view: One, to please another, and the other to please oneself by one's way of pleasing. The third way is the true feeling of respect which rises from one's heart, and if one tried to express it one could not express it enough. If one were not able to express it fully it can always be felt, because it is a living spirit of respect.

The mark of people having tradition behind them, by birth, nation or race, shows in their respectful tendency. To them disrespect either on their part or on the part of another means absence of beauty. Life has many beautiful things -- flowers, jewels, beauty of nature, of form, of line, of color -- but beauty of manner excels all, and all good manner is rooted in a respectful tendency.

ESOTERIC PAPERS - GATHA III - MORALS - Adab (Respect) (2)

GAYAN 212 - BOULA -171 – Simplicity of nature is the sign of saints.

All is mystery when we do not know it; when we know it all is simple. The true seekers after truth are lovers of simplicity. The right road is simple, clear and distinct. There is nothing vague about it.
The Mysticism of Sound and Music - The Mystery of Color and Sound

A spiritual person is considered very evolved, but in his appearance the spiritual person may be the most simple, the most innocent one. He is not ignorant but less complicated, broader in outlook, keener in perception, with lofty ideals, with a high consciousness; and yet humble and democratic in the true sense of the word.
The Alchemy of Happiness – The Art of Personality

Man today has made life so complex that whatever he seeks after, he wants to find in complexity. All things in life, which have importance, beauty, and value, are simple; and simplest of all things is the divine truth. The one who cares little for it thinks it is too deep water to go into, and the one who cares much for it thinks that it is so difficult that it would be very hard to find it. In this way both the lover of truth and the one who does not care look for complexity. Knowing his nature, the wise have guided man gradually to the truth. Nevertheless, Jesus Christ, the Prophet Mohammed, Moses, all the different prophets who in their time have given the message of God and truth, have given it in perfect simplicity. Today man with all his knowledge complicates that truth and gives it a form that is not understood. The general tendency is that when a man does not understand something, he believes by the very fact of his not understanding it, that there must be something in it.
IN AN EASTERN ROSE GARDEN - Simplicity and Complexity

GAYAN 213 - BOULA -172 – The heart is the gate of God; as soon as you knock upon it, the answer comes.

      The second kind of intuition is that of which it is said in the Bible, 'Knock, and it shall be opened unto you'. Knocking at the door is asking within one's own self, 'What will become of this particular business, or aim, or object that I am thinking of?' As soon as one knocks at the gate of God, which is one's heart, from there the answer comes, and it is a truer answer than any other person can give. There is no one who can know as much about our life, affairs, objects, motives as we do ourselves. And therefore nobody can advise us better than ourselves.

IN AN EASTERN ROSE GARDEN – Intuition

GAYAN 214 - BOULA -173 – Every impression of an evil nature should be met with a combative attitude.

The best way of keeping the mind free from all undesirable impressions is not to partake them at the moment when they fall upon the mind. For instance, if someone is disagreeable, instantly his influence produces the same thing in another person with whom he is disagreeable. The best way to avoid it would be to stand on one's guard that one may not catch his infectious disagreeableness. All such things as pride, prejudice, jealousy, intolerance, coldness, have a great influence upon a person.

When speaking, working or walking with someone, one can easily partake one's companion's disagreeable impulse, because as a rule a person thinks there is justification for giving it back, a word for a word, a frown for a frown. A person feels satisfied in boasting, "He said two words to me, but I have given him back the same in four words." He feels very glad for the moment, thinking, "I have given back what I had received." But he does not know that if he had not given it back, the same that the other person had thrown upon him would have returned to that person a thousandfold.

The psychological point of view therefore differs from the ordinary point of view, for in the psychological point of view there is a science, it teaches one not to take in one's mind what is disagreeable, inharmonious. By understanding this one can maintain the purity of mind, and it requires fortifying oneself with will-power, making the heart as a stone wall, for all that is thrown at it not to pierce through, but to fall down.

The psychological effect of every impression is such that each impression has a tendency to be held by the mind; all we see during the day has, consciously or unconsciously, an influence upon our life. All good or bad things, or things with beauty or ugliness, they remain with us and flourish in our minds. If it was an impression of beauty, that would flourish; if it was an impression of ugliness, that would flourish. This is the principal reason why dreams have effect upon our life. It is the impression that the dream has made upon us that works out its destiny in the waking state. Therefore, if by being on one's guard, instead of resisting evil one would only slide it over, it would run away by its own force.

The one who is strong enough to keep away from his mind all undesirable impressions will in time radiate harmony and will create the atmosphere of peace; thus making himself happy, he will bring happiness to others.

ESOTERIC PAPERS - GATHA II - EVERYDAY LIFE - Keeping the Mind Free From All Undesirable Impressions

GAYAN 215 - BOULA -174 – There is no greater phenomenon than love itself.

When man analyses the objective world and realizes the inner being, what he learns first and last is that this whole vision of life is created of love; love itself being life, all will in time be absorbed in it.

THE WAY OF ILLUMINATION - Some Aspects of Sufism - Suma, the Music of the Sufis

GAYAN 216 - BOULA -175 – Those guilty of the same fault unite in making a virtue out of their common sin.

It must be remembered that one shows lack of nobleness of character by love of gossiping. It is so natural, and yet it is a great fault in the character to cherish the tendency to talk about others. One shows a great weakness when one makes remarks about someone behind his back. In the first place it is against what may be called frankness, and also it is judging another, which is wrong according to the teaching of Christ, who says, 'Judge not, that ye be not judged'. When one allows this tendency to remain in one, one develops love of talking about others. It is a defect which commonly exists, and when two people meet who have the same tendency, they gossip together. One helps the other, one encourages the other. And when something is supported by two people of necessity it becomes a virtue, if only for the time being.

THE ART OF PERSONALITY - CHARACTER AND PERSONALITY –
Character-Building

GAYAN 217 - BOULA -176 – Life can be full of blessings when one knows how to receive them.

The same is with all things in life. Every moment in our lives is an opportunity which brings a benefit and blessing. And the one who knows how to be benefited by it, and how to be blessed by it, receives the benefit and the blessing. Everyone seems living and awake, but few souls really are living and awake. There are opportunities of benefit and blessing on every plane of one's life--on the physical plane, on the mental plane, on the spiritual plane--and every opportunity is invaluable. But often one realizes the truth when it is too late. There is no greater and better opportunity than the moment that can give a spiritual illumination, a moment when one can receive the blessing of God. It is a priceless moment. Who knows it and understands it and tries to be benefited by it is blessed.

THE UNITY OF RELIGIOUS IDEALS - PROPHETS AND RELIGIONS – Gatha 2 –The Sufi's Conception of God – The Ten Virgins

GAYAN 218 - BOULA -177 –Where the body goes the shadow goes also; so is truth followed by falsehood.

As there is water in the depths of the earth so there is truth at the bottom of all things, false or true. In some places one has to dig deep, in other places only a short distance, that is the only difference, but there is no place where there is no water. One may have to dig very, very deep in order to get it, but in the depths of the earth there is water, and in the depths of all this falsehood which is on the surface there is truth. If we are really seeking for the truth we shall always find it at some time or other. The one who wants to protect himself from being misguided shows a certain tendency, a kind of weakness, which comes from thinking deep in himself that there is no right guidance. If he realizes that right guidance is to be found in himself, he will always be rightly guided; and his power will become so great that if his guide is going wrong, the power of the pupil will help him to go right, because the real Teacher is in the heart of man.

The Path of Initiation - THE PATH OF INITIATION AND DISCIPLESHIP - The Path of Initiation

GAYAN 219 - BOULA -178 –Life in the world is false, and its lovers revel in falsehood.

The life in the world is such that it is as difficult for the rich as for the poor. A world such as this, made by falsehood, has its blows, continual blows, that a person of good heart has to stand. And there is only one safety from all these blows that might destroy the heart altogether: it is to learn how to tolerate, to learn how to forgive. For everyone says or does or thinks only according to his own particular evolution, and he cannot do better. Why not, therefore, tolerate? Why not, therefore, forgive? And if there is intolerance, then there must be a continual reciprocity; it is giving and taking intolerance. It means killing the element of love and giving life to the element which is death itself.

THE UNITY OF RELIGIOUS IDEALS - RELIGION - The Religion Heart

GAYAN 220 - BOULA -179 – Nothing false will succeed, and if it apparently succeeds, it can only bring a false benefit.

What people want to do today is to get spiritual insight and power and use it for their material advantage. They think that if they can make things more profitable in their worldly life, it is worth doing. This is like spending pearls to buy pebbles. They would do better to pay for pebbles with pennies than to spend spiritual pearls on pebbles. Business and industry and all other concerns require effort, perseverance, qualifications, intelligent work. If one does it that way one is successful. But the belief that spiritual attainment should only be used for worldly success would make of it a very small aim to be accomplished. Spiritual attainment is success itself, all things come to the spiritual person. If he is a business man, he will be more successful; but he should not try to attain spiritually in order to succeed in business. The accent must be on spiritual attainment and all things will follow as a matter of course. As Christ has said, 'Seek ye first the kingdom of Heaven and all these things shall be added unto you.' Therefore whatever a man's profession, be he a writer, a poet, a politician, or an inventor, whatever the profession, spiritual attainment will always help, in every direction.

IN AN EASTERN ROSE GARDEN - Sublime Knowledge

GAYAN 221 - BOULA -180 – All that produces longing in the heart deprives it of its freedom.

If one asks what kind of captivity it is, the answer is that for a spider the thin threads of the web are a captivity, and for an elephant iron chains are a captivity. The stronger a person is the greater the captivity; the greater power he has the greater are his difficulties; the stronger the soul is the heavier the load it has to carry. Therefore in captivity we are all equal. When a person sees only the surface, it appears as if one has an easy life and another has to toil all day; as if one has a gay life and another is miserable. But that is the outside. When we look deeply into life, in some way or another, whether a person looks cheerful or sad, some captivity is always hidden there. We do not know. In order to understand their life's situation it is not enough to cast a glance at people from the outside. We only see the prisoners; if we saw the prisons we would be shocked.

I have met numberless people who do not know what they want to do next week; they only think of today. Life is becoming uncertain, and its burden greater. They say that we are progressing, but towards what? Freedom? No, towards captivity. A greater and greater load of duty and responsibility is put on our shoulders. Perhaps it is worse in the West, perhaps it is worse in the East; but the cause of it all is the lack of understanding of freedom. One must look in another direction to see the sun or the moon; one must not look at the earth. How to die before death is something that man today does not know; and he does not care to know. The central theme of life today is self-assertion. When a person speaks about himself he wants to make himself ten times more important than he is. He cannot help it; if he does not do so the others will not understand. I even heard one man say to another, 'Your modesty is your greatest misfortune'.

Every man has to be self-asserting, continually guarding his interests in order to live. There are many who toil from morning till evening, guarding their self-interest and thinking about nothing else. And what is it all for? In order to exist. But even germs and grubs exist and enjoy life much better! Birds fly in the air and are quite happy; but man is loading his heart with a thousand troubles, making his responsibilities greater and greater. And in the end he gains nothing; his health is spoiled, his spirit wrecked. He does not know any more where he is, nor where his spirit is; and if he has nothing here he has nothing in the hereafter. Many die without ever having given a thought to the deeper side of life. Not that they did not care for it; but they could not find time for it; they had too much to do in life.

IN AN EASTERN ROSE GARDEN - The Freedom of the Soul (2)

GAYAN 222 - BOULA -181 – Possibility is the nature of God, and impossibility is the limitation of man.

There is no such thing as impossible. All is possible. Impossible is made by the limitation of our capacity of understanding. Man, blinded by the law of nature's working, by the law of consequences which he has known through his few years life on earth, begins to say, "This is possible and that is impossible." If he were to rise beyond limitations, his soul would see nothing but possible. And when the soul has risen high enough to see all possibility, that soul certainly has caught a glimpse of God.

They say God is all-mighty; and I say, God is all-possible. Possibility is the nature of God, and impossibility is the art of man. Man goes so far, and cannot go any further. Man makes a flower out of paper, giving it as natural a color as possible, yet he says it is not possible to make it fragrant, for he has his limitations. But God, Who is the Maker of the flower and who is the Giver of the fragrance, has all power, and man, who is weakened by his limitedness, becomes more and more limited the more he thinks of it. In this is created the spirit of pessimism.

Man who is conscious of God Almighty, and who in the contemplation of God loses the consciousness of his own self, inherits the power of God, and it is in this power and belief that the spirit of optimism is born

ESOTERIC PAPERS - GITHA II - THE PATH OF ATTAINMENT - Spirit of Optimism

GAYAN 223 - BOULA -182 – It is the exaltation of the spirit which is productive of all beauty.

Exaltation depends upon purity. The body cleansed gives an exaltation which is experienced by all living beings on the physical plane. The heart cleansed of all impurities gives a much greater exaltation, which is experienced in the inner plane and is reflected on the outer plane.

Most people little realize the meaning of exaltation. In point of fact all things man seeks for and becomes occupied with are most often methods adopted to obtain an exaltation, through food, perfume, music, or through the beauty of color and line. No method, however, succeeds in giving the experience of a fuller exaltation in the absence of purity of heart. In plain words it is the pure-hearted who enjoy the beauty of music, color or perfume more fully than those without purity of heart; although the pure-hearted seem to need these things which bring about exaltation less, sometimes for the very reason that the very purity of the heart gives them that exaltation which others strive to achieve by different methods.

Amir, the mystic poet, says, "Their eyes refused the wine, her generous offer, saying, 'We do not need thee, we are intoxicated perpetually.'" The reason behind the refusal of the pious, at times, of music, art, gaiety, or merriment was that they already had the exaltation which others try to gain by these things. It does not at all mean that the pious are always against things of beauty and pleasure. It only means that they are rich by the feeling of exaltation which comes from within, without adopting for it any other methods. Nevertheless the pious are the ones who are capable of enjoying beauty in all its aspects fully. As Hafiz says, "If the pious ones would hear the song I sing they would get up and dance unrestrainedly."

ESOTERIC PAPERS - GITHA III – Everyday Life - Exaltation

GAYAN 224 - BOULA -183 – One virtue can stand against a thousand vices.

A person may realize all the various weaknesses in himself, and be very sorry about them, and he would like to give them up if he could; but he finds that whether he likes some little weakness or not, he cannot hold himself back from doing certain things, whether it is weakness of mind or weakness of action. This shows that though the desire of the soul is always to direct man on the right path, on the path of virtue, on the good path, yet at the same time he has lost his control, and he is led away by some force he cannot control. This weakness of character is shown when a person says, 'I do not wish to be angry; after being angry I am very sorry, but at the same time I cannot help it. I do not wish to hurt others, but when the moment comes I cannot help myself, I am abrupt.' Then even vices such as drink, or thieving, or any weakness, are all caused by weakness of mind. When the mind has no control over its thoughts and feelings, when it is not mastered, all these things come to pass.

From all this it is plain that man has two aspects of being: the servant aspect and the master aspect. When only the servant aspect is nourished and the master aspect is not, then the master aspect of his being longs to be master, and cannot be; and the whole conflict in life depends on that. When a person is interested in the master aspect and wishes to be master, then he becomes master of himself, and he becomes not only master of his thoughts, feelings, and actions, but he becomes master of his affairs.

In an Eastern Rose Garden - The Master Mind

GAYAN 225 - BOULA -184 –Wickedness manifesting from an intelligent person is like a poisonous fruit springing from a fertile soil.

Man's contact with the outer world is such that there is a continual mechanical interchange going on; every moment of his life he is partaking of all that his senses allow him to receive. Therefore very often the man who is looking for faults in others, who is looking for evil, even though he may not be a wicked person, is yet partaking unknowingly of all that is evil. Once deceived, a person is always on the look-out; even with someone who is honest he will look for deceit, as he holds that impression within himself. Thus a hunter who, comes from the forest where he has just received a blow from a lion, will shrink even from the caress of his mother; and when we consider how many impressions, agreeable and disagreeable, we receive from morning till evening, we realize how someone may become wicked without meaning to.

For in point of fact nobody is born wicked. Although the body belongs to the earth, yet the soul belongs to God, and from above man has received nothing but goodness. With the wickedest person in the world, when one can touch the deepest depths of his being one finds nothing but goodness there. So if there is any such thing as wickedness or badness, it is only what man has acquired; and he has not acquired it willingly but simply because he is open to all impressions, as it is natural for every man to be open to impressions.

The Alchemy of Happiness - The Interdependence of Life Within and Without

GAYAN 226 - BOULA -185 – Failure in life does not matter; the greatest misfortune is standing still.

Remember that every soul that raises its head in life gets much opposition from the world. It has been so with all the prophets, saints and sages, so one cannot expect to be exempt. In this is the law of nature, and also God's plan working and preparing something desirable. No one is either higher or lower than oneself. In all sources that fulfill one's need, one may see one source, God, the only source; and in admiring and in bowing before and in loving anyone, one may consider one is doing it to God. In sorrow one may look to God, and in joy one may thank Him. One does not bemoan the past, nor worry about the future; one tries only to make the best of today. One should know no failure, for even in a fall there is a stepping-stone to rise; but to the Sufi the rise and fail matter little. One does not repent for what one has done, since one thinks, says, and does what one means. One does not fear the consequences of performing one's wish in life, for what will be, will be.

THE WAY OF ILLUMINATION – Some Aspects of Sufism - Life In This World

GAYAN 227 - BOULA -186 –Consideration is born in the heart and developed in the head.

If we inquire of our self within for what purpose we have come on earth and why we have become human beings, wondering whether it would perhaps have been better to remain angels, the answer will certainly come to the wise, from his own heart, that we are here to experience a fuller life, to become fully human. For it is through being considerate that we become fully human. Every action done with consideration is valuable, every word said with consideration is precious. The whole teaching of Christ --'Blessed are the meek... the poor in spirit'--teaches one thing: consideration. Although it seems simple, yet it is a hard lesson to learn. The more we wish to act according to this ideal, the more we realize that we fail. The further we go on the path of consideration, the more delicate do the eyes of our perception become; we feel and regret the slightest mistake.

It is not every soul that takes the trouble to tread this path. Everyone is not a plant; there are many who are rocks, and these do not want to be considerate, they think it is too much trouble. Of course the stone has no pain, it is the one who feels who has pain. Still, it is in feeling that there is life; life's joy is so great that even with pain one would rather be a living being than a rock, for there is a joy in living, in feeling alive, which cannot be expressed in words. After how many millions of years has the life buried in stones and rocks risen to the human being! Even so if a person wishes to stay a rock, he had better stay so, though the natural inclination in every person should be to develop the human qualities fully.

THE PATH OF INITIATION - THE PATH OF INITIATION AND DISCIPLESHIP - Discipleship

GAYAN 228 - BOULA -187 – Indifference is the key to the whole secret of life.

It is the interest of the bird which enables it to build its nest, and in the same way it is the interest of man which enables him to make all that he makes. If man did not have this faculty of taking interest the world would never have evolved; this is why the secret of manifestation and the mystery of evolution are to be found in interest. But at the same time I do not deny the power of indifference. The power of indifference is a greater one still, provided that the indifference is not an artificial one. When a person chooses indifference only because he thinks 'it is a good principle, then it is not a virtue; and also there will be no power, for such a man is a captive: on one side he is drawn by interest, and on the other side he wants to show indifference. It is a mistake on his part, for he neither accomplishes anything by the power of interest, nor does he gain the advantages that can be derived from indifference.

Seen from the point of view of metaphysics, why is the power of indifference greater than the power of interest? Because although motive has a power, yet at the same time motive limits power. Man is endowed at birth with much greater power than he ever imagines, and it is motive that limits this power: any motive and every motive; yet it is motive that gives man the power to accomplish things. If there were no motive there would be no power. But when one compares the original power of man with the power of motive, one will find it is just like the difference between the ocean and a drop. The motive reduces the power to a drop. Without a motive the power of the soul is like an ocean; but at the same time that ocean-like power cannot be used without a motive, while as soon as one wants to use it for a purpose it becomes less.

THE ALCHEMY OF HAPPINESS- Interest and Indifference

GAYAN 229 - BOULA -188 – Life is differentiated by the pairs of opposites.

When we look at the dual aspect of nature we shall find this to be even more important. The dual aspect is also to be seen in all things and in every being, for instance the two sides, the right and the left, the head and the feet, the top and the bottom, two points in one line, the two eyes which enable us to see, the necessity of the pairs of opposites. The dual aspect is manifest to our view when we see the sun and the moon, when we see the male and the female aspect in nature, and when we see good and not good. When we experience joy and sorrow, when we realize that there is birth and death, we know what is to be known about the dual aspect of nature. The earth and the water, above and below, everything in nature distinctly shows two opposite aspects.

Furthermore there are opposite qualities in every human being, call them male and female, call them positive and negative, call them free and gross; no one can exist without opposite qualities. Besides the more power one has in one quality, the greater capability one has for the opposite quality; in other words the higher a person stands, the deeper is the space before him to fall into.

There is a hidden quality, and there is a quality which is manifest. What is manifest we recognize; what is hidden we do not see. There is going forward and there is going backward, there is success and there is failure, there is light and there is darkness, there is joy and there is sadness, there is birth and there is death. All things that we can know, feel, and perceive have their opposites. It is the opposite quality which brings about balance. The world would not exist if there were not both water and earth. Every thing and every being needs these two opposite qualities in order to exist, to act, and to fulfil the purpose of life; for each quality is incomplete without the other. No man has a complete personality if he does not have some little touch of the fineness that belongs to the female nature; woman is only complete in her character when there is some little touch of the male nature.

PHILOSOPHY, PSYCHOLOGY, MYSTICISM - PHILOSOPHY - The Threefold, Dual, and Unique Aspects of Nature

GAYAN 230 - BOULA -189 – There is nothing we take in this bazaar of life that we shall not sooner or later have to pay for.

We have many debts to pay in our lives, debts we do not always know of. We only know our money debts, but there are many others: of the husband to his wife and of the wife to her husband; of the mother to the child and of the child to the mother; the debts to pay to our friends and acquaintances, to those who stand above us and to those who are dependent upon us. There are so many different kinds of debts we have to pay; and yet we never think about them. In ancient times even those not taking the spiritual path, for instance noblemen and warriors, had the law of chivalry, and there were strict rules about paying one's debts. The ancient people thought, 'My mother has brought me up from infancy, she has sacrificed her sleep, rest, and comfort for me and loved me with a love which is beyond any other love in this world, and she has shown in life that mercy to me which is the compassion of God.' The child thought a great deal about the debt it owed to its mother.

Someone went to the Prophet Mohammed and asked him, 'Prophet, you said there is a great debt to be paid to one's mother. Suppose that I gave my mother all that I have earned, would that pay her back?' The Prophet said, 'No, not in the least. If you served her your whole life, even then you could not pay the debt of what she has done for you in one day. She brought you up with the thought always in her mind that even when she was gone you would live; she has not only given her service and heart and love to you, but also her life. That you will live after her, that has been all her thought. And what is your thought? If you are a kind and good person your thought is, "So long as my poor mother is living, I will take care of her to the end; one day she will die, and then I shall be free." It is a different thought from her thought.'

This is only one example; but there are many other debts, to our neighbors, to strangers, to those who depend upon us or who expect from us some help, some counsel, a word of advice, some service. They are all debts we have to pay. There is also much to pay to God, but God can forgive. The debt to the world, however, must not be forgotten before entering upon the spiritual path. The spirit feels a great release when it pays its debts as it goes further. Do people think of these simple things nowadays? As soon as a person starts thinking about spiritual matters the first question is what occult books shall he read in order to obtain the key to the path. He never thinks about these little things and how much depends upon them. But there is a condition that must be fulfilled, and that condition is our consideration for every soul.

THE ALCHEMY OF HAPPINESS - The Inner Life and Self Realization

GAYAN 231 - BOULA -190 – A diamond must be cut before its light can shine out.

Expressing the art of personality is the sign of the great. Knowingly or unknowingly a person may develop that manner in himself and it is wonderful to watch it….

One may ask: If we have a personality, why must we develop it? But even a diamond must be cut! It has light in it, yet cutting is required to awaken it. It cannot show its glow and brilliancy before it has been cut. It is the same with the personality.

SUFI TEACHINGS - THE PRIVILEGE OF BEING HUMAN - The Art of Personality

GAYAN 232 - BOULA -191 –Beyond goodness is trueness, which is a divine quality.

... There is, however, a standard of inner purity of which the principle is that anything in speech or action which causes fear, brings confusion, or gives a tendency to deception, extinguishes that little spark in the heart, the spark of trueness which only shines when the life is natural and pure.

A man may not always be able to tell when an action is right in regard to particular circumstances, or when it is wrong; but he can always remember this psychological principle, and judge as to whether the action or word robs him of that inner strength and peace and comfort which form his natural life. No man can judge another; it is a man's self that must be his judge. Therefore it is no use to make rigid standards of moral or social purity. Religion has made them, schools have taught them, yet the prisons are full of criminals and the newspapers are daily more eloquent about the faults of humanity. No external law can stop crime. It is man himself who should understand what is good for him and what is not; he should be able to discriminate between what is poison and what is nectar. He should know it, measure it, weigh it and judge it; and that he can only do by understanding the psychology of what is natural to him and what is unnatural. The unnatural action, thought, or speech is that which makes him uncomfortable before, during, or after it has taken place; for his sense of discomfort is proof that in this case it is not the soul which is the actor. The soul is forever seeking something which will open a way for its expression and give it freedom and comfort in this physical life. In reality the whole life is tending towards freedom, towards the unfoldment of something that is choked up by physical life and this freedom can be gained by true purity of life.

THE ALCHEMY OF HAPPINESS - Purity of Life

GAYAN 233 - BOULA -192 – A guilty conscience robs the will of its power.

Power depends greatly upon the consciousness and the attitude of mind. A guilty conscience can turn lions into rabbits. They lose their power once they feel guilty; and so it is with man. When a man is impressed by what others think, if that impression is of disappointment or distress or shame, his power is diminished; but when he is inspired by a thought, a feeling, an action he performs, then he is powerful. It is the power of truth that makes one stronger.

HEALING AND THE MIND WORLD - MENTAL PURIFICATION - The Power Within Us

GAYAN 234 - BOULA -193 – The answer that uproots the question from its ground is truly inspired.

It is the problem of life in the crowd which he has to solve, and yet not solve it intellectually, as everyone wishes to do, but spiritually, by keeping that instrument, the heart, in proper tune to the Infinite, that he may get the answer for all questions arising at every moment of the day.

It is therefore that even the presence of the Prophet is the answer to every question: without having spoken one word, the Prophet gives the answer; but if a mind, restless and confused, cannot hear it, then that mind receives the answer in words. The answer of the Prophet uproots every question; but the answer always comes from the heart of the Prophet without his even having been asked a question. For the Prophet is only the medium between God and man; therefore the answer is from God. It is not true that the Prophet answers a question because he reads the mind; it is the mind of the one who asks the question that strikes, in the inner plane, the divine bell, which is the heart of the Prophet; and God, hearing the bell, answers. The answer comes in a manner as if words were put into the mouth of the Prophet.

THE UNITY OF RELIGIOUS IDEALS - THE SPIRITUAL HIERARCHY - The Attunement of the Prophet

GAYAN 235 - BOULA -194 – A jest lightens the intelligence and clears away the clouds of gloom that surround man's heart.

Without humor life is dull and depressing. Humor is the reflection of that divine life and sun which makes life like a day full of sunshine. And a person who reflects divine wisdom and divine joy adds to the expression of his thought when he expresses his ideas with mirth.

THE PATH OF INITIATION - SUFI POETRY - Muslih-ud-din Sa'di

GAYAN 236 - BOULA -195 – If man only knew what is behind his free will, he would never call it "my will," but "Thy Will."

In the Qur'an one reads in clear words, "For everything we have appointed a time," and in another place, "Not one atom moves (which always moves) without the command of God;" in a third place, "We have the power to raise and to bring down any soul, whatever be his position in life." And this shows that not only are all things appointed to happen at a certain time, but they are directed by the One so perfect in power and wisdom. When man says, "I have done this," or "I can do it," or "I will do it," the one perfect in power and wisdom smiles as a grown-up person would smile at a child saying, "I will remove mountains." It does not mean there is no free will, but if one only knew what is behind one's free will he would never call it free will, he would call it His Will.

Esoteric Papers - Sangatha II

GAYAN 237 - BOULA -196 –The service of God means that we each work for all.

...We can see on the face of a man who takes a dislike to another that his own soul despises him, because in disliking the other he dislikes his own soul. His own soul is not a different soul; it is the same soul as that of the other, the same soul as the soul of the prophet, the same soul as the soul of the greatest sinner, the same soul as the Soul of the whole world.

The most essential lines of a poem of Hafiz are these: "To friends be faithful and loving, to enemies serviceable and courteous. This is the secret of the two worlds".

This was taught in all ages by all the prophets, saints and those who have served the world, and it is because we have forgotten it that we suffer all the ills we suffer; all our lacks come from our forgetting it. It is the secret of happiness and peace. What is done for a return is not service, otherwise all the people in the city working with their machines would be called servants of God. That which is done, not for fame or name, not for the appreciation or thanks from those for whom it is done, but only for love, is service of God.

SUFI TEACHINGS - THE PRIVILEGE OF BEING HUMAN - Moral Culture

Gayan #338 - Boula #197 – His trust is of no value, to him or others, who has no trust in himself.

Whatever be the faith or belief of one who has no confidence in himself, it will not be substantial. If a person came to a wise man and said, 'I believe in you, I trust you, but I cannot trust in myself', he would say, 'I appreciate very much your trust and belief, but I cannot depend upon you'. If, however, another person comes and tells him, 'I trust myself, but do not yet know if I can trust you', he will say "There is hope for that man', for he will know that that person has already taken his first step; he has now to take the next step. The man who cannot trust his own intuition is perplexed, he does not know what he wants. He will always depend upon outer things which give him reasons; but the things of the outer life which are subject to continual change, to death and destruction, are not dependable.

IN AN EASTERN ROSE GARDEN - Intellect and Wisdom

GAYAN 239 - BOULA -198 – If you wish to probe the depths of a man's character, test him with that which is his life's greatest need.

What is character? Character is, so to speak, a picture with lines and colors which we make within ourselves. It is wonderful to see how the tendency of character-building springs up from childhood, just as one sees in a bird the instinct of building a nest. A little child begins to notice all kinds of things in grown-up persons and to adopt all that seems best to it: words, manners, movements, ideas. Everything that it grasps from the grown-up it attracts and gathers, and builds, so to speak, a building with it which is its character. It is being built all through life.

By this we understand that, when a person is absorbed in himself, he has no time for character-building, because he has no time to think of others: then there is no other. But when he forgets himself, he has time to look here and there, to collect what is good and beautiful, and to add it naturally to his character. So the character is built. One need not make an effort to build it, one has only to forget oneself. For instance, actors and actresses with great qualifications cannot act if they do not forget themselves. If the musician cannot forget himself when he is playing, he cannot perform music satisfactorily; the singer's voice will not come out. And so it is with the poet and all other artists.

Think then how the whole work of building oneself, and everything else, depends on how much one is able to forget oneself. That is the key to the whole life, material and spiritual, and to worldly and spiritual success. It seems such a simple thing, and yet it is so difficult.

TEACHINGS - THE PRIVILEGE OF BEING HUMAN - Character-Building

GAYAN 240 - BOULA -199 –It is the lack of personal magnetism that makes a man look for magnetism in others.

The question is, how can this magnetism be developed? This magnetism is developed by study, by concentration, by a keen observation of life, and by the knowledge of repose. Very many intelligent persons, because they do not know how to concentrate and how to take repose in their lives, in time blunt their intelligence; because there is a certain fund of energy which is preserved and which is limited, and when there is too much pressure put upon that limited energy in the end what happens? A person becomes less and less intelligent, and his power of mind diminishes every day. Whenever you find a very intelligent man becoming duller every day, it always proves that the amount of energy that was there has been spent. It is, therefore, by knowing how to preserve one's energies by repose, and how to concentrate and sharpen one's intellect, that this magnetism remains in a right condition. What generally happens is that great responsibility falls on the intelligent person. Much more is asked of him than of others who lack intelligence. If he does not give his mind a rest by knowing how to repose, and if he does not concentrate and thus sharpen his intellect, naturally, just like a knife which is continually used, it will become blunted; naturally the continual use of intellect will make him short of words.

The third aspect of magnetism is perhaps a higher kind than the two which have been described above, for this magnetism is more profound and it affects another person more deeply. This is the magnetism of love, of sympathy, of friendliness. A person who by nature is sympathetic; a person who tolerates, who forgets, who forgives; a person who does not keep bitterness nor malice in his mind against anyone; a person who admires and appreciates beauty, who loves it in art, in nature, in all its forms, and who goes out to friend and foe, to the acquaintance, the stranger, to all; the person who can endure and who can suffer, and who has the power to have patience through all conditions of life, who feels the pain of another in his heart and who is always willing to become a friend, it is that person whose magnetism is greater than all the other magnetisms that we know of. We do not need to go far to see this. If only we look for good things in people we shall find this. Among our surroundings we can find many in whom we can appreciate this quality....

HEALING AND THE MIND WORLD - MENTAL PURIFICATION - Magnetism

GAYAN 241 - BOULA -200 – Love develops into harmony, and of harmony is born beauty.

Beauty is born of harmony. What is harmony? Harmony is right proportion, in other words, right rhythm. And what is life? Life is the outcome of harmony. At the back of the whole creation is harmony, and the whole secret of creation is harmony. Intelligence longs to attain to the perfection of harmony. What man calls happiness and comfort, or profit and gain - all he longs for and wishes to attain - is harmony. In smaller or greater proportion he is longing for harmony; even in attaining the most mundane things he always wishes for harmony. But often he does not adopt right methods. Often his methods are wrong. The object attained by both good and bad methods is the same, but the way one tries to attain it turns the object into right or wrong. It is not the object which is wrong, it is the way one adopts to attain it. No one, whatever his station in life, wishes for disharmony, for all suffering, pain and trouble are disharmony.

THE MYSTICISM OF SOUND AND MUSIC - MUSIC - Spiritual Attainment by the Aid of Music

GAYAN 242 - BOULA -201 – Devotion is proved by sacrifice.

When a person thinks, 'I am too good or too kind to you, I have been too devoted to you', that person forgets that kindness, goodness and devotion are larger than the horizon. No one can be too good, no one can be too kind, and no one can be too devoted. And when there is a discussion between friends, and one says, 'I have done so much for you, I have suffered so much for you, I have had so much pain on your account, I have had such a difficult life for your sake,' then he is entering into business. He wants to keep a diary of what he has given in the form of love and kindness and goodness and sacrifice. A true friend makes every sacrifice he can and never thinks about it; he does not even allow his mind to ponder upon the subject. Real friendship means regard, a deep regard for the pleasure and displeasure of the friend. Is there anything in life which is more delicate than friendship-taking care that no words should hurt the friend, that no action should harm him, that not the slightest shade of coldness may fall on his heart? It is most difficult. If a person has learnt the manner of friendship he need not learn anything more; he knows everything. He has learnt the greatest religion, for it is in this same way that one will make a way to God. The one who has never learnt the manner of friendship will never know the way to God. He may be God's worshipper, but he cannot be the friend of God.

IN AN EASTERN ROSE GARDEN - Friendship (2)

GAYAN 243 - BOULA -202 – It is God who, by the hand of man, designs and carries out His intended plan in nature.

By learning the mystery of attainment one learns the divine mastery which is suggested in that phrase of the Bible, 'Thy will be done on earth as it is in heaven.' This phrase is a veil which covers the mystery of attainment. On coming to earth, man, who is the instrument of God, loses connection with that divine power whose instrument he is, thus keeping not only himself but even God from helping His will to be done. When man, who is born to be the instrument of God, does not perform his mission properly he naturally feels dissatisfied. It does not mean that he does not accomplish what he desires, but it is the reason why he is unhappy. This condition is like a hand out of joint: it is not only the hand that suffers, but the person whose hand it is, not being able to use it, suffers also. Therefore in accomplishing the work he undertakes, in attaining to the aim he has in life, man not only helps himself but he also serves God.

THE ALCHEMY OF HAPPINESS - The Path of Attainment (1)

GAYAN 244 - BOULA -203 – As fire can cook food or burn it, so also does pain affect the human heart.

Krishna is pictured in Hindu symbology with a crown of peacock's feathers, playing the flute. Krishna is the idea of divine love, the god of love. And the divine love expresses itself by entering in man and filling his whole being. Therefore the flute is the human heart, and a heart which is made hollow, which becomes a flute for the god of love to play. When the heart is not empty, in other words when there is no scope in the heart, there is no place for love. Rumi, the great poet of Persia, explains the idea more clearly. He says the pains and sorrows the soul experiences through life are holes made in a reed flute, and it is by making these holes that the player makes out of a reed a flute.

Which means, the heart of man is first a reed, and the suffering and pain it goes through make it a flute, which can then be used by God as the instrument to produce the music that He constantly wishes to produce. But every reed is not a flute, and so every heart is not His instrument. As the reeds need to be made into flutes, so the human heart can be turned into an instrument and can be offered to the God of love. It is the human heart which becomes the harp of the angels, it is the human heart which is the lute of Orpheus. It is on the model of the heart of man that the first instrument of music was made, and no earthly instrument can produce that music which the heart produces, raising the mortal soul to immortality.

The crown of peacock's feathers leads to a further revelation, that it is the music of the heart which can be expressed through the head; it is the knowledge of the head and the love of the heart that express the divine message fully. Peacock's feathers have in all ages been considered as a sign of beauty, as a sign of knowledge; beauty because they are beautiful, knowledge because they are in the form of an eye. It is by keen observation that man acquires knowledge. Knowledge without love is lifeless. So with the flute the crown of peacock's feathers makes the symbol complete.

THE UNITY OF RELIGIOUS IDEALS - PROPHETS AND RELIGIONS - The Sufi's Conception of God - The Flute of Krishna

GAYAN 245 - BOULA -204 – Every desire increases the power of man to accomplish his main desire, which is the purpose of every soul.

Every man seems to have his purpose, but this purpose is nothing but a step to that which is the one purpose, which is the purpose of God. Our small desires, if they are granted today, to-morrow we will have another wish. Whatever be the desire, when it is granted, next day there is another desire. This shows that the whole of humanity, that every soul, is directed towards one desire, and that is the object of God: a fuller experience of life within and without, a fuller knowledge of life, the life above and below. It is the widening of the outlook: that it may be so wide that in the soul, which is vaster than the world, all may be reflected; that the sight may become so keen that it may probe the depths of the earth and the highest of the heavens. It is herein that lies the fulfillment of the soul. And the soul who will not make every effort possible, with every sacrifice for the attainment of this, that soul has not understood religion. What is the Sufi message? It is esoteric training, working and practicing through life towards that attainment which is as the fulfillment of the object of God.

The Smiling Forehead - Man the Seed of God

GAYAN 246 - BOULA -205 – The word which is not heard is lost.

Many holy scriptures give evidence of the power of the word. But a science so well known to the prophets of all times where has it gone? That science has been lost to the view of the generality. The reason for this is that man engaged himself in the things of the earth and the knowledge of material things, and in this way he lost the art of the ancient times. By losing that great science, that mystical secret, what has the soul attained? The soul has attained an increasing deafness, and this increasing deafness prevailed with the prevailing of material life. Nevertheless, at every time there have been some thinkers, and in every period there have been some servants of God, working known or unknown to the world, who have admitted that the word was lost. It was not lost for them they saw that for the generality that word was lost. By the loss of this word is meant that the secret of the whole life was lost. This is however an exaggerated saying. The word which is existent cannot be lost, but man has lost his capability of knowing, of hearing that word.

Besides this, man did not hear that word from the sky: he heard that word from the earth, the outcome of which is the great progress and awakening of material science. All the great inventions of this time, which are like miracles, have come to the great minds who have, so to speak, communicated with matter, and matter has spoken with them face to face. All such great inventions are answers from the earth to the communication of these minds with matter. In this way the word was not lost, but the direction was lost.

THE MYSTICISM OF SOUND AND MUSIC - THE POWER OF THE WORD - The Power of the Word #5

GAYAN 247 - BOULA -206 – Consideration is the sign of the wise.

Khatir means consideration for someone, which is shown in the form of respect, help or service. Very often it wants a sacrifice, it may even need self-denial. However, consideration is the highest quality that can be found in human nature. Consideration of age, of experience, of knowledge, of position, consideration of some good done by a person, also consideration of somebody's feebleness, weakness, it is all included in the word Khatir. This spirit of consideration, when developed, extends not only to the person for whom one has consideration, but also, for that person's sake, to another who is related or connected with that person in some way or other. When a king is respected and not his ambassador, that means lack of consideration to the king.

For a Sufi this quality becomes his moral. The Sufi learns consideration beginning with his Murshid, but this culminates in consideration for God. When one arrives at that tenderness of feeling one considers every person in the world. To the Sufi the missing of an opportunity of considering another is a great disappointment, for he does not consider it to be a fault toward a human being but to God. Verily, he is pious, who considers human feeling. No doubt it needs no end of endurance to consider everybody and to be considerate always, it wants no end of patience. However, by being considerate nothing is lost, if seemingly nothing is gained. The reward of this virtue is always in store. Consideration is the sign of the wise.

GATHA III – MORALS - Khatir (Consideration)

GAYAN 248 - BOULA -207 – Faith in oneself must culminate in faith in God, for faith is a living trust.

Very often a man is afraid of losing his common sense. He would rather be ordinary than become extraordinary. He is afraid of losing himself, but he does not know that losing himself means gaining himself. A person may say, 'To think about these things is like moving in the air.' But if we were not in the air what would become of us? Air is the substance on which we live, more important for us than the food we eat and the water we drink. Belief, therefore, is the food of the believer; it is the sustenance of his faith. It is on belief that he lives, not on food and water.

Faith is so sacred that it cannot be imparted, it must be discovered within oneself; but there is no one in the world who is without faith, it is only covered up. And what covers it? A kind of pessimistic outlook on life. There are people who are pessimistic outwardly, there are others who are pessimistic unconsciously, they themselves do not know that they are pessimistic. Man can fight with the whole world, but he cannot fight with his own self, he cannot break his own doubts; and the one who can disperse these clouds has accomplished a great thing in the world.

Is faith attainable by perseverance in belief? Things of heaven cannot be attained by perseverance, they are the grace of God. No perseverance is required to ask for the grace of God, to believe in the grace of God, and to open oneself for the grace of God, to trust in it. It is this which strengthens belief into faith. Everything belonging to the earth costs us more or less, we purchase it; there is only one thing which does not cost anything, because we can never pay its price, and that is the grace of God. We cannot pay for it in any form, in any way, by our goodness, by our piety, by our great qualities, merits or virtues, nothing. For what does our goodness amount to? Our lifelong goodness is nothing more than a drop of water compared with the sea. We as human beings are too poor to pay for the grace of God in order to purchase it; it is only given to us.

HEALING AND THE MIND WORLD – HEALTH

GAYAN 249 - BOULA -208 – Man's attitude is manifest in the expression of his countenance.

Man's expression is more indicative of his nature and character than his form or features. In the Qur'an it is said that man's eyes and gestures will confess what he tries to hide in his heart. The strength, the weakness, the power, the fear, the happiness, the joy, the uneasiness, the praise or blame, the love or hatred, all these are shown by the expression. The more capable one becomes of reading the expression the more clearly one can read character.

This shows that there is a mystery that lies behind movement. There are certain vibrations which take a particular direction under certain conditions, and the visible signs of all vibrations can be seen in man's movements or the expression of his countenance. It does not take one moment for the expression to change from pleasure to pain, from calm to horror, from love to hate. That shows that all the atoms of man's body, the veins, tubes and muscles, and the lines formed by their movements, are under the control of the heart, and every change that takes place in the heart shows on man's face, so that one who knows the language can read it. People who see each other often can read such changes from the expression, because each grows accustomed to know and recognize the changes of facial expression in the others, but it is the development of intuition which gives the clearness of vision by which one can see more completely.

The eyes are more expressive of thought and feeling than anything else. A person who can read the language of the eyes, their appearance and their movement, has the key to character. The eyes can ask and answer questions, and it is in the grade of speed and direction of the glance that the mystery of expression lies.

Esoteric Papers – Gatha 1 – Insight - The Mystery of Expression

GAYAN 250 - BOULA -209 – Happiness alone is natural and is attained by living naturally.

It is a great pity that the mechanical and artificial life we live today in this world is depriving us of that natural experience of deep sleep. Our first fault is our gathering and living in one city, all crowded together. Then there are motorcars, there are houses of twenty stories shaking every moment of the day and night, every vehicle shaking it. We are a race at the present time which is unaware of the comfort and bliss of the life known to the ancient people who lived simply, who lived with nature, far removed from this mechanical and artificial life. We are so far away from natural life that it has become our habit; we do not know any other comfort except the comfort we can experience in this kind of life we live. At the same time it shows that the soul is capable of attaining to greater comfort, pleasure and joy, to greater peace, rest and bliss only by living naturally.

THE SMILING FOREHEAD – Sufi Teachings

GAYAN 251 - BOULA -210 – The mind must be one's obedient servant; when it is a master life becomes difficult.

Then comes the discipline of the mind. That is done by concentration. When you wish the mind to think on one thought that you have before you while the mind is thinking about something else, then the mind becomes very restless. It does not want to stand on one spot, because it has always been moving about without discipline. As soon as you discipline it, it becomes like a wild horse. Very often people tell me that during the day they do not have such difficulty as at the moment that they want to concentrate: at that time the mind jumps, at other times it moves. This is because the mind is an entity. It becomes restive. It feels as a wild horse would feel: 'Why should I be troubled by you?' At the same time this mind is meant to be an obedient servant. This body is meant to become your tool with which to experience life. If mind and body are not in order, if they do not act as you wish them to, then you cannot hope for real comfort, for real happiness in this world.

THE MYSTICISM OF SOUND AND MUSIC Cosmic Language - Will

GAYAN 252 - BOULA -211 – Every experience, good or bad, is a step forward in man's evolution.

No sooner does the soul begin to unfold and experience in life the purpose which is hidden within itself, than it begins to feel the joy of it; it begins to value the privilege of living; it begins to appreciate everything; it begins to marvel at everything. For in every experience, good or bad, it finds a certain joy, and that joy is in the fulfillment of life's purpose. That joy is not only experienced in pleasure but even in pain, not only in success but also in failures; not only in the cheerfulness of the heart but even in the breaking of the heart there is a certain joy hidden. For there is no experience which is worthless; and specially for that soul who is beginning to realize this purpose, there is no moment wasted in life. For under all circumstances and in all experiences that soul is experiencing the purpose of life.

THE WAY OF ILLUMINATION; THE INNER LIFE; THE SOUL WHENCE AND WHITHER?; THE PURPOSE OF LIFE - The Purpose of Life Chapter XII

GAYAN 253 - BOULA -212 – It is no use saying you know the truth; if you knew the truth, you would keep silent.

To the class of people who claim that they are God, the answer may be given in the words of the Urdu poet, who says, 'Man is not God, but man is not apart from God.' One drop cannot call itself the ocean, yet the drop is a part of the ocean. Those who lay claim to this should bear witness to it in their lives, and if they can do this, then they will keep silent and not speak one word about it in the presence of others.

SPIRITUAL LIBERTY - PEARLS FROM THE OCEAN UNSEEN

GAYAN 254 - BOULA -213 – The trust of the one who trusts another and does not trust himself is profitless.

Now arises the question: how can one find faith in oneself, how can one develop it? One can find faith by practicing self-confidence as the first thing, by having self-confidence even in the smallest things. To-day most people have the habit to say with everything "perhaps". It seems as if a new word has come in use; they say "perhaps it will happen". It is a kind of polite expression, or a word of refined people to show themselves pessimistic. I can see their reason; they think that it is fanatic, presumptuous, and simple to say, "It will be", or "It will come", or "It will be accomplished", or "It will be fulfilled". To say "perhaps", - so they think - makes them free from the responsibility of having committed themselves. The more pessimistic a person, the more "perhaps" he uses, and this "perhaps" has gone so deep in souls to-day that they cannot find faith.

After self-confidence is developed, the second step is to trust another with closed eyes. One might think that this is not always practical, and one might think that it might lead to great loss. But at the same time even that loss would be a gain, and a thousand gains compared with the loss of faith would be as nothing. A person is richer if he has trusted someone and lost something than if he had not trusted someone and preserved something - that one day will be taken away from him! He could just as well have given it up.

One might say that every simple person is inclined to trust another. Yes, but the difference between the wise person who trusts bravely and the simple person who trusts readily is great. The wise man who trusts, if he is influenced by another that he may not, or must not, trust a certain person, even if he is given a certain proof, even then that habit of trusting will remain with him. As to the simple man, as soon as anyone says, "Oh, what are you doing, you trust somebody who is not trustworthy", his trust will change. That is the difference between the wise and the foolish person. The foolish person trusts because he does not know better; the wise person trusts because he knows that to trust is best.

The Unity of Religious Ideals – The Sufi's Conception of God - The Symbol of the Sun

GAYAN 255 - BOULA -214 – Human suffering is the first call we have to answer.

Question: In focusing our mind on beauty alone, is there not a danger of shutting our eyes to the ugliness and suffering we might alleviate?

Answer: In order to help the poor we ought to be rich, and in order to take away the badness of a person we ought to be so much more good. That goodness must be earned, as money is earned. That earning of goodness is collecting goodness wherever we find it, and if we do not focus on goodness we will not be able to collect it sufficiently. What happens is that man becomes agitated by all the absence of goodness he sees? Being himself poor he cannot add to it, and unconsciously he develops in his own nature what he sees. He thinks, "Oh poor person! I should so much like you to be good but that does not help that person. His looking at the badness, his agitation, only adds one more wicked person to the lot. When one has focused one's eyes on goodness one will add to beauty, but when a man's eyes are focused on what is bad he will collect enough wickedness for him to be added himself to the number of the wicked in the end, for he receives the same impression.

Besides, by criticizing, by judging, by looking at wickedness with contempt, one does not help the wicked or the stupid person. The one who helps is he who is ready to overlook, who is ready to forgive, to tolerate, to take disadvantages he may have to meet with patiently. It is he who can help.

A person who is able to help others should not hide himself but do his best to come out into the world. "Raise up your light high" it is said. All that is in you should be brought out, and if the conditions hinder you, break through the conditions! That is the strength of life.

THE SMILING FOREHEAD Answers to Questions—Aphorisms

GAYAN 256 - BOULA -215 – Sin is the fuel for virtue's fire.

Everything a person does, spiritual or material, is only a stepping-stone for him to arrive at the inner purpose, if he can only take it to be so. If he is mistaken, the mistake is in himself; he is working towards the inner purpose just the same. For all is created to work as one scheme, and therefore each individual is acting towards the accomplishment of the divine purpose.

THE WAY OF ILLUMINATION; THE INNER LIFE; THE SOUL WHENCE AND WHITHER?; THE PURPOSE OF LIFE - THE PURPOSE OF LIFE - Chapter I

GAYAN 257 - BOULA -216 – The first lesson that the seeker after truth must learn is to be true to himself.

There are subtleties of ideas, of spiritual, moral, or philosophical ideas, which cannot be given to everyone at first, but they are given gradually to those who are serious enough to walk in the path of truth. But every seeker after truth must remember one thing: that the first step in the path of truth is to become true to oneself.

Religious Gathekas - The Message of Unity

GAYAN 258 - BOULA -217 – Subtlety is the art of intelligence.

Subtlety of nature is the sign of the intelligent. If a person takes the right direction he does good with this wealth of intelligence, but a person who is going in a wrong direction may abuse this great faculty. When someone who is subtle by nature is compared with the personality which is devoid of it, it is like the river and the mountain. The subtle personality is as pliable as running water, everything that comes before that personality is reflected in it as clearly as the image in the pure water. The rocklike personality, without subtlety, is like a mountain, it reflects nothing. Many admire plain speaking, but the reason is they lack understanding of fine subtlety. Can all things be put into words? Is there not anything more free, more subtle than spoken words? The person who can read between the lines makes a book out of one letter. Subtlety of perception and subtlety of expression are the signs of the wise. Wise and foolish are distinguished by fineness on the part of the one and rigidness on the part of the other. A person devoid of subtlety wants truth to be turned into a stone; but the subtle one will turn even a stone into truth.

THE ART OF PERSONALITY - CHARACTER AND PERSONALITY - Character-Building

GAYAN 259 - BOULA -218 –As the Sun-glass reflects the heart of the sun, so the contemplative heart reflects the divine qualities.

Then comes mastery of the feelings, of the heart. There must be no feeling of revenge, of unkindness, of bitterness against anyone in the heart. When such a feeling comes, one must say: this is rust coming into my heart. When all such feelings are cleared off the heart, it becomes like a mirror. A mirror without rust reflects all that is before it; then everything divine is reflected in the heart, then all inspirations, intuitions, impressions come, and what we call clairvoyance. There is no need to go after such things; they come of themselves.

SUFI TEACHINGS - HEALTH AND ORDER OF BODY AND MIND - Self-Control

Contemplation is not much different from concentration, the difference being only that in concentration the mind holds an object, in contemplation the object holds the mind. Concentration itself, when mastered, turns into contemplation. The contemplative person is he who easily holds in mind all he thinks about. The mystics contemplate upon the sacred names which signify the different attributes of God. By contemplating upon divine attributes man wakens the same attributes within himself, his heart reflects the light of that divine attribute which he contemplated upon.

Esoteric Papers - SANGATHA II

GAYAN 260 - BOULA -219 – People build four walls around their ideas, lest their minds escape out of the prison bars.

The deeper the person, the more friends he has. It is smallness, narrowness, lack of spiritual development which makes a person exclusive, distant and different from others. He feels superior, greater and better than others; his friendly attitude seems to have been lost. In that way he cuts himself apart from others, and in this lies his tragedy. That person is never happy.

The one who is happy is he who is ready to be friends with all. His outlook on life is friendly. He is not only friendly to persons, but also to objects and conditions. It is by this attitude of friendship that man expands and breaks down those walls which keep him in prison. And by breaking down those walls he experiences at-one-ment with the Absolute. This at-one-ment with the Absolute manifests as the music of the spheres, and this he experiences on all sides: beauties of nature, color of flowers, everything he sees, everyone he meets. In the hours of contemplation and solitude, and in the hours when he is in the midst of the world, always the music is there, always he is enjoying the harmony.

THE MYSTICISM OF SOUND AND MUSIC - The Music of the Spheres

GAYAN 261 - BOULA -220 – It is easy to become a teacher, but difficult to become a pupil.

The idea is this, that when one thinks that, "What I think is right," and one finds arguments and reasons to make it right; and "What another person thinks is wrong," and one finds reasons to make it wrong, this person will always remain in the same place. But one who is ready to accept even from a child, if there is anything that one says that is wrong and one thinks, 'Yes, even the child says it, it is a profit for me to accept it." For God has not only spoken through His prophets, but He speaks through every person if we open our heart to listen to it. The difficulty is that we become teachers. If we kept ourselves a pupil.... Through our whole life we can keep ourselves a pupil, and the teaching will come all the time from within and without. As soon as we become teachers we close our heart from Him Who alone is our Teacher.

THE SUPPLEMENTARY (DUTCH) PAPERS - MISCELLANEOUS VI - Q & A After the Lecture on "Resist Not Evil"

GAYAN 262 - BOULA -221 – The soul is either raised or cast down by the effect of its own thought, speech, and action.

The mind covering the soul is as a globe: a sinful mind makes the soul sinful, a virtuous mind makes the soul virtuous, not in nature but in effect, as a red globe on the light makes the light red, and a green globe makes it look green, though in reality the light is neither green nor red; it is void of color, color being only its garb.

The soul becomes happy when there is happiness in the heart; it becomes miserable when there is misery in thought. The soul rises high with the height of imagination; the soul probes the depths with the depth of thought. The soul is restless with the restlessness of the mind, and it attains peace when the mind is peaceful. None of the above conditions of mind changes the soul in its real nature, but for the time being it seems to be so. The soul is a bird of paradise, a free dweller in the heavens. Its first prison is the mind, then the body. In these it becomes not only limited, but captive. The whole endeavor of a Sufi in life is to liberate the soul from its captivity, which he does by conquering both mind and body.

SPIRITUAL LIBERTY - METAPHYSICS - Our Constitution - The Soul with the Mind

GAYAN 263 - BOULA -222 – Love rises in emotion and falls in passion.

When the life-force acts in the soul it is love, when it acts in the heart it is emotion, and when in the body it is passion. Therefore the most loving person is the most emotional, and the most emotional is the most passionate, according to the plane of which he is most conscious. If he is most awake in the soul he is loving, if awakened in the heart he is emotional, if he is conscious of the body he is passionate. These three may be pictured as fire, flame, and smoke. Love is fire when in the soul, it is a flame when the heart is kindled by it, and it is as smoke when it manifests through the body.

SPIRITUAL LIBERTY - LOVE, HUMAN AND DIVINE - The Philosophy of Love

GAYAN 264 - BOULA -223 – As poison acts as nectar in some cases, so does evil.

A stone is not only used to break another person's head or to break one's own head, but is also used to build houses. Use everything where it will be most useful, where it will be of some advantage. All such things as passion and anger and irritation one looks upon as very bad, as evil; but if that evil were kept in hand it could be used for a good purpose, because it is a power, it is an energy. In other words evil, properly used, becomes a virtue; and virtue wrongly used becomes an evil. For instance, when a person is in a rage, or when he really feels like being angry, if he controls that thought and does not express it in words, that gives him great power. Otherwise the expression has a bad effect upon his nerves. His control of it has given him an extra strength which will remain with him. A person who has anger and control is to be preferred to the person who has got neither.

THE ALCHEMY OF HAPPINESS – Reaction

GAYAN 265 - BOULA -224 – The whole course of life is a journey from imperfection to perfection.

Life is a journey from one pole to another, and the perfection of the conscious life is the final destiny of the imperfect life. In other words, every aspect of life in this world of variety gradually evolves from imperfection to perfection; and if life's evolution were not so in its nature, there would be no difference between life and death, for life on the surface is nothing but the phenomena of contrast. This, then, is another way of expressing what is the purpose of life.

THE WAY OF ILLUMINATION - Some Aspects of Sufism - The Purpose of Life

GAYAN 266 - BOULA -225 – Every virtue is but an expression of beauty."

The world is a dome, where every action is the echo of another. Do good: it will come back; if not from one person, it will come from another. That is the echo. You do not know from which side it will come. It will come a hundredfold more than you give.

If we give love, will we get coldness? If we do good, can we get evil? We cannot be a judge of the action of another until we ourselves are selfless. Only then will justice come to us; only then will we understand the nature of justice. Self is the wall between us and justice. There is only one thing that is truly just, and that is to say, 'I must not do this'. But when we say this to another we may be wrong.

The mystic develops his mind in this manner, purifying it by pure thought, feeling, and action, only following this one line of thought. Pure means free from sense of separateness. Whatever difference in principles of right and wrong religious faith may show, no two individuals will ever differ in this one natural principle. Every soul seeks after beauty; and every virtue, righteousness, good action, is nothing but a glimpse of beauty.

Once having this moral, the Sufi does not need to follow a particular belief or faith, to restrict himself to a particular path. He can follow the Hindu way, the Muslim way, the way of any Church or faith, provided he treads this royal road: that the whole universe is but an immanence of beauty. We are born with the tendency to admire it in every form, and we may not blind ourselves by being dependent on one particular line of beauty. We will not get it from another. Give it. Let us make our action, our thought beautiful, and let others profit by it.

IN AN EASTERN ROSE GARDEN – Mind, Human and Divine

Gayan #267 – Bola #226 Every soul has its own way in life; if you wish to follow another's way, you must borrow his eyes to see it.

When the followers of diverse religions dispute over their ideals--the sacred ideals which they have not known, but of which they have only had a tradition--and wish to prove one better than the other, they merely lose time and destroy that sacred sentiment which can only be preserved in the heart. The religious ideal is the medium by which one rises towards perfection. Whatever name a person gives to his ideal, that name is most sacred for him. But that does not mean that that name limits that ideal. There is only one ideal, the divine ideal. Call him Christ, and let the same Christ be known by different names, given to him by various communities.

For instance, a person who has great devotion, great love and attachment for his friend, speaks about friendship in high words and says what a sacred thing it is to become friends. But then there is another who says, "Oh, I know your friend; he is no better than anybody else." The answer to this idea is given by Majnun in the story told by the ancients. Someone said to Majnun, "Leila, you beloved, is not so beautiful as you think." He said, "My Leila must be seen with my eyes. If you wish to see how beautiful Leila is, you must borrow my eyes." Therefore, if you wish to regard the object of devotion of whatever faith, of whatever community, of whatever people, you will have to borrow their eyes and you will have to borrow their heart. There is no use in disputing over the points of each tradition in history; they are made by prejudice. Devotion is a matter of heart, and is made by the devotee.

RELIGIOUS GATHEKAS - The Coming World Religion (1)

Gayan #268 – Bola #227 The one who lives in his finer feelings lives in heaven; when he puts them into words, he drops down to earth.

The spirit of feeling is lost when a sentiment is expressed in words. If words did not exist, the power of man's feeling would be a thousand times greater. The heart of man is vaster than the ocean. Every feeling therein is a wave rising in the sea, and when it is put into a word it becomes a pebble. Yes, there is a beauty in words, as there is beauty in flowers. But the flowers may be called the angels of the earth. They live only in Heaven; on the earth they appear for a moment and fade away. The feelings are like angels.

The one who lives in his feelings lives in Heaven, when he puts them into words he drops down on the earth. And, however beautiful his imagination and his choice of words, he turns angels into flowers. A person who really has some feeling, a person who has imagination, when he is silent it becomes a power, an ever increasing power. Do you think a person who really loves need say "I love you?" No, the word "love" cannot express his feeling, it is too small in comparison to what love means to him who truly loves.

Expression of sentiment is an outlet given to the energy of the heart, which if it had been conserved would have been a power in itself. A person who expresses an opinion about another readily, a mist is produced by his word before his own eyes; he can see no further than what he sees. If he controlled that impulse of expressing his opinion, it would be an effort at that moment, but it would open before him the vision revealing all that he would wish to know.

Esoteric Papers - Sangatha 1 - METAPHYSICS

Gayan #269 – Bola #228 Man's personality reflects his thoughts and deeds.

There are four sources from which the human face and form are derived, and these account for the changes which take place in them. These are: the inherent attributes of his soul; the influence of his heritage; the impressions of his surroundings; and lastly the impression of himself and of his thoughts and deeds, of the clothes he wears, the food he eats, the air he breathes, and the way he lives.

In the first of these sources man is helpless for he has no choice. It was not the desire of the tiger to be a tiger, neither did a monkey choose to be a monkey, and it was not the choice of the infant to be born a male or a female. This proves that the first source of man's form depends upon the inherent attributes brought by his soul. Words never can express adequately the wisdom of the Creator who not only fashioned and formed the world, but has given to each being the form suited to his needs. The animals of the cold zone are provided with thick fur as a protection against the cold; to the beasts of the tropics a suitable form is given; the birds of the sea have wings fit for the sea, and those of the earth are provided with wings suitable for the earth. Birds and animals have forms which accord with their habits in life. The form of man proclaims his grade of evolution, his nature, his past and present, as well as his race, nation and surroundings, character and fate.

In the second instance man inherits beauty or its opposite from his ancestors, but in the third and fourth his form depends upon how he builds it. The build of his form depends upon the balance and regularity of his life, and upon the impressions he receives from the world; for in accordance with the attitude he takes towards life his every thought and action adds, or takes away, or removes to another place the atoms of his body, thus forming the lines and muscles of form and feature. For instance the face of a man speaks his joy, sorrow, pleasure, displeasure, sincerity, insincerity, and all that is developed in him. The muscles of his head tell the phrenologist his condition in life. There is a form in the thoughts and feelings which produces a beautiful or ugly effect.

THE MYSTICISM OF SOUND AND MUSIC - THE MYSTICISM OF SOUND – Form

Gayan #270 – Bola #229 Reason is learned from the ever changing world, but wisdom comes from the essence of life.

...the inner life makes one richer, the outer life poorer. With all its richness and treasures that the earth can offer man is poor; and very often the richer, the poorer, for the greater the riches, the more the limitation he finds in his life. The inner life makes one powerful, whereas the outer life, its consciousness makes one weak. It makes one weak because it is the consciousness of limitation. The consciousness of the inner life makes one powerful, because it is the consciousness of perfection.

The outer life keeps one confused. However intellectual or learned a person may be, he is never clear. His knowledge is based upon reasons which are founded upon outer things, things that are liable to change and destruction. That is why, however wise that person may seem to be, his wisdom has limitations. What today he thinks right, after four days he thinks, perhaps, wrong. The inner life make the mind clear. The reason is that it is that part of one's being which may be called divine, the essence of life, the pure intelligence.

The phenomena of it is that where ever the light of pure intelligence is thrown things become clear. The absorption in the outer life without what the inner life gives makes one blind, all one says, thinks, or does is based upon outer experiences; and no one can realize to what extent the power gained by the inner life enables man to see through life. There existed the belief of the third eye. In reality the third eye is the inner eye, the eye that is opened by one's wakening to the inner life.

SOCIAL GATHEKAS - The Inner Life

Gayan #271 – Bola #230 Finding apt words to express one's thought is like shooting at a target.

It is the heart of the spiritual worker which must speak, not his lips. All that is necessary as conversation is a word of consolation to the downhearted, a word of courage to the weak, a word of sympathy to the suffering heart, and a word of enlightenment to the seeker. The word of a spiritual person must be like shooting at the target, that one answer may uproot the question and a thoughtful person may become satisfied with that one answer instead of a long argument...

ESOTERIC PAPERS - SANGITHA I - Teaching

Gayan #272 – Bola #231 A true life enables man to realize God.

In selfishness there is an illusion of profit, but in the end the profit attained by selfishness proves to be worthless. Life is the principal thing to consider, and true life is the inner life, the realization of God, the consciousness of one's spirit. When the human heart becomes conscious of God it turns into the sea and it spreads; it extends the waves of its love to friend and foe. Spreading further and further it attains perfection.

THE SMILING FOREHEAD - The Liberal and the Conservative Point of View

Gayan #273 – Bola #232 The whole of life is a chemical process; and the knowledge of its chemistry helps man to make life happy.

Sometimes when it is difficult for love to take away some impressions that are disagreeable, which block the way of the love-stream, they may be washed away by some element that can destroy them. The whole life is a chemical process, and the knowledge of its chemistry helps man to make life happy. An unhappy person, being himself unhappy, cannot make others happy. It is a wealthy person who can help the one who is hard up, not a poor person, however much desire of helping he may have. So it is with happiness, which is a great wealth; and a happy person can take away the unhappiness of another, for he has enough for himself and for others.

ESOTERIC PAPERS - GATHA II - EVERYDAY LIFE - Purity of Mind (2)

Gayan #274 – Bola #233 The domain of the mystic is himself; over it he rules as king.

...one must picture oneself as two beings, one the king and the other the servant. When one of them expresses a wish, it is the king who wishes; and the part that says, 'I cannot', is the servant. If the servant has his way, then the king is in the place of the servant. And the more the servant has his way, the more the servant rules and the king obeys. In this way naturally conflict arises and that reflects upon the outer life; one's whole life becomes unlucky. One may be pious or good or religious, it makes no difference. If man does not realize the kingdom of God within himself nor realize his spirit to be a king, he does not accomplish the purpose of life.

THE ALCHEMY OF HAPPINESS - The Path of Attainment (1)

Gayan #275 – Bola #234 The water that washes the heart is the continual running of the love-stream.

Purity of mind is the principal thing upon which the health of both body and mind depend. The process of purifying the mind is not much different from the process of cleaning or washing any object. Water poured upon any object washes it, and if there is a spot which cannot be washed away by the water, some substance which can take away that spot is applied, to wash it thoroughly. The water which washes the heart is the continual running of the love-stream. When that stream is stopped, when its way is blocked by some object which closes the heart, and when the love-stream is no longer running, then the mind cannot keep pure. As water is the cleansing and purifying substance in the physical world, so love is on the higher plane.

ESOTERIC PAPERS - GATHA II - EVERYDAY LIFE - Purity of Mind (2)

Gayan #276 – Bola #235 The moment a person becomes straightforward a straight way opens before him.

One has only to make one's vision keener, in other words, to explore one's self; but that is the last thing one does. People are most pleased to explore the tomb of Tut-ank-Amen in Egypt, in order to find mysteries, regardless of the mystery hidden in their own heart. Tell them about any mystery existing outside themselves: they are delighted to explore it. But when you tell them to see in themselves, they think it is too simple; they think, 'I know myself. I am a mortal being. I don't want to die, but death awaits me.' Difficulties they make; complexities they raise by their own complex intelligence. They do not like the straight way; they like the zigzag way; they enjoy puzzles. Even if there is a door before them, they say, 'No, I do not look for it.' If a door opens before them, they do not wish to go out by that door; they prefer to be in the puzzle. It is a greater joy not to be able to find the door for a long time. One who is thus enjoying the puzzle, is horrified when he sees the way out.

THE WAY OF ILLUMINATION; THE INNER LIFE; THE SOUL WHENCE AND WHITHER?; THE PURPOSE OF LIFE - THE PURPOSE OF LIFE - Chapter II

Gayan #277 – Bola #236 No one can be human and not make a mistake.

All that we see before our eyes, and all objects made by the skill of man, every condition brought about in life, whether favorable or unfavorable, all are the creation of the human mind; of one mind or of many minds. Man's failures in life, together with his impression of limitation, keep him ignorant of that great power which is hidden in the mind. Man's life is the phenomenon of his mind; man's happiness and success, his sorrows and failures, are mostly brought about by his own mind, of which he knows so little. If this secret had been known by all, no one in this world would have been unhappy, no soul would have had failure..'

THE WAY OF ILLUMINATION– THE SOUL, WHENCE AND WHITHER? - Manifestation

Gayan #278 – Bola #237 A humiliated conscience dims the radiance of the countenance.

Question: What to do when the feeling of humiliation has entered the mind?

Answer: To take it as a lesson, to take poison as something that must be. However, poison is poison. What is put in the mind will grow. It must be taken out. Every impression, if it remains, will grow: humiliation, fear, doubt. When it is there it remains; there will come a time when the person will be conscious of it. It will grow, and because it is growing in the subconscious mind it will bear fruits and flowers.

SUFI TEACHINGS - HEALTH AND ORDER OF BODY AND MIND - The Control of the Mind

Only if one studies it keenly, then one gets accustomed to read by the different actions and conditions of the face a person's thought. Besides, that very often when a person is telephoning someone, you only hear this person speaking, not the other person. But by hearing this person you can hear what the other person is saying. And in the same way, by seeing the action of the face, the change of countenance, and as it takes place continually you can trace the thought which is going on, and which is reacting in the face. No sooner you read this, no one can tell a lie before you.

You at once know it, because words cannot hide then the thought. Mostly words are the cover over thought, but when one can read it in the face, then the words have no power to contradict. You can see it just like a mirror. Besides, there is a thought of humility, there is a thought of guilty conscience, there is a thought of shame; and how much powerful a person may be he cannot hide it. It is so strong and you can see it in his face just like a moving picture.

ESOTERIC PAPERS - SANGATHA II

Gayan #279 – Bola #238 The development of one's personality is the real purpose of human life.

When the spirit of art develops, this development does not produce anything outwardly, but it does so inwardly. And what is this? It is the art of personality. In a real artist a distinct personality is developed which expresses itself in everything he does. In other words, an artist need not paint a picture in order to prove himself an artist. When he has reached a certain stage of art his thought, his speech, his word, his voice, his movements, his action, everything he does becomes art. The value of the art of personality is so great that no one in this world, whatever be his occupation, can say that he does not need to develop or to learn it. If he is a business man, if he is a lawyer, if he is in industry, if he is a shopkeeper, or working in an office or factory, whatever be his position, this art of personality will help him. If he is a soldier he has a chance to become a general, if he is a worker in a factory he may one day be the head of it. Besides success he has the magnetism to win everyone he meets because of the art of personality. The art of personality shows in one's movements, in one's manner, in words, in speech, in thought, and in feeling. On the other hand, an awkward person does everything wrong. His movements are awkward, and every move he makes is unattractive. The one who has not yet acquired the art of speaking will offend even without intending to; and in everyday life do we not see people insulting others unintentionally because they do not know the art of saying without saying?

THE PATH OF INITIATION - ART: YESTERDAY, TODAY, AND TOMORROW - Divinity of Art

Gayan #280 – Bola #239 Man expresses his soul in everything he does.

One thinks, speaks, and acts according to the pitch to which one's soul is tuned. The highest note one could be tuned to is the divine note; once one has arrived at that pitch, one begins to express the manner of God in everything one does. What is the manner of God? It is a kingly manner, yet a manner which is not known even to kings. Only the king of heaven and earth knows that manner; the soul who is tuned to God expresses it. This manner is void of narrowness, free from pride and conceit, and not only beautiful but beauty itself, for God is beautiful and God loves beauty.

The soul tuned to God also becomes as beautiful as God and begins to express God through all one does, expressing in life the divine manner. Why is it a kingly manner? The word kingly signifies someone who possesses power and wealth in abundance. The soul tuned to God, before whom all things fade away and in whose eyes the importance of the little things of which every person thinks so much is lessened, begins to express divine manner in the form of contentment.

Gatheka 27   Divine Manner, I

Gayan #281 – Bola #240 Out of the shell of the broken heart emerges the newborn soul.

One sees that those in the world who have really suffered, who have been disappointed, who are broken-hearted, do not wish to tell anybody about their experiences, they do not want any company but wish to be alone. And then it is as if there were someone waiting with open arms, waiting for such a soul to come as a child comes to its mother. This shows that there is somewhere a consoler greater than any in the world, a friend dearer than anyone else, a protector stronger than any earthly one. Knowing that the world is not to be depended upon, the one who has gone through all this looks for that great one in himself.

The friend who is a friend in life and after death, in pleasure and pain, in riches and poverty, one upon whom one can always depend, who always guides rightly, who gives the best advice, that friend is hidden in one's own heart. One cannot find a better one. Who is this friend? Man's own being, this true inner being. That friend is the origin, source, and goal of all.

But the question arises: if that friend is one's own being, why then call him a friend, why not call him one's self? The answer is that no doubt this friend is really one's own being, but when the greater Self is compared with the present realization one finds oneself smaller than a drop in the ocean. Man cannot very well call that friend himself until he has forgotten himself, until he is no more himself. Until and unless one has arrived at the state of perfection one had better be quiet and not insolent, talking about that which one has not yet become.

THE ALCHEMY OF HAPPINESS - The Journey to the Goal (2)

Gayan #282 – Bola #241 "In beauty is the secret of divinity."

What does music teach us? Music helps us to train ourselves in some way or other in harmony, and it is this which is magic, or the secret behind music. When you hear music that you enjoy, it tunes you and puts you in harmony with life. Therefore man needs music; he longs for music. Many say that they do not care for music, but these have not heard music! If they really hear music it will touch their souls, and then certainly they cannot help loving it. If not, it only means that they have not heard music sufficiently, and have not made their heart calm and quiet in order to listen to it, to enjoy and appreciate it. Besides, music develops that faculty by which one learns to appreciate all that is good and beautiful. In the form of art and science, in the form of music and poetry, in every aspect of beauty one can then appreciate it. What deprives man of all the beauty around him is his heaviness of body, or heaviness of heart. He is pulled down to earth, and by that everything becomes limited. When he shakes off that heaviness and feels joyous, he feels light. All good tendencies, such as gentleness and tolerance, forgiveness, love and appreciation - all these beautiful qualities - come by being light, light in mind, soul and body.

Where does music come from? Where does the dance come from? It all comes from the natural spiritual life which is within. When that spiritual life springs forth, it lightens all the burdens that man has. It makes his life smooth, floating on the ocean of life. The faculty of appreciation makes one light. Life is just like the ocean. When there is no appreciation, no receptivity, man sinks like a piece of iron to the bottom of the sea. He cannot float like the boat which is hollow, which is receptive."

THE MYSTICISM OF SOUND AND MUSIC – MUSIC - Spiritual Attainment by the Aid of Music

Gayan #283 – Bola #242 There is no better companion than solitude.

All the prophets, all the great ones have sought solitude. Christ was in solitude for a long time in the caves of the mountains. Moses was in solitude on Mount Sinai. Buddha had to have solitude for a long, long time before he could give his message to the world. The Prophet Muhammed was for a long time in solitude on Mount Hira. Why this solitude?

You may see by the experience of your own life what solitude does. If you try to go out all day to talk with acquaintances and friends, you will find that each day so much is gone from your speech; first because of your exaggeration, for if you speak you begin to exaggerate. Then, if you speak to amuse people, you may say what is not true: you add to what you are saying. Then out of politeness you embellish what you say: you say what you do not mean.

To everyone the wish comes to go home, to be with one or two people whom one likes, or to be alone. When you are silent thoughts are less, feelings are less, and the mind has a rest. When people come - people whom you like or undesirable people - the impression of their words and actions falls upon you and your peace of mind is broken.

A part of your time should be given to solitude. The more you cultivate solitude, the more you will like it, but when very much time is spent in solitude, people become unbalanced. The madzubs in India are very great people, often they are Nabi or Qutub. They attain a very high degree of spirituality, they have control over the elements, but part of their power, as the world demands it of them, is lost to the external world. I think that it is most desirable to be well-balanced: to spend so much time with others, and so much time in solitude.

SUFI TEACHINGS - HEALTH AND ORDER OF BODY AND MIND - Balance in Solitude

Gayan #284 – Bola #243 He who realizes the effect of his deed upon himself begins to open his outlook on life.

Whatever we do comes back to us. It may not come back from the same side, it may come from another side. But how does it come? Suppose we speak very badly to a servant, we insult him, we hurt his feelings. We think, "I am quite safe; he cannot do me any harm." But subconsciously our mind is impressed by the insult, the unkindness and that impression we take with us; we take it before whomever we meet and it calls forth the insulting tendency, the unkindness of him with whom we come in contact. The element attracts the same element, our coldness attracts his unkindness. We may meet many people who cannot insult us: their situation makes it impossible for them. But when we meet someone who can do so, our superior for instance, he will insult us, he will hurt our feelings.

If we do someone a kindness we ourselves are impressed by kindness and this impression draws out kindness from those before whom we come. The cruel will not be so very cruel with us because of this impression of kindness, and when we meet someone who is kind his kindness towards us will be increased a thousand times.

A sin without its reaction is just like a drop of poison in one's system which awaits its chance until it is developed enough to break out throughout one's life as a disease arising in time from that one drop. And such is the case with virtue, but an unanswered flame of virtue may enlighten one's whole life so that the world may see the illumination.

We make sins and virtues according to our idealization. What we have been taught from our childhood as good, we think good. What we have been taught from our childhood as bad, we think bad. It is not that God, from there, without the experience of manifestation, has made certain things virtues and others sins. It is God who sees with our eyes, who hears with our ears.

Every thing we do, every little good deed or bad deed has its effect upon every soul. It has always been said, "If you wish to see your children happy, do good deeds, give to the poor, be charitable. If you wish to see your fathers, your ancestors happy in the life beyond, do good actions, because the effect of your deeds will reach them, is felt by them."

THE SMILING FOREHEAD - The Law of Action

Gayan #285 – Bola #244 Life is what it is; you cannot change it, but you can change yourself.

In Sufi terms the crushing of the ego is called Nafs Kushi. And how do we grind it? We grind it by sometimes taking ourselves to task. When the self says, 'O no, I must not be treated like this', then we say, 'What does it matter?' When the self says, 'He ought to have done this, she ought to have said that,' we say, 'What does it matter, either this way or that way? Every person is what he is; you cannot change him, but you can change yourself'. That is the grinding.

When a thorn shows itself and you grind it as soon as you notice it, that same thorn by being crushed will turn into a rose, for the thorn also belongs to the rose bush. And when a person says, 'I will not occupy this position, I will not eat this, I hate it, I despise it, I cannot bear it, I cannot look at it, I cannot endure it, I cannot stand it,' these are all little thorns. A person may not know it, but they are thorns, and when they are crushed, then the rose comes out of it. How easy it is for people to say they want to know about mysticism and occultism. If there were an even bigger name, they would like to take an interest in that, and they believe that by reading books one can understand it, by learning lessons one can learn it, or by doing certain practices one can know it. But it is the everyday life that teaches us from morning till night. Every moment of the day and night we are up against something that our Nafs rebels against; and if we took that opportunity to crush it, to put it down, in some years' time our personality would become a rose.

IN AN EASTERN ROSE GARDEN - Human Evolution

Gayan #286 – Bola #245 To be alone with one's self is like being with a friend whose company will last forever.

When the lips are closed, then the heart begins to speak; when the heart is silent, then the soul blazes up, bursting into flame, and this illuminates the whole of life. It is this idea which demonstrates to the mystic the great importance of silence, and this silence is gained by repose. Most people do not know what repose means, because it is something they feel they need when they are tired, while if they were not tired they would never see the necessity for it.

Repose has many aspects. It is one kind of repose when a person retires from the activity of everyday life and finds himself alone in his room. He draws a breath of thankfulness as he feels, after all his interesting or tiresome experiences, 'At last I am by myself'. It is not an ordinary feeling, for there is a far deeper feeling behind it; it expresses the certainty that there is nothing to distract his mind and nothing which demands his action. At that moment his soul has a glimpse of relief, the pleasure of which is inexpressible; but the intoxication of life from which every man suffers is such that he cannot fully appreciate that moment of relief, which everyone expects, when it is time to retire after the activities of his daily life, whether he be rich or poor, tired or not.

…To explain in simple words what the spiritual path is, I would say that it begins by living in communication with oneself, for it is in the innermost self of man that the life of God is to be found. This does not mean that the voice of the inner self does not come to everyone. It always comes, but not everyone hears it. That is why the Sufi, when he starts his efforts on this path, begins by communicating with his true self within; and when once he has addressed the soul, then from the soul comes a kind of reproduction, like that which the singer can hear on a record which has been made of his own voice.

THE PATH OF INITIATION - Sufi Mysticism - Repose

Gayan #287 – Bola #246 Speech is the sign of living, but silence is life itself.

What can we learn from this? Every activity which we call 'life' has sprung from a source that is silent, and will always be silent; and every activity, however different in aspect, peculiar to itself, and unlike others in its effect, is still the activity of a tiny part of that life which is as wide as the ocean. Call it world, universe, nation, country, race, community, one individual, or only a particle, an atom--its activity, its energy springs in each case from one inseparable and eternal silent aspect of life. And it has not only sprung from it, but it also resolves itself into it. One throws a pebble into the water, water that is still and calm; there comes an activity, it comes for one moment, and then it vanishes. Into what does it vanish? It vanishes into the same silence in which the water was before. Water is a substance that is active by nature, and the silence, the stillness, the calmness that it shows is just the original state, the effect of its original source. This means that the natural inclination of every thing and every being is silence, because it has come from silence, and yet it is active, because it is activity that produces activity; and its end is silence.

IN AN EASTERN ROSE GARDEN - Silent Life

Gayan #288 – Bola #247   He who keeps no secret has no depth; his heart is like a vessel turned upside down.

And now coming to the other aspect of personality which belongs to speech. The more we understand about this, the more we shall know that for every word there is a time and for every word there is a place. And everything you say in its own place and which is a fitting thing, it will be good. It becomes wrong when it is spoken in a place which is not its place. People generally do not think about it. Very often people are outspoken, they do not mind when they speak, what they speak, where they speak. A person who has no control over his speech becomes like a kind of machine which goes on and goes on and goes on, without any will at the back of it.

Remember that not only they do not gain the affection of others, the approbation of others, but they repel others, they cannot keep any secret because they have to say it, they have the habit to say, they have no control about it. Once a woman went to a healer and said: "Can you help me, I am in a distress." The healer asked: "What is the matter?" She said: "When my husband comes home, he is in such a state that there always is a disagreement." "O," said the healer, "that is the easiest thing to do. I will just give you these magnetized lozenges. When your husband comes home, you take one in the mouth and keep it." When the husband came home, tired and fatigued, he was inclined to war as usual, but she was quiet and did not answer. He was grumpy for a little while but then became quiet. And so the home became more harmonious. Then, before the lozenges were finished, she went to the healer and said : "Give me one more packet of these," and he answered: "Lady, learn from this that it is not the lozenges, it is the keeping quiet, it is the closed lips. When your husband is tired, he does not know his mind. And when you do not encourage him to quarrel, he will not quarrel."

THE SUPPLEMENTARY PAPERS - PSYCHOLOGY - PSYCHOLOGY III - The Art of Personality

Gayan #289 – Bola #248 Wisdom is attained in the solitude.

Raja Yoga is the best one for life in the Western world. This is because life in the West is so full of responsibilities and there is so little time to devote to solitude and practices. You have to practice wisdom and deep thought in all your affairs from morning till night; in this way you make your life into a teaching for yourself. Therefore whatever your work or business or profession, let that be your mode of progress, so that you advance through your every duty. At the same time, if you will only devote ten or twenty minutes to a practice it will prepare you for something better, and it will also help you in your work. Thus Raja Yoga, the yoga of life's experiences, is certainly the best for Western life, but if a person prefers a life of retirement, let him take it.

THE VISION OF GOD AND MAN – Discipleship (2)

Gayan #290 – Bola #249   It is the tongue of flame that speaks the Truth, not the tongue of flesh.

There is a stage in the life of a Seer when the tongue of flame becomes, not only an interpretation of the mystery, but as a reality, as his own experience. The head is the center of knowledge, and, when this organ opens, the light which was covered becomes manifest, not only in idea, but even in form.

THE UNITY OF RELIGIOUS IDEALS - PROPHETS AND RELIGIONS - The Sufi's Conception of God - Tongues of Flame

Gayan #291 – Bola #250 Every desire in life has its answer; if it were not so, creation would not have gone on.

Which is the most desirable thing in life, to seek for the goal or to dwell in this changing life? The answer is that every person's desire is according to his evolution. That for which he is ready is desirable for him. Milk is a desirable food for the infant, other foods for the grown-up person. Every stage in life has its own appropriate and desirable things. The desire to attain to a goal must be there before reaching it; when he does not feel the desire, it is not necessary for a man to seek it.

All things are worth while when we seek after them; then only do we appreciate their value; then only are we happy to have them. We do not need the things we do not know and do not desire. We need them when we know them and desire them. The law of nature is that this 'external life develops gradually, stage by stage, through rocks, through vegetables, through animals, through man. Its depth is intelligence, which is named 'Ilm by the mystic. The joy of the whole life is the fullness of intelligence, and intelligence comes to its fullness in the human kingdom. It is there that life and the primitive intelligence have their eyes opened to see and understand and think. 'God slept in the mineral kingdom, dreamed in the vegetable, woke in the animal, and became self-conscious in the human'. But in the human stage we find that not everyone has the same capability of thinking and understanding and knowing. It is his thinking quality that distinguishes man, that is why the real man is the thinker, he who is capable of thinking. The more thoughtful, the more awakened the mind, the more can be found in man the fullness of that attribute for which the whole world was created.

When he begins to think, the question arises why all this was created. And the answer is that all this gradual development is towards one single development, that of human life; and in human life towards the development of mind. Throughout the whole universe that which has really developed is the mind, which begins to know the use of all things and all forms, their secret and the way in which all things and all forms are controlled.

IN AN EASTERN ROSE GARDEN - The Journey to the Goal

Gayan #292 – Bola #251 He to whom life's purpose is clear is already on the Path.

In everyone, whatever be the position of life, someone very rich or one very poor, one full of life and the other ill, in all conditions, man is continually yearning and waiting for something to come, he does not know what, but he is waiting. The real explanation of life is waiting; waiting for something. And what is it that man awaits? It is the fulfillment of the purpose of life, which comes when the soul strikes that note; that note which is meant to be his note. And this he seeks, whether in the outer plane or the inner plane. And man has not fulfilled his life's purpose until he has struck that note which is his note.

And the greatest tragedy in life is the obscurity of purpose. When purpose is not clear, man suffers, he cannot breathe. He knows not what is the purpose, what he must do. This life will present to him things that will interest him for the moment, but the moment he possesses that thing he will say, "no this is not it, it is something else." So man goes on, in an illusion, constantly seeking, and yet not knowing what he seeks. Blessed is he who knows his life's purpose, for that is the first step toward fulfillment.

And how are we to know life's purpose? Can anybody tell us? No. No one can tell us: for life in its very nature is self-revealing, and it is our own fault if we are not open to that revelation which life offers to us. It is not the fault of life, because the very nature of life is revealing. Man is the offspring of nature, therefore his purpose is nature. But the artificiality of life brings obscurity, which prevents him from arriving at that knowledge which may be called the revelation of one's own soul.

And if you ask me how one should proceed, I would advise you to study every object, whether false or true, which holds and attracts you, to which you are outwardly attracted and also inwardly attracted. And do not be doubting and suspicious. What Christ taught from morning till night was faith, but the interpretation of this word is not made clear. People have said faith in priest, in church, or in sect. That is not the meaning. The true meaning of faith is trust in one's self. A person came to me and said, "I wish to follow your ideas. Will you receive me? Will you let me follow you?" I said, "yes, but will you tell me if you have faith?" This person looked perplexed for a moment, then he said, "well, I have faith in you." I asked, "have you faith in yourself?" He said, "well, I am not sure." I said, "your faith in me would be of no use to me. What I need is your faith in you."

SOCIAL GATHEKAS - Shaikh Muslih-ud-din Sa'adi (CON'T)

Gayan #293 – Bola #252 In the complete unfoldment of human nature is the fulfillment of life's purpose.

It is in unfoldment that the purpose of life is fulfilled, and it is not only so with human beings but also with the lower creation; even with all the objects that exist the fulfillment of their existence lies in their unfoldment. When the clouds gather the purpose of their gathering is shown when it is raining: it is the unfoldment of that gathering of clouds which shows itself in the rain. Not in the gathering of the clouds was a purpose accomplished, it was accomplished in the raining; the gathering was a preparation. One finds the same thing in nature which works the whole year long and brings forth its fruits in the autumn. Not only human beings but even birds and animals can watch and be delighted to see the purpose of nature's continual working fulfilled in the spring.

We learn from this that every being and every object is working towards that unfoldment which is the fulfillment of its purpose. There is a saying of a Persian poet, Sa'adi, that every being is intended to be on earth for a certain purpose, and the light of that purpose has been kindled in his heart.

In all different purposes which we see working through each individual, there seems to be one purpose which is behind them all, and that is the unfoldment of the soul.

THE SMILING FOREHEAD - The Unfoldment of the Soul

Gayan #294 – Bola #253   What God makes man mars; what man makes God breaks.

All that man considers beautiful, precious and good, is not necessarily in the thing or the being; it is in his ideal; the thing or being causes him to create the beauty, value and goodness in his own mind. Man believes in God by making Him an ideal of his worship, so that he can commune with someone whom he can look up to; in whom he can lay his absolute trust, believing Him to be above the unreliable world; on whose mercy he can depend, seeing selfishness all round him. It is this ideal when made of a stone, and placed in a shrine, which is called an idol of God; and when the same ideal is raised to the higher plane and placed in the shrine of the heart, it becomes the ideal of God with whom the believer communes and in whose vision he lives most happily, as happily as could be, in the company of the sovereign of the whole universe.

When this ideal is raised still higher it breaks into the real, and the real light manifests to the godly; the one who was once a believer now becomes the realizer of God.

THE WAY OF ILLUMINATION - Some Aspects of Sufism - Suma, the Music of the Sufis

Gayan #295 – Bola #254 All things are good; but all things are not good for every person, nor right at all times.

That way is best which suits you best. The way of one person is not for another person, although man is always inclined to accuse another person of doing wrong, believing that he himself is doing right. In reality, the purpose is beyond all these four things. Neither in paradise nor in the ideal, neither in pleasures nor in the wealth of this earth is that purpose accomplished. That purpose is accomplished when a person has risen above all these things. It is that person then who will tolerate all, who will understand all, who will assimilate all things, who will not feel disturbed by things which are not in accordance with his own nature or the way which is not his way. He will not look at them with contempt, but he will see that in the depth of every being there is a divine spark, which is trying to raise its flame towards the purpose.

THE PURPOSE OF LIFE - Chapter XI

Gayan #296 – Bola #255 If in truth we shall not build our hope, in what shall we build?

Our life of limitation in the world, and the nature of this world's comforts and pleasures which are so changeable and unreliable, and the falseness that one finds in everything everywhere, if one complained about it, a whole lifetime would be too short to complain about it fully; every moment of our life would become filled with complaints. But the way out is to look at the cheerful side of it, the bright side. Especially those who seek God and truth, for them there is something else to think about; they need not think how bad a person is. When they think who is behind this person, who is in his heart, then they will look at life with hope. When we see things which are wrong, if we only give thought to this: that behind all workings there is God, who is just and perfect, then we will certainly become hopeful.

THE ART OF PERSONALITY - CHARACTER AND PERSONALITY - Character-Building

Gayan #297 – Bola #256   Life is progress, and ceasing to progress is death.

The mind cannot act properly when it is hindered by impressions which have a paralyzing effect upon it. Life is progress, and stopping from progress is death. Failure does not matter in life for a progressive person, even a thousand failures do not matter. He has before his view success, and success is his even after a thousand failures. The greatest pity in life is the standstill when life does not move further. A sensible person prefers death to such a life. It is as a paralysis of the soul, of the spirit, and is always caused by holding bad impressions in mind. No soul is deprived of happiness in reality.

ESOTERIC PAPERS - GATHA II - EVERYDAY LIFE - Purity of Mind (1)

Every belief and every experience for a wise person is a step of a staircase; he has taken this step, there is another step for him to take. The steps of the staircase are not made for one to stand there. They are just made for one to pass, to go further. Because life is progress. Where there is no progress there is no life. One should go on. Death and disappointment; two things are one. And if there is a hereafter, then the death was a passing stage; and so is disappointment. It only has made one more steady, more wise, more . . . .

ESOTERIC PAPERS - GATHA III - INSIGHT - Three Ways To Develop Insight

Gayan #298 – Bola #257 Truth is hidden in the heart of nature; therefore, man naturally hides all that is precious.

When the soul begins to see the truth it is, so to say, born again, and to this soul all that appears true to an average person appears false, and what seems truth to this soul is nothing to an average person. All that seems to an average person important and precious in life has no value nor importance for this soul, and what seems to this soul important and valuable has no importance nor value for an average person. Therefore such a one naturally hides himself in a crowd which lives in a world quite different from that in which he lives. Imagine living in a world where nobody uses your language! Yet he can live in the world for he knows its language. And yet to him life in the world is as unprofitable as to a grown-up person the world of children playing with their toys.

ESOTERIC PAPERS - GATHA I - SYMBOLOGY - The Symbol of the Cross

Gayan #299 – Bola #258 The false ego is a false god; when the false god is destroyed, the true God arrives.

The way to perfection for the mystic is by the annihilation of the false ego. He understands that in man there is a real ego, that this ego is divine, but that the divine ego is covered by a false ego; and every man has a false ego because it begins to grow from his birth.

Man develops in himself a false idea, and that false idea is identification with something which he calls himself. He says, 'I am a professor, a lawyer, a barrister, a doctor,' or, 'I am a king, a lord, or something.' But whatever he claims, he is not that. His claim may be humble or proud, but in reality he is not that.

The mystic on the spiritual path perseveres in wiping out this false ego as much as he can, by meditation, by concentration, by prayer, by study, by everything he does. His one aim is to wipe out so much, that one day reality, which is always there buried under the false ego, may manifest. And by calling on the Name of God, in the form of prayer, or in Zikr, or in any other form, what the mystic does is to awaken the spirit of the real ego in order that it may manifest. It is just like a spring which rises out of the rock and which, as soon as the water has gained power and strength, breaks even through stone and becomes a stream. So it is with the divine spark in man. Through concentration, through meditation, it breaks out and manifests; and where it manifests it washes away the stains of the false ego and turns into a greater and greater stream, which in turn becomes the source of comfort, consolation, healing, and happiness for all who come into contact with that spirit.

THE PATH OF INITIATION – SUFI MYSTICISM - Mysticism

Gayan #300 – Bola #259 The lover of nature is the true worshipper of God.

Most people consider as sacred scriptures only certain books or scrolls written by the hand of man, and carefully preserved as holy, to be handed down to posterity as divine revelation. Men have fought and disputed over the authenticity of these books, have refused to accept any other book of similar character, and, clinging thus to the book and losing the sense of it, have formed diverse sects. The Sufi has in all ages respected all such books, and has traced in the Vedanta, Zendavesta, Kabah, Bible, Qur'an, and all other sacred scriptures, the same truth which he reads in the incorruptible manuscript of nature, the only Holy Book, the perfect and living model that teaches the inner law of life: all scriptures before nature's manuscript are as little pools of water before the ocean.

To the eye of the seer every leaf of the tree is a page of the holy book that contains divine revelation, and he is inspired every moment of his life by constantly reading and understanding the holy script of nature.

When man writes, he inscribes characters upon rock, leaf, paper, wood or steel; when God writes, the characters He writes are living creatures.

It is when the eye of the soul is opened and the sight is keen that the Sufi can read the divine law in the manuscript of nature; and that which the teachers of humanity have taught to their followers was derived by them from the same source; they expressed what little it is possible to express in words, and so they preserved the inner truth when they themselves were no longer there to reveal it.

THE WAY OF ILLUMINATION - Sufi Thoughts

Gayan #301 – Bola #260 - One who worships God and despises man worships in vain.

    A complete believer is he, who does not only believe in himself, but respects the beliefs of others. For a Sufi, in this world there is no one, neither heathen nor pagan, who is to be despised. For he believes in that God, who is not the God of one chosen sect, but the God of the whole world. He does not believe in a God of one nation, but of all nations. To him God is in all the different houses where people worship Him. Even if they stand in the street and pray, it makes no difference to Him; that is the holy place--where he is worshipped. The Sufi leaves sectarianism to the sects. He has respect for all. He is not prejudiced against any--does not despise any. He feels sympathy for all.

    The idea of the Sufi is that the one who does not love his fellowman cannot love God. He thinks, as Christ has said, "love your neighbor; love your enemy." And what does it mean? It means not, "love him, because you consider him as your enemy," but "love him, because in God you are related to him." If humanity had believed in this simple and most valuable teaching, these wars would not have taken place. Is it the work of political people, to bring this home to men--or the work of commerce? No, it is the work of the church, of religion. But as long as the religious authorities will make of themselves a sect, and divide religion, and look upon each other with prejudice; this truth, brought by Christ, is not practiced.

THE UNITY OF RELIGIOUS IDEALS - THE MESSAGE AND THE MESSENGER - The Sufi's Aim in Life

Gayan #302 – Bola #261 - We give way to our faults by being passive towards them.

Often, when man does wrong, it is not that he likes to do wrong, but that he is not able to prevent himself from acting in that way. In the first place, wrongdoing is almost always the consequence of the appetites and passions, or for the gratification of vanity. Fasting and special postures are often practiced by the mystics for the same reason. The more man gives way to the appetites and passions the more he is enslaved by them, until he reaches a state where he speaks and acts against his own conscience. Such faults as treachery, flattery, falseness, and all others of the kind come from lack of will-power and from giving way to the passions.

For training the ego it is not absolutely necessary to abstain from all physical desires; the idea is to master the desire instead of allowing it to master one. The complaint of every soul and the remorse of every soul is always of the same thing, the enslavement of man through yielding to his desires. One allows the desire to master one when one identifies oneself with the desire; and one pities oneself, which makes things worse. And the desire for the momentary joy becomes an excuse for having given way. For instance, a person who gets up later makes the cold an excuse; he had to, he says, because it was cold. Reason always supplies an excuse for everything. But one cannot escape the consequences, and the remorse that follows proves that a fault has been committed.

And once a person has accustomed himself to his faults, the sense of his fault becomes less keen; then he no longer troubles about them. Then he becomes a slave to his faults, he is like a worm, and his faults become his life. That is why in the language of the Hindus the word for hell means a place full of worms. In other words, he feeds on his faults and his faults find their nourishment in him. To a keen sight such cases are not rare. There are some cases that everyone can see, others are hidden.

Those who know its value consider the training of the ego the most important thing in life. The first lesson in this training is to ask, "Why must I have a certain thing? Why must I not have it? If it is not good for me why should I have it? And if it is good for me why should I not have it?" What a person has acquired the habit of speaking with his ego in this way about every physical appetite, he will always be able to do what he ought to do.

Gatha II - Morals - The Ego Is Trained As a Horse

Gayan #303 – Bola #262 - When a person does not listen to us, we must know it is because we ourselves do not believe.

Someone asked a Brahmin, 'Why do you worship a god of rock, an idol of stone? Look, here I am, a worshipper of the God who is in heaven. This rock does not listen to you, it has no ears.' And the Brahmin said, 'If you have no faith, even the God in heaven will not hear you; and if you have faith this rock will have ears to hear.'

THE PATH OF INITIATION - THE PATH OF INITIATION AND DISCIPLESHIP - Four Kinds of Discipleship

Gayan #304 – Bola #263 - When a defect becomes common, it is considered as the normal state by the generality.

When one allows this tendency [to gossip] to remain in one, one develops love of talking about others. It is a defect which commonly exists, and when two people meet who have the same tendency, they gossip together. One helps the other, one encourages the other. And when something is supported by two people of necessity it becomes a virtue, if only for the time being.

THE ART OF PERSONALITY - CHARACTER AND PERSONALITY - Character-Building - IX

The nature of most people is like that of sheep; wherever sheep are taken, there all the other sheep will follow. One should realize that although it is the nature of sheep to move in a flock this is not the real nature of man. He will always deny that he has this tendency and he will disapprove of it, and yet he will do the very thing without knowing that he does it. If you want to see it, just stand in the street and look up with surprise, acting as if you were absorbed in what you see, and soon twenty persons will be standing by your side, not only foolish people but wise ones too!

THE PATH OF INITIATION - THE PATH OF INITIATION AND DISCIPLESHIP - The Different Steps on the Path

Gayan #305 – Bola #264 - Love in its beginning lives only on reciprocity, but when fully developed it stands on its own feet.

Today our activity which is called the World Brotherhood is more than necessary, for the activities in bringing about a brotherly feeling in humanity are of more value than any other activity in the line of culture; and although there are many societies and institutions which are established and working along this line of brotherhood, yet our contribution to this great service of God and humanity has its peculiarity, owing to its ideas being based on spiritual ideals. We believe that the brotherhood brought about by coming to an understanding of exchanging the good of one another in the interest of one another is not sufficient.

The reason is that the nature of life is changeable; where there is a day there is a night, and there is light and darkness, and therefore the interest in life is not always even. If two persons are friends with one another and they make a condition; that, we shall be friends and we shall love one another, if each wishes to regard justice and fairness by the others interests they will quarrel a thousand times a day. Because who is to be the judge? When two people quarrel both are just, both think they are in the right; and a third person has no right to interfere. Therefore brotherhood cannot be brought about satisfactorily on by teaching the law of reciprocity based upon self-interest.

Because even if they said, "I will give you a pound in gold, and you will give me in return a pound in notes paper;" and the exchange is made, there is a dispute. Because: "I gave you the pound in gold and you gave me the pound in notes." A friendship which is based upon selfishness is to secure, it is not dependable; because seemingly they may be friends, of the other, they are the friend of themselves. However greatly they show friendship to one another in reality they are showing friendship to themselves. No, the brotherhood, from the spiritual point of view that may be learned is the brotherhood of rivalry in kindness, in goodness. It is not weighing:"what good have you done to me," but it is trying to do more for another and not thinking "what he will do for me."

The ideas of the Sufis in all times have been different from those of the man in the world, and yet not too difficult for a man to practice. The Sufi ideas are that when one does an act of kindness for another it is because he wishes to do it, because the action itself is his satisfaction, not looking for a return even in the form of appreciation. Any form of appreciation or any return he thinks consumes, takes away that act of goodness or kindness that one has done. And when one thinks that one does some good expecting that another must return it, then it is a business.

SOCIAL GATHEKAS #39- Our Activity Which is Called the World Brotherhood

Gayan #306 – Bola #265 - The present spirit of humanity has commercialism as its crown and materialism as its throne.

No nation, race, or section can be considered a separate part of humanity. Today education, politics, and all directions in life seem to work from an individualistic view, but where must such a tendency end and where will it lead humanity? If each says, "I must get the better of another," where will be the harmony and peace for which all are longing, no matter what race or religion they belong to?

This condition has been brought about by long-continued materialism and commercialism, which have taught every soul the spirit of competition and rivalry. The whole life of each is absorbed in guarding his own interests and trying to take the best in life for himself. Life is one continual fight, and only one thing can ease this fight: consideration for others, reciprocity, and give and take of good, instead of selfishness.

The world's progress, with selfishness as the central theme, will never lead to the soul's desire and aim; it will culminate in destruction. Just as at one time there was a call from everywhere to guard self-interest, now the moment has come for the message to be given for men to understand and consider one another. The happiness and peace of each individual depends on the happiness and peace of all.

Religious Gatheka #17 - The Message of Unity

Gayan #307 – Bola #266 - Without humor human life is empty.

And how few of us in this world know what real, true mirth means, humor that is not vulgarized, not abused. it shows the rhythm and tune of the soul. Without humor life is dull and depressing. Humor is the reflection of that divine life and sun which makes life like the day. And a person who reflects divine wisdom and divine joy, adds to the expression of his thought when he expresses his ideas with mirth.

THE PATH OF INITIATION - SUFI POETRY - Muslih-ud-din Sa'di

Gayan #308 – Bola #267 - To see life as a whole is beyond the power of the generality.

To see life as a whole is beyond the power of the generality of mankind. The outlook of the average man is bounded by the consideration of the welfare of the race or community to which he happens to belong. In the cycles that form the history of civilization man evolves and degenerates and often his gain in the eyes of succeeding generations has been quite outweighed by a corresponding loss. Man sees no further than he sees; and ever and again the turn of the cycle has brought a period of cruelty, of intolerance, and of degeneration.

THE ART OF PERSONALITY - LIFE'S CREATIVE FORCES: RASA SHASTRA - Polygamy

Gayan #309 – Bola #268 - All aspects of life meet and share in common in that one central point which is the Divine Mind.

...There is one treasure-house where all knowledge collected, experienced, learned, and discovered by human beings is stored; and that treasure-house is the Divine Mind, a mind with which all minds are linked. There is no experience we go through that does not remain or that is not recorded in that treasure-house. Every good or bad experience we have, every new thing we learn, every discovery we make, is all stored in that treasure-house. But one might ask, 'How does one find in it what one wants? If we have a large store, perhaps hundreds and thousands of things, it is difficult to find anything we want at a moment's notice!' The power of the mind, the willpower, is such that if one has enough of it one can find anything one wants to find. It is related that someone with great willpower wanted to buy a certain piece of furniture. In the first street he went to after leaving his house he saw exhibited in the showroom the very piece of furniture he desired. He was guided towards it.

What one really wants is attracted by one, and one is attracted by what one wants. It is the same with the poet, the musician, the thinker. When he is deeply interested in what he is doing, then he has only to wish; and by the automatic action of the desire his wish becomes a light. This light is thrown on the divine store-house, and it is projected on the object he wants. Such is the phenomenon of will and inspiration that no sooner is an inspired person moved by the beauty and harmony of life and wishes to express his soul, than the light of his soul shines on that particular object or on that particular knowledge. It comes instantly to his mind, expressing itself outwardly through his mind. All that is brought from within in this way is perfect, harmonious, beautiful, and has a wonderful effect.

THE ALCHEMY OF HAPPINESS: Communicating with Life

Gayan #310 – Bola #269 - Patient endurance is the strongest defense.

The greater the object of your pursuit, the greater patience it requires, and there is a side in human nature which keeps one impatient and which makes one feel that he should mount to the top immediately; and therefore when he rushes impatiently toward the accomplishment of his object, he often falls. In climbing there are steps, and one should climb gradually. One must hold before one's mind the object, but one must at the same time see the steps that one has to climb.

If patience will not help in climbing the steps and in journeying the necessary distance, there will come a fall. This shows that there are three chief things in the path of attainment: Steadiness of concentration in holding the object of concentration firmly before oneself; at the same time noticing with open eyes the many steps that one must climb to reach the object; and the third thing is patient perseverance.

Patience is the most difficult thing in life, and once this is mastered, man will become the master of all difficulties. Patience, in other words, may be called the power of endurance during the absence of the desired things or conditions. They say death is the worst thing in life, but in point of fact, patience is often worse than death. One would prefer death to patience, when patience is severely tried. Patience is a life power; it is a spiritual power and the greatest virtue that one can have.

ESOTERIC PAPERS - GITHA I - THE PATH OF ATTAINMENT - Patience

Gayan #311 – Bola #270 - All that is good and worthwhile is difficult to obtain.

And now we come to the question of the Sufi Message. There are mureeds who are interested in their own advancement. And there are mureeds who are interested in the furtherance of the Message. Those who are interested in their own advancement, they may just as well have indifference for the furtherance of the Cause. But those who are interested in the Movement, in Murshid, in the furtherance of the Message, they think that they can contribute; and the contribution that can be most valuable is a continued interest without the slightest shadow of indifference.

Those who have the interest of the Message at heart, one day they are enthusiastic, saying, "I would like to do everything in my power, it does not matter how little I can do, but I would like to do all I can," and the other day they say, "What does it matter if I did it or someone else did it? It is the Message of God for humanity; somebody will do it if I do not do it. What am I? I am a poor, humble person; I occupy no position in the Movement. Besides, to do something, it wants great resources which I lack, it wants quality, it wants capability, which I do not know if I have. I have a great desire to work for the Message, but at times I feel, can I really do it?" Looking at the thousand difficulties which discourage one from doing anything. When such a thought rises in the heart of the worker, it comes as a shadow that darkens the path that he wishes to tread.

It is such mureeds and workers who will be able to accomplish something worthwhile who will not mind what position they are placed in, what work they have to do in the Order, small or great; but they wish to do it, without being discouraged, with patience and endurance, in spite of all difficulties. Is there any difficulty that cannot be surmounted? No doubt, those who have every desire to serve the Cause, but at the same time cannot, owing to such difficulties which may seem insurmountable, they may give their thought, and help the Cause by their prayers. But those who have time at their disposal, strength and health granted by God, and opportunity before them, for them it is necessary to know the nature and the power of motive, and to know the danger of the shadow of indifference falling upon it. It is in this way, with united effort, we shall be able to bring that Message before humanity which we are destined to bring."

Interest and Indifference August 18, 1925

Gayan #312 – Bola #271 - The more you make of your gifts, the less becomes the value of something which is priceless.

Man's greatest enemy is his ego which manifests itself in selfishness. Even in his doing good, in his kind actions, selfishness is sometimes at work. When he does good with the thought that one day it may return to him and that he may share in the good, he sells his pearls for a price. A kind action, a thought of sympathy, of generosity, is too precious to trade with. One should give and, while giving, close the eyes. Man should remember to do every little good action, every little kindness, every act of generosity with his whole heart, without the desire of getting anything in return making a trade out of it. The satisfaction must be in doing it and in nothing else.

SUFI TEACHINGS - THE PRIVILEGE OF BEING HUMAN - Man, the Purpose of Creation

Gayan #313 – Bola #272 - Lack of understanding of human nature brings about all conflicts and disagreements.

One might ask why one cannot understand self by studying human nature in general. Why must one study self by trying to understand oneself? The answer is that to study human nature is most interesting, but one can only study it well after one has studied oneself, for that enables one to understand human nature. As long as one remains ignorant of self one cannot study human nature properly. Often we hear people say, 'I am so disappointed in my friends,' 'I am so disheartened by my neighbors,' 'I have lost my faith in mankind,' 'I can bear animals, I can stand trees and plants better than human beings; I always try to avoid places where there are people.' Why do these thoughts come? Where do they come from and what causes them? It is the lack of understanding of oneself. The more one understands oneself, the more one finds that everything that is lacking in others is also lacking in oneself. Does a person become less by finding faults in himself? No, he becomes greater, for he not only finds that all the faults which are in others are also to be found in him, but that all the merits of the others are also his own merits. With faults and merits he becomes more complete; he does not become less.

PHILOSOPHY, PSYCHOLOGY, MYSTICISM - MYSTICISM IN LIFE - Self-Knowledge

Gayan #314 – Bola #273 - The more a man explores himself, the more power he finds within.

The first thing to do is to get control of the glance. The next is to get control of the feelings. And the third is to get control of the consciousness. If these three things are attained then one begins to look within. Looking within helps a person very much in looking outside; then the same power with which the heart and eyes are charged begins to manifest outwardly. And the one who looks within finds, when he looks without, that all that is within manifests without. His influence is healing and consoling, uplifting and soothing. His sight, too, becomes penetrating, so that not only human beings but even objects begin to disclose to him their nature, character, and secret.

HEALING AND THE MIND WORLD - MENTAL PURIFICATION - Insight (1)

Gayan #315 – Bola #274 - The secret of life is balance, and the absence of balance is life's destruction.

"In balance lies the whole secret of life, and the lack of it explains death. All that is constructive comes from balance, and all destruction comes from lack of balance. It is when balance goes that sickness and death come. There are many people who are sickly and ill for years, yet their life is prolonged because they have some balance. They are physically on the decline, but to counterbalance this they have an ambition in life that keeps them alive. It may be the desire to see the success of a loved son, or the happiness of a daughter.

All religions and philosophies have laid down certain principles such as kindness, truthfulness, and forgiveness, but the mystic lays no stress on principles, he allows everyone to have his own principles, each according to his point of view and evolution. For example, there are two men, one is so merciful that he will not even harm an insect, and he could not draw a sword to kill another human being, while the other man for the sake of his people is content to fight and to die.

These are two opposite points of view, and both are right in their way. The Sufi therefore believes one should let each hold on to the principle suited to his evolution, but for himself he looks beyond the principle to that which is at the back of it, the balance; and he realizes that what makes one lose balance is wrong, and what makes one keep it is right. The main point is not to act against one's principles. If the whole world says a thing is wrong, and you yourself feel that it is right, it is so, perhaps, for you.

The question of balance explains the problem of sin and virtue, and he who understands it is the master of life. There should be a balance in all our actions; to be either extreme or lukewarm is equally bad. There is a saying, 'Jack of all trades, and master of none'. This is very true, as there has been too little effort given, so that no one thing has been done thoroughly.

A balance in repose and activity is necessary, as too much weight on the side of repose leads to idleness, and even sickness, whereas an unbalanced activity results in nervousness, and frequently in a mental or physical breakdown.

Spiritual Liberty – Pearls from the Ocean Unseen - Balance

Gayan #316 – Bola #275 - All that is from God is for all souls.

The Message, whenever, at whatever period it came to the world, did not come to a certain section of humanity; it did not come to raise only some few people who perhaps accepted the faith, the Message, or a particular organized Church. No, all these things came afterwards. The rain does not fall in a certain land only; the sun does not shine upon a certain country only. All that is from God is for all souls. If they are worthy, they deserve it; it is their reward; if they are unworthy, they are the more entitled to it. Verily, blessing is for every soul; for every soul, whatever be his faith or belief, belongs to God.

THE UNITY OF RELIGIOUS IDEALS - Religion - Religion

Gayan #317 – Bola #276 - It is not our situation in life, but our attitude towards life that makes us happy or unhappy.

...Man is mostly selfish and what interests him is that which concerns his own life, and not knowing the troubles of the lives of others, he feels the burden of his own life even more than the burden of the whole world. If one could only think in his poverty that there are others, who are poorer than he; in his illness that there are others whose sufferings are perhaps greater than his; in his troubles that there are others whose difficulties are perhaps greater than his. Self-pity is the worst poverty. It overwhelms man and he sees nothing but his own troubles and pains and it seems to him that he is the most unhappy person--more than anyone in the world.

There is a story of a great thinker of Persia, Sa'adi. He writes in the account of his life: "once I had no shoes and I had to walk in the hot sand barefoot and I though how very miserable I was; then I met a man who was lame, for whom to walk it was very difficult. I bowed down at once to Heaven and offered thanks that I was much better off than he, who had not even feet to walk upon." This shows that it is not the situation in life, but it is man's attitude toward life, that makes him happy or unhappy. And this attitude can even make such a difference between men that one in a palace would be unhappy and another in a humble cottage, could be very happy.

SOCIAL GATHEKAS - The Privilege of Being Human (1)

Gayan #318 – Bola #277 - Gain by the loss of another is not profitable in the end.

In the path of attainment, many lose their way and go astray, especially those who are regardless of consideration. There are objects which cannot bring anything but harm, and there are many in this world who would never stop to think of the harm to another, as long as they think that they are safe. But since the very nature of the world is give and take, and as every action has its reaction, and as every cause has its own similar effect, how can one really think that he can be safe by causing harm to another?

Often, in many attainments through life, there is found a benefit for one by the loss of another. And thus we see it go up and down through life, like a scale. And this is a matter of time and experience, and often one finds that a momentary gain is more disastrous than the loss would have been. Therefore, the wise have a greater gain as their object through life than the objects of sense of the average man, who is ever in pursuit of transitory gain, and in success and in failure both he is at a loss, because in the end both may get little. The wise, therefore, fix their eyes on that divine attainment, divine ideal, which is the best object possible, and by the attainment of that object they enjoy eternal bliss.

ESOTERIC PAPERS - GITHA I - THE PATH OF ATTAINMENT -
Necessity of Common Sense

Gayan #319 – Bola #278 - Speaking wisdom is much easier than living it.

God is not the Father of one sect; God is the Father of the whole world, and all are entitled to be called His children, whether worthy or unworthy. And in fact it is man's attitude toward God and Truth which can bring him closer to God, Who is the ideal of every soul. And if this attitude is not developed, then, whatever a man's religion be, he has failed to live it. Therefore, what is important in life is to try and live the religion to which one belongs, or that one esteems, or that one believes to be one's religion.

THE UNITY OF RELIGIOUS IDEALS – RELIGION – Religion

Gayan #320 – Bola #279 - Charity is the expansion of the heart.

The spirit of generosity in nature builds a path to God, for generosity is outgoing, is spontaneity; its nature is to make its way towards a wide horizon. Generosity, therefore, may be called charity of heart. It is not necessary that the spirit of generosity be shown always by the spending of money; in every little thing one can show it. Generosity is an attitude a person shows in every little action that he does for people that he comes in contact with in his everyday life. One can show generosity by a smile, by a kind glance, by a warm handshake; by patting the younger soul on the shoulder as a mark of encouragement, of showing appreciation, of expressing affection. Generosity one can show in accommodating one's fellow-man, in welcoming him, in bidding farewell to one's friend. In thought, word, and deed, in every manner and form one can show that generous spirit which is the sign of the godly.

The Bible speaks of generosity by the word 'charity', but if I were to give an interpretation of the word 'generosity' I would call it nobility. No rank, position, or power can prove one noble; truly noble is he who is generous of heart. What is generosity? It is nobility, it is expansion of heart. As the heart expands, so the horizon becomes wide, and one finds greater and greater scope in which to build the kingdom of God.

Depression, despair, and all manner of sorrow and sadness come from lack of generosity. Where does jealousy come from? Where does envy, aching of the heart come from? It all comes from lack of generosity. A man may not have one single coin to his name, and yet he can be generous, he can be noble, if only he has a large heart of friendly feeling. Life in the world offers every opportunity to a man, whatever be his position in life, to show if he has any spirit of generosity.

The changeableness and falsehood of human nature, besides lack of consideration and thoughtlessness for those whom he meets through life, and furthermore the selfishness and grabbing and grafting spirit that disturbs and troubles his soul, all these create a situation which is itself a test and trial through which every soul has to pass in the midst of worldly life. And when through this test and trial a man holds fast to his principle of charity, and marches along towards his destination, not allowing the influences that come from the four corners of the world to keep him back from his journey to the goal, in the end he becomes the king of life, even if when he reaches his destination there is not left one single earthly coin to his name.

It is not earthly wealth that makes man rich. Riches come by discovering that gold-mine which is hidden in the human heart, out of which comes the spirit of generosity.

Art of Personality – Personality and Character-Building - part 10

Gayan #321 – Bola #280 - All that is not plain is a puzzle; therefore, wisdom is a puzzle to the ordinary mind.

In the Sufi literature, which is known to the world as the Persian literature, there is much talk about the "curls of the Beloved," and many have often wondered what it means. The curl is a symbol of something which is curved and round. The curve denotes the twist in the thought of wisdom. Very often a straight word of truth hits upon the head harder than a hammer. That shows that truth alone is not sufficient, the truth must be made into wisdom. And what is wisdom? Wisdom is the twisted truth. As raw food cannot be digested, and therefore it is cooked, although raw food is more natural than cooked food, so the straight truth is more natural, but is not digestible, it needs to be made into wisdom.

And why is it called the Beloved's curl? Because truth is of God, the Divine Beloved, and truth is God, and that twist given to His Own Being, which is truth, amplifies the divine beauty, as the curl is considered to be the sign of beauty. Then what is not straight is a puzzle. So wisdom is a puzzle to the ordinary mind. Besides, the curl hangs low down; so the heavenly beauty which is wisdom is manifested on earth. In other words, if someone wishes to see the beauty of the heavenly Beloved he may see it in wisdom.

Wisdom is traced not only in the human being, but even in the beasts and birds, in their affection, in their instinct. Very often it is most difficult for man to imitate fully the work which birds do in weaving their nests. Even the insects do wonderful work in preparing a little abode for themselves which is beyond man's art and skill. Besides this, if one studies nature, after keen observation and some contemplation upon it one will find that there is perfect wisdom behind it. Once man has thought on the subject, he can never, however materialistic he may be, deny the existence of God. Man's individuality is proved by his wisdom and distinguished by comparison. The wisdom of God, being perfect, is unintelligible to man. The glass of water cannot imagine how much water there is in the sea. If man would realize his limitation he would never dare question the existence of God.

The symbol of the curl also signifies something which is there, attractive, and yet a puzzle, a riddle. One loves it, admires it, and yet one cannot fathom its length and breadth. It is that which is wisdom. Its surface is human, but its depth is divine. It could be hell or heaven, and the knowledge of it can enable man always to keep in touch with his heaven, instead of waiting for it till the hereafter.

Gatha 2 – Symbology - Number 6 - The Curl of the Beloved

CHALAS

(Chala: An iluminated word.)

Gayan #322 – Chala #1 - The spiritual guide performs the role of Cupid in bringing the seeking souls closer to God.

According to the Sufi point of view there is only one teacher, and that teacher is God Himself. No man can teach another man. All one can do for another is to give him one's own experience in order to help him to be successful. For instance if a person happens to know a road, he can tell another man that it is the road which leads to the place he wishes to find. The work of the spiritual teacher is like the work of Cupid. The work of Cupid is to bring two souls together; and so is the work of the spiritual teacher: to bring together the soul and God. But what is taught to the one who seeks after truth? Nothing is taught. He is only shown how he should learn from God. For no man can ever teach spirituality; it is God alone who teaches it. And how is it learned? When these ears which are open outwardly are closed to the outside world and focused upon the heart within, then instead of hearing all that comes from the outer life one begins to hear the words within. Thus if one were to define what meditation is, that also is an attitude: the right attitude towards God.

THE ALCHEMY OF HAPPINESS - The Secret of Life

Gayan #323 – Chala #2 - The Sufi's tendency is to look at everything from two points of view: from his own and that of another.

Is it not amusing to think that the foolish person disagrees more with others than the wise? One would think that he knows more than the wise one. The wise one agrees with both the foolish and the wise; he is ready to understand everybody's point of view. It may not be his ideal his way of looking, but he is capable of looking at things from the point of view of others. It is not one eye that sees fully; to make the vision complete two eyes are needed, and so the wise one can see from two points of view. If we do not keep away our own thoughts and preconceived ideas, if we cannot be passive and desirous of seeing from the point of view of another, we make a great mistake.

THE SMILING FOREHEAD - The Soul, its Origin and Unfoldment

Gayan #324 – Chala #3 - The true religion, to the Sufi, is the sea of truth, and all different faiths are as its waves.

The principal thing that the Sufi message has brought to the world is tolerance for all faiths existing in the different parts of the world, followed by different people. This can be done by giving the idea of that one truth which stands as the stem of religion, and all different faiths as its branches. The true religion to a Sufi is the sea of truth and all the different faiths are as its waves. The message of God from time to time comes as tides in the sea, but what remains always is the sea, the truth. Those who consider anther on the wrong track they themselves are also not on the right track, for the one who is on the right track finds every road leading to the same goal sooner or later. The Sufi mission does not make converts to a certain faith to the exclusion of all faiths. A convert to the Sufi orders means a convert to all faiths of the this world and bound by no particular faith. Faith to a Sufi is a free ideal, not a captivity.

SOCIAL GATHEKAS - The Mission of Sufism to the World

Gayan #325 – Chala #4 - The pure truth not every man can see; if he can, he needs no more teaching.

The prophet can never tell the ultimate truth, which only his soul knows and no words can explain. His mission is therefore to design and paint and make the picture of the truth in words that may be intelligible to mankind.

Not every man can see the bare truth. If he can see it he needs no more teaching. The prophet, so to speak, listens to the words of God in the language of God and interprets the same words in the human tongue. He speaks to every man in his own language; he converses with every man, standing on his own plane. Therefore he has little chance to disagree, unless there were someone who wanted disagreement and nothing else: there he cannot help.

RELIGIOUS GATHEKAS - The Prophet

Gayan #326 – Chala #5 - The Creator is hidden in his own creation.

Granting that we see nature, and also admitting its original cause, upon what grounds do we consider the cause to be a personal God, meriting worship? The answer is that nature itself consists of different personalities, and each of them has its peculiar attributes. The sum total of all these personalities is One, the only real personality. In relation to that One all other personalities are merely an illusion. Just as, in a limited form, a nation or a community is the sum of many personalities, just as nature manifested in numerous names and forms is still called nature, singular not plural, just as the individual combines within himself the different parts of his body, arms, limbs, eyes, ears, and is possessed of different qualities yet is one person, so the sum total of all personalities is called God.

He is the possessor of all the visible and invisible attributes of the Absolute, and has different names in different languages for the understanding of man. It may be said that the personality of a man is quite comprehensible, since his actions exhibit him as a single individual, whereas God's personality has no clear identification of its own. The answer is, that variety covers unity. 'Hidden things are manifested by their opposites, but as God has no opposite He remains hidden. God's light has no opposite in the range of creation whereby it may be manifested to view' (Jelal-ud-Din Rumi).

The wise man by studying nature enters into the unity through its variety, and realizes the personality of God by sacrificing his own. 'He who knows himself knows Allah' (Sayings of Mohammed). 'The Kingdom of God is within you' (Bible). 'Self-knowledge is the real wisdom' (Vedanta).

God's relation to nature may be understood by analyzing the idea expressed in the words, 'I myself'. This affirmation means the one individual; at the same time it identifies the dual aspect of the One. In this phrase 'I' is the possessor, and 'myself' is the possessed. So also God, the unmanifested, is the possessor; and nature, the manifestation, is the possessed, which has its source hidden within itself.

The possessed could not have been created from anything other than the possessor's own self, as there existed none but the possessor. Although the possessor and the possessed are considered to be two separate identities, in reality they are one. The possessor realizes the possessed through the medium of his own consciousness, which forms three aspects, the Trinity, of the one Being. The German philosopher Hegel says, 'If you say God is one, it is true; if you say He is two, that is also true; and if you say He is three, that is true too, because it is the nature of the world.'

Spiritual Liberty – The Sufi Message of Spiritual Liberty – The Personal Being

Gayan #327 – Chala #6 - Natural religion is the religion of beauty.

It would be no exaggeration to say that all these disagreeable things which go on in this world--wars, diseases and the like--all come from the lack of artistic attitude in life the lack of a sense of beauty, and the lack of that vision which unites the whole humanity in one center; and this center is God. When man closes his eyes to beauty, he will never think of looking for the beautiful, although beauty is constantly beside him. Behind the beauty, as Qur'an says, God is. "God is beautiful and He loves beauty." The natural tendency to love and admire beauty is a divine inheritance; it is the spiritual thing which leads to spirituality. Through this tendency one accomplishes one's spiritual duty in life. When that tendency has gone and religion is left without art, then the religion may be perhaps useful for an inartistic society, but it turns into a sort of formality. One does one thing, one does another. As one does weekday work, so one also does Sunday duty.

The Dutch Papers – Art and Music #4 – The Divinity of Art

Gayan #328 – Chala #7 - The same light which is fire on earth and the sun in the sky, is God in heaven.

Light has the greatest attraction for the human soul. Man loves it in the fire and in things that are bright and shining, and that is why he considers gold and jewels as precious. The Cosmos has a greater attraction for him than the earth, because of the light. As man evolves, he naturally ceases to look down on earth, but looks up to the Cosmos, the Heavens. The most attractive object that he sees is the sun in the heavens, the sun which is without any support and is more luminous than anything else in the heavens. Therefore, as man is attracted to beauty and surrenders to beauty, he bows to the sun as being the greatest beauty in heaven, and man took the sun as Nature's symbol of God.

This symbol he pictures in different forms. In Persia, China, Japan, India, Egypt, whenever God was pictured, it was in the form of the sun. In all ages man has pictured his Prophet, Master, Savior, with a sun around his head. In ancient Persia there used to be a golden disc behind the head of the king, picturing him as the sun, and they used to call this disc Zardash. The name Zarathustra has the same origin; the word simply meant the golden disc. In Hindu temples and Buddhist temples around the image of different Avataras there is this sign of the sun, and this symbol was used both in the East and in the West in turbans and hats. There are now people in India who put on their turbans a brass band, which represents the sun.

A deeper study of the sun suggests the four directions of lines that are formed around it. It is this sign that is the origin of the symbol of the cross. The ancient traditions prove that the idea of the cross existed in the East long before the coming of Christ, especially among the Brahmans. It is from this sign that the two sacred arms were made, Chakra and Trissoun. Islam, the religion which allows no symbolism, has in the building of the mosques the same symbolism of the sun. Whether the name of the sun be written in Persian or in Arabic, it makes the form of the mosque.

Man, as happens to be his nature, has blamed the sun worshipers and mocked at them, but he has never been able to uproot the charm, the attraction for human souls held by the sun.

Unity of Religious Ideals – The Sufi's Conception of God - The Symbol of the Sun

Gayan #329 – Chala #8 - All surrender to beauty willingly and to power unwillingly."

Beauty, which a knower appreciates and a lover admires, is worshipped by the mystic. It is useless to try and put into words what beauty is; but if anything can explain it, it is the other word for beauty and that is harmony. It is the harmonious combination of colors, the harmonious grouping of lines, and the harmonious blending of the objects of nature which suggest to us the idea of beauty. In order to be beautiful an object must be harmonious, for in point of fact harmony is beauty. If there is anything in the world that makes man unconscious of himself, in other words that makes man lose his self-consciousness, if there is anything that makes man humble, that makes him surrender willingly, it is beauty. Beauty is something that conquers without a sword, that holds without hands, that is more tender than the petals of a flower and stronger than anything in the world. The Prophet has said, 'God is Beauty, and He loves what is beautiful.

Philosophy, Psychology, Mysticism – Mysticism in Life - Beauty

Gayan #330 – Chala #9 - The creation is not only the nature of God, but also His art.

People belonging to different faiths very often make the mistake of considering art as something outside of religion. The fact is that the whole creation is the art of the Creator, and one sees the perfection of His art in divine man. This shows that the source of the whole creation has the spirit of art at the back of it. In all ages man has developed his artistic faculty, and he has tried to progress in art. But, in the end, where does he arrive? He remains far from touching either the beauty of nature or the art of creation. Man's art always fails to equal the art of God.

This shows that the source of every soul is the spirit of art, and art is spirit, that everything which has come out from that spirit has manifested in the form of art. Did man look more at nature--at the heavens, the beauty of the stars and planets, of the clouds and the sun, its rising and setting, and when the sun is at its zenith, the waxing and waning of the moon, the different shades of color which we can see in the sky--the more would man always marvel at the art at work behind it all.

The Dutch Papers - ART AND MUSIC IV - The Divinity of Art

Many think that art is something different from nature, but, if I were to say, art is the finishing of nature. And one may ask, "can man improve upon nature which is made by God." But the fact is that God Himself, through man finishes his creation in art. As all different elements are God's vehicles, as all the trees and plants are His instruments to create through, so art is the medium of God, through which God Himself creates and finishes His creation.

Social Gatheka #40

Gayan #331 - Chala #10 - Vanity is the impetus hidden behind every impulse, that brings out both the worst and the best in man.

At the back of this tendency [of intolerance] there is a most wonderful secret hidden, the depths of which are fathomed by the mystic. The mystic who sees God within and without, both, who recognizes God in unity and in variety both, the mystic realizes that it is the One Who has known Himself to be One, Who does not know of two, Who feels uncomfortable and agitated, and shows a revolt on knowing that "There exists another besides Me." And it is therefore that the birds have the tendency to fight with their own element, and so the same thing one finds among the beasts. Among men, man is the enemy of man, and woman of woman. The rivalry that exists between professions and between people of the same position and between nations shows the same thing, that one principle that the nature of the ego, through every name and form, revolts against another, especially of the same name and form, in some way or other. One may give a thousand reasons for intolerance. They exist too, but the inner reason is one and the same in all aspects of intolerance. The Sufis have called it Kibriyy, which means "vanity," vanity of the One to Whom alone it belongs.

ESOTERIC PAPERS - GATHA III - METAPHYSICS – Tolerance

Gayan #332 - Chala #11 - Time and space are but the length and breadth of the infinite.

...Now coming to the other side of the subject, how can one be in tune with the infinite? The nature of being in tune with the infinite can be seen by comparing one's soul to the string of an instrument. It is tied at both sides: one is the infinite and the other is the finite. When a person is conscious all the time of the finite then he or she is tuned with the finite, and the one who is conscious of the infinite is tuned with the infinite. Being in tune with one makes us limited, weak, hopeless, and powerless: by being in tune with the other we obtain the power and strength to pull through life under all adverse conditions.

The work that a Sufi considers his or her sacred work has nothing to do with any particular creed nor with any particular religion; it is only this simple thing which I have just said: to be in rhythm with life's conditions and to be in tune with the infinite.

Gatheka 30   Sufi Initiation

Gayan #333 - Chala #12 - It is presumption on the part of man when he demands in words an explanation of God.

An ordinary person reads about the kingdom of God and heaven, but does not know where heaven is; the ordinary person feels there is a God, but there is no evidence. Therefore, a large number of intellectual people who really are seeking the truth are going away from outer religion, because they cannot find the explanation; consequently they become materialistic.

The mystic says the explanation of the whole of religion is the investigation of the self. The more one explores oneself, the more one will understand all religions in the fullest light and all will become clear. Sufism is only a light thrown upon your own religion, like a light brought into a room containing all the things you want; the one thing needed was light.

Yet the mystic is not always ready to give his or her answer to every person. Can parents always answer every question of their infant children? No. There are questions which can be answered, and there are some which should wait until the person comes to a point of understanding. I used to be fond of a poem which I did not understand; I could not find a satisfactory explanation. After ten years, all of a sudden in one second's time, a light was thrown upon it and I understood. There was no end to my joy. Does it not show that everything has its time? When people become impatient and ask for an answer, something can be answered, but something cannot be answered; the answer will come in its time. One has to wait. Has anyone in the world been able to say fully what God is, all the scriptures and prophets notwithstanding? God is an ideal too high and great for words.

Religious Gatheka 19   Sufi Mysticism, V: Realizing the Truth of Religion

Gayan #334 - Chala #13 - Truth is the evidence of God, and God is the evidence of truth.

When a person thinks about many effects, to his view manifest many causes, but when he is capable of looking at one effect, then he is able to know the one single cause. It is the one single cause which is the evidence of God. How true it is as it is said in a song, "The night has a thousand eyes, the day has but one. The mind has a thousand eyes, the heart has but one." The mind has a thousand eyes because it produces a thousand reasons, perhaps, for each effect, and the heart overlooks the thousand effects, for it sees the sum total of a thousand effects in one effect.

This is supported by a sura of the Qur'an, which says, "Every atom has its action directed by God," which may be expressed in other words as that every activity seen is directed by some unseen activity behind it. And nobody can deny the logic of this truth, that everything is directed by one activity and purposed for one effect. Therefore it is necessary that in attraction and in repulsion, in harmony and in faction, there is one activity which is the cause and each atom is working, affected by the others, harmoniously for the whole.

ESOTERIC PAPERS - GITHA III - MYSTICISM - The Knowledge of Past, Present and Future

Gayan #335 - Chala #14 - Among a million believers in God, there is scarcely one who makes God a reality.

    The first and principal thing in the inner life is to establish a relationship with God, making God the object with which we relate ourselves, such as the Creator, Sustainer, Forgiver, Judge, Friend, Father, Mother and Beloved. In every relationship we must place God before us, and become conscious of that relationship so that it will no more remain an imagination; because the first thing a believer does is to imagine. He imagines that God is the Creator, and tries to believe that God is the Sustainer, and he makes an effort to think that God is a Friend, and an attempt to feel that he loves God. But if this imagination is to become a reality, then exactly as one feels for one's earthly beloved sympathy, love and attachment, so one must feel the same for God. However greatly a person may be pious, good or righteous, yet without this his piety or his goodness is not a reality to him.

    The work of the inner life is to make God a reality, so that He is no more an imagination; that this relationship that man has with God may seem to him more real than any other relationship in this world; and when this happens, then all relationships, however near and dear, become less binding. But at the same time, a person does not thus become cold; he becomes more loving. It is the godless man who is cold, impressed by the selfishness and lovelessness of this world, because he partakes of those conditions in which he lives. But the one who is in love with God, the one who has established his relationship with God, his love becomes living; he is no more cold; he fulfills his duties to those related to him in this world much more than does the godless man.

THE INNER LIFE - The Object of the Journey

Gayan #336 - Chala #15 - The God-ideal is the flower of creation, and the realization of truth is its fragrance.

The existence of God is a question which arises in every mind, whether in the mind of the believer in God or in the mind of the unbeliever. There are moments when the greatest believer in God questions His existence--whether there really is a God? He finds it, at the second thought, sacrilegious to have a notion such as this, and he tries to get rid of it. But often the question rises in the heart of the unbeliever if it is really true; if there is such a thing as God? The idea of God is inborn in man. The God-Ideal is the flower of the human race; and this flower blooms in the realization of God.

THE UNITY OF RELIGIOUS IDEALS - THE GOD IDEAL - The Existence God

Gayan #337 - Chala #16 - A true worshipper of God sees His person in all forms, and in respecting man he respects God.

This ideal of brotherhood develops, taking different forms. In the first stage the mystic becomes respectful to all beings, both to the saint and the sinner, to the wise and the foolish. In the next stage his sympathy goes out to everyone he meets, no matter who it is. The third stage is when he understands the condition of every person because of his sympathy and respect. The fourth stage is when he tolerates and forgives; he cannot help doing it for the very reason that he understands. One who cannot tolerate, who cannot forgive, is not able to understand; tolerance and forgiveness come from understanding. And the fifth stage is that he sees himself united with all, not only in God but even in himself; in each being he sees himself. No one can sympathize more than one sympathizes with oneself, and so it is natural that, when the self of the mystic is at the same time all people, he can then sympathize with everyone as he would with himself.

THE MYSTICISM OF SOUND - PHILOSOPHY, PSYCHOLOGY, MYSTICISM – MYSTICISM IN LIFE – Brotherhood

Gayan #338 - Chala #17 - The hidden desire of the Creator is the secret of the whole creation.

A deep study of anything shows the seer that there is a purpose beneath it all. Yet, if one could look beyond every purpose, there would seem to be no purpose. This boundary is called the Wall of Smiles, which means that all purposes of life, which seem at the moment to be so important, fade away as soon as one looks at them from that height called the Wall of Smiles*.

But as deeply as the purpose of life can be traced, there seems to be one ultimate purpose working through all planes of life and showing itself through all planes of existence; that is as if the Knower, with His knowing faculty, had been in darkness, desiring to know something; and in order to know something He created all things. Again, it is the desire of the Creator that has been the power which created; and, too, it is the materialized substance of the spirit, a part of Himself, that has been turned into a creation, yet leaving the Creator behind as the absolute Spirit, constantly knowing and experiencing life through all different channels, some developed, some undeveloped for the purpose.

This Knower, through His final creation, man, realizes and knows more than through any other channel of knowledge, such as bird, beast, worm, germ, plant, or rock. This one Spirit, experiencing through various channels, deludes Himself with the delusion of various beings; and it is this delusion which is the individual ego. He experiences, therefore, two things in His delusion: pain and pleasure; pleasure by the experience of a little perfection, and pain by the lack of it. As long as the cover of this delusion keeps His eyes veiled He knows, yet does not know; it is an illusion; He experiences all things, and yet everything is confusion. But as time goes, when this veil becomes thinner and He begins to see through it, the first thing that comes to Him is bewilderment; but the next is knowledge, culminating in vanity, which is the purpose of life.

SPIRITUAL LIBERTY - METAPHYSICS - The Destiny of the Soul - The Purpose of Life

* There is a well known Eastern legend giving the idea of a soul who had found truth. There was a wall of laughter and of smiles. This wall existed for ages and many tried to climb it, but few succeeded.

Those who had climbed upon it saw something beyond, and so interested were they that they smiled, climbed over the wall and never returned. The people of the town began to wonder what magic could there be and what attraction, that whoever climbed the wall never returned. So they called it the wall of mystery. Then they said, 'We must make an enquiry and send someone who can reach the top, but we must tie him with a rope to hold him back.' When the man they had thus sent reached the top of the wall, he smiled and tried to jump over it, but they pulled him back. Still he smiled, and when the people eagerly asked, 'what did you see there?' he did not answer, he only smiled.

This is the condition of the seer. The man who in the shrine of his heart has seen the vision of God, the one who has the realization of truth, can only smile, for words can never really explain what truth means.

SUFI TEACHINGS - THE PRIVILEGE OF BEING HUMAN - Truth

Gayan #339 - Chala #18 - Vanity is the sum total of every activity in the world.

The whole of manifestation is the expression of that spirit of the Logos which in Sufi terms is called Kibria. Through every being this spirit is manifested in the form of vanity, pride, or conceit. Vanity expressed crudely is called pride. Had it not been for this spirit working in every being as the central theme of life, no good or bad would have existed in the world, nor would there have been great or small. All virtues and every evil are the offspring of this spirit. The art of personality is to cut off the rough edges of this spirit of vanity, which hurts and disturbs those one meets in life. The person who says 'I,' the more he does so, the more he disturbs the minds of his listeners.

Many times people are trained in politeness and are taught a polished language and manner; yet if this spirit of vanity is pronounced, it will creep up in spite of all good manners and beautiful language, and express itself in a person's thought, speech, or action, calling aloud, 'I am, I am!' If a person be speechless, his vanity will leap out in the expression of his glance. It is something which is the hardest thing to suppress and to control. For adepts the struggle in life is not so great with the passions and emotions, which sooner or later by more or less effort can be controlled; but vanity, it is always growing. If one cuts down its stem then one cannot live, for it is the very self, it is the I, the ego, the soul, or God within; it cannot be denied its existence. But struggling with it beautifies it more and more, and makes more and more tolerable that which in its crude form is intolerable.

Vanity may be likened to a magic plant. If one sees it in the garden growing as a thorny plant, and one cuts it down, it will grow in another place in the same garden as a fruit-tree; and when one cuts it down again, in another place in the same garden it will spring up as a bush of fragrant roses. It exists just the same, but in a more beautiful form which gives happiness to those who touch it. The art of personality, therefore, does not teach the rooting out of the seed of vanity, which cannot be rooted out as long as man lives; but its crude outer garb may be destroyed in order that, after dying several deaths, it may be manifested as the plant of desires.

THE ART OF PERSONALITY - CHARACTER AND PERSONALITY - The Art of Personality - V

Gayan #340 - Chala #19 - Beauty is the object which every soul pursues.

But in order to develop art in the real sense of the word, one need not be an artist, one need not have that particular vocation in life. Whatever be one's vocation, art is necessary just the same. It is wrong to think that art is not needed in one's social or domestic life, in business, in industry, in one's profession. It is because of the division that people have made between art and other walks of life that life has become devoid of beauty. And in this way art has been very much neglected, except by those who pretend to appreciate it and who have perhaps some leisure in which to give thought and time to it. But even they are very often ignorant of the real beauty and value of art; they take an interest in it only because they want to be able to say that they are fond of art. It is because of this that artists sometimes lack the opportunity of expressing their soul through their art, being hampered by this lack of appreciation.

Others want to commercialize their art, but art is always above material values. When art has to be limited by material values and by seeking the approbation of those who do not understand it, it has to suffer; instead of evolving it declines. But even in practical life art has great scope. Think for instance how much a woman can do in her everyday life in her home with her artistic gifts. She can make it beautiful and comfortable; she can train her children to have better taste; and whatever her means may be, even her manner can produce beauty, harmony, and happiness in her home. It is the same thing in one's office, in industry, in business, in whatever one does. If there is a regard for beauty and harmony one can make one's own business or profession, one's life and one's work, more beautiful, thereby producing greater happiness for oneself and for others.

THE PATH OF INITIATION - ART: YESTERDAY, TODAY, AND TOMORROW - The Divinity of Art

Gayan #341 - Chala #20 - Beauty is the life of the artist, the theme of the poet, the soul of the musician.

The object of worship of the Sufi is beauty; not only beauty in form and color and line, but beauty in all its aspects, from gross to fine. The moral for the Sufi is the understanding of harmony: in what way one can harmonize with one's soul and how one can harmonize with one's fellow human being. Instead of labeling one action as a sin and another action as a virtue, instead of arguing on the subject of the right and wrong of certain actions, the Sufi trains him or herself, as a musician trains his or her ear, to see what is harmonious and what lacks harmony in oneself and in one's dealings with others.

Gatheka 22   The Ideals and Aim of the Sufi Movement

Gayan #342 - Chala #21 - A charming personality is as precious as gold and as delicious as perfume.

Therefore the first necessity for those who are seeking after truth is to develop the spirit of personality. Gold and jewels are worthless if one has no personality; nothing is valuable then. Personality is more valuable than wealth. How strange it is that there is such a large population in this world and that there are so few personalities! Think of that Greek philosopher who went about with a lighted lantern in daytime. People asked, 'What are you looking for?' He said, 'For a human being.'

THE ALCHEMY OF HAPPINESS - The Development of Personality

Gayan #343 - Chala #22 - A dancing soul shows its graceful movements in all its activities.

It was natural that with Persian thinkers of all periods, who thought deeply on life, its nature and character, their expressions should become subtle, artistic, fine, and picturesque. In short, it is the dancing of the soul. In all other living beings, the soul is lying asleep, but when once the soul has awakened, called by beauty, it leaps up dancing, and its every movement makes a picture, whether in writing, poetry, music or whatever it may be. A dancing soul will always express the most subtle and intricate harmonies in the realm of music or poetry.

When we read the works of Hafiz and of many other Sufi poets, we shall find that they are full of the same imagery and this is partly because that was the time of Islam. The mission of Islam had a particular object in view, and in order to attain that object it had strict rules about life. A free-thinker had difficulty in expressing his thoughts without being accused of having done a great wrong towards the religion and the State. And these freethinkers of Persia, with their dancing soul and continual enthusiasm, began to express their soul in this particular imagery, using words such as 'the beloved', 'wine', wine-press', and 'tavern'. And this poetry became so popular that not only the wise derived benefit from it, but also the simple ones enjoyed the beauty of its wonderful expressions which make an immediate appeal to every soul. There is no doubt that the souls which were already awakened and those on the point of awakening were inspired by these poems. Souls which were opening their eyes after the deep slumber of many years began to rise up and dance; as Hafiz says, 'If those pious ones of long robes listen to my verse, my song, they will immediately begin to get up and dance'. And then he says at the end of the poem, 'Forgive me, O pious ones, for I am drunk just now!'.

Path of Initiation – Sufi Poetry - Sufi Poetic Imagery

Gayan #344 - Chala #23 - A charming personality is like a magnificent piece of art with life added.

There is a difference between individuality and personality, just as there is a difference between nature and art. However much nature is near to man's soul, art is closer to his heart. If it were not so man would have preferred to live in the forest; he would have roamed about in nature and would have been quite satisfied in the wilderness; he would have found the greatest charm in what the wilderness can offer and in the beauty to be seen in the forest. Instead of all this man has created a world - a world which he has made for himself- and in that world he has made a nature of his own imagination, a nature which he calls art. If that is art then on this art much depends. People may say, "Is it not an imitation of nature?" Yes, it is an imitation of nature. You might say, "Then it is not as great as Nature", but I say: both nature and art are made by the same Artist. Nature is made directly by the Artist, and art is made indirectly through the pen of the Artist. Art is the finishing of that beauty which begins to manifest itself in nature. A person who has not come to this conception of art does not yet know the divinity of art.

Now as to the question what art has to do with personality, personality is art itself, and the greatest art. Once a lady told me, "My parents brought me up just like a plant grows in the wilderness". When I replied, "It is a great pity", she was surprised. What is education, what is culture, what is self-development? It is all art, it is the way for individuality to culminate into personality.

In ancient times the religious education and human culture in every form mainly had the culture of the personality as their central theme. To-day we are expected to learn mathematics, geography, history and other things, but never the art of personality which is of the greatest use in life. Apart from its spiritual significance, we see in our everyday life that a salesman who is pleasant, courteous and well-mannered is successful. If he lacks manner he will be repellent; he may have all kinds of beautiful things in his shop, he will have no success. If a clerk in an office, a secretary, an assistant, a supervisor has a charming personality, a kindly manner, a sympathetic attitude, he will win the affection of all; everything will be light, everything will go smoothly. If he lacks the art of personality, he may have all qualifications, he may be a most capable person, yet things will not run smoothly. A person, whether man or woman, may be a barrister, a solicitor, a doctor, a most qualified individual, but if the art of personality is not developed he will be disagreeable and unpleasant - in his own home and in all walks of life. The art of personality is the main thing to develop; if not, a person misses a great deal.

Sufi Teachings – The Privilage of Being Human – The Art of Personality

Gayan #345 - Chala #24 - Life is the principal thing to consider, and true life is the inner life, the realization of God.

In selfishness there is an illusion of profit, but in the end the profit attained by selfishness proves to be worthless. Life is the principal thing to consider, and true life is the inner life, the realization of God, the consciousness of one's spirit. When the human heart becomes conscious of God it turns in the sea and it spreads - extends the waves of its love to friend and foe - spreading further and further, it attains perfection.

SOCIAL GATHEKAS - Different Points of View

Gayan #346 - Chala #25 - The soul of Christ is the life of the universe.

The divine message has always been sent through those fitly endowed. For instance when wealth was esteemed the message was delivered by King Solomon; when beauty was worshipped, Joseph, the most handsome, gave the message; when music was regarded as celestial David gave his message in song; when there was curiosity about miracles Moses brought his message; when sacrifice was highly esteemed Abraham gave the message; when heredity was recognized, Christ gave his message as .the Son of God; and when democracy was necessary, Mohammad gave his message as the Servant of God, one like all and among all; this put an end to the necessity for more prophets, because of the democratic nature of his proclamation and message. He proclaimed la elaha ill 'Allah (none exists but God). God constitutes the whole being, singly, individually and collectively, and every soul has the source of the divine message within itself. This is the reason why there is no longer the need for mediation, for a third person as a savior between man and God. For man has evolved enough to conceive the idea of God being all and all being God, and has become tolerant enough to believe in the divine message given by one like himself, who is liable to birth, death, joy, and sorrow, and all the natural vicissitudes of life.

All Masters from the time of Adam till the time of Mohammad have been the one embodiment of the Master-ideal. When Jesus Christ is represented as saying, 'I am Alpha and Omega, the beginning and the end,' it is not meant that either the name or the visible person of Jesus Christ is the Alpha and Omega, but the Master-spirit within. It was this spirit which proclaimed this, moved by its realization of past, present, and future life, confident of its eternity. It is the same spirit which spoke through Krishna, saying, 'We appear on earth when Dharma is corrupted,' which was long before the coming of Christ. During his divine absorption Mohammad said, 'I existed even before this creation and shall remain after its assimilation.' In the holy traditions it is said, 'We have created thee of Our light and from thy light We have created the universe.' This is not said of the external person of Mohammad as known by this name. It refers to the spirit which spoke through all the blessed tongues and yet remained formless, nameless, birthless and deathless.

THE WAY OF ILLUMINATION - Some Aspects of Sufism - The Masters

Gayan #347 - Chala #26 - The mother was the stepping-stone of Jesus to Christhood.

It is the mother's fear that gives the child fear; her anger gives it anger; her contempt gives it contempt. Her bad surroundings and impressions give the child bad impressions; her good and desirable impressions give the child good and desirable impressions. It is she who molds the human race. From her are born the prophets and murshids. The credit for all good and great people is hers; but at the same time children are often born weak and defective because of her want of control and foolishness. By putting too many coals on the fire, the fire may be covered up and the flame cannot come out.

Krishna is often represented with his mother Devaki, and Christ with his mother the Virgin Mary. This is woman's greatest merit and glory. In the Gayan it is said, 'The mother was the stepping-stone of Jesus to Christhood.' This means that human nature is such that man often forgets, seeing the great glory of the Master, that modest and humble help given at the time of need which enabled the Master to show forth his divine glory. The soul which was to expand as Christ was enabled to come on earth by the mother; and that is why in every case thought and consideration for the mother are important. Even Jesus Christ, the manifestation of the Almighty God, was dependent on his mother for his manifestation.

SPIRITUAL LIBERTY - AQIBAT, LIFE AFTER DEATH - The Law of Heredity

Gayan #348 - Chala #27 - God speaks to the prophet in His divine tongue, and the prophet interprets it in the language of man.

But besides, the prophet is the message-bearer; the prophet is master and servant at the same time; the prophet is a teacher and at the same time a pupil. There is a great deal that he must learn from his experience through life, not in order to make himself capable to receive the message, but in order to make himself efficient enough to give the message. For God speaks to the prophet in his divine tongue, and the prophet interprets it in his turn in the language of men, making it intelligible to them and trying to put the finest ideas in the gross terms of worldly language.

Therefore all that the prophet comes to give is not given to the world in words, but all that cannot be given in words is given without words. It is given through the atmosphere; it is given by the presence; it is given by the great affection that gushes forth from his heart; it is given in his kind glance; and it is given in his benediction. Yet most is given in silence that no earthly sense can perceive. The difference between human language and divine words is this, that a human word is a pebble: it exists, but there is nothing further; but the divine word is a living word, just like a grain of corn. One grain of corn is not one grain; in reality, it is hundreds and thousands. In the grain there is an essence which is always multiplying and which will show the perfection in itself.

RELIGIOUS GATHEKAS - How the Wise Live in the World (2)

Gayan #349 - Chala #28 - The evidence of prophecy is the personality of the prophet.

There are some who receive the knowledge from the Divine Mind indirectly, and some receive it directly. Souls who happen to receive the central current of the Spirit of Guidance, in such souls the spirit of prophecy is conceived. The Messengers of all times, of whom we hear in the histories and traditions of the world, have been souls in whom the central current of the Divine Light has functioned. In other words, the Prophets of all ages have been the reflections of the Divine Mind on earth. No one has ever seen God, and if the evidence of God has ever been manifested, it was in man who reflected God. Besides all the Prophets have taught, it was the personality of the Prophets which proved their prophecy. In their thought, speech, and word they reflected God, which was more than morals, doctrines, and teachings could do.

THE UNITY OF RELIGIOUS IDEALS - THE SPIRITUAL HIERARCHY - The Spirit of Guidance

Gayan #350- Chala #29 - The true sword of Mohammed was the charm of his personality.

The power of character is like the power of an army. With Christ there was an army of angels. With Mohammed there was also an army of angels. He stood, while thousands of people were running away. When an enemy came near to the great Khalif to behead him, the enemy was afraid. But this fear was simply a result of the Prophet's power of control. Personality shows what has been sown in it. One cannot pretend to be righteous and good unless one's spirit has practiced it and that strength has really come. One's appearance and one's atmosphere can tell what one is, because man is the picture of his thoughts. Whatever he thinks, whatever he is about, that speaks in his atmosphere, in his voice, in his movements. In everything he expresses himself as he is, how far he has evolved, and how far he has not evolved. Whatever he is, he shows.

IN AN EASTERN ROSE GARDEN - Character and Fate

Gayan #351 - Chala #30 - As the whole of nature is made by God, so the nature of each individual is made by himself.

As the whole nature is made by God; so the nature of each individual is made by himself. And as the Almighty has the power to change His nature, so the individual is capable of changing his nature if he only knew it. Among all the creature of this world, man has the most right to be optimistic, for man represents on earth God. God as Judge, as Creator and as Master of All His Creation. So is man Master of his life; master of his own affairs if he only knew it. A man with optimism will help another drowning in the sea of fear and disappointment; but on the contrary a pessimistic person if to him some one goes ill, or downhearted he will pull him down and make him sink to the depths with him. On the side of the one is Life, on the side of the other death.

SOCIAL GATHEKAS - Optimism and Pessimism

Gayan #352 - Chala #31 - When the personality of an artist is absorbed in his art, it becomes art itself.

… Mental magnetism, which depends on the power and harmony of thought. This can be obtained by being fully absorbed in beautiful and harmonious thoughts, and by suppressing all irritable tendencies, such as anger, passion, greed, attachment, jealousy and pride. The reason why an artist, poet, musician and sculptor, or a thinker proves to have a more arresting personality than a politician or a businessman is because his interest keeps his mind absorbed in the thought of beauty, love, and harmony. While several other occupations of life distract the mind from these thoughts. Just like physical culture brings new life to the body, so in the same way thought culture brightens one's personality.

The Dutch Papers – Psychology 1 - Magnetism 2

Gayan #353 - Chala #32 - Vanity is a mask over the hidden object that attracts every soul.

Always consider that this is the one thing that you will meet on this path, and the one enemy you will avoid: vanity. You must be on your guard against it from which ever side it comes. It comes so swiftly and so subtly that it is difficult to recognize. When you are on your guard you will see that even your humble words and your meek actions will prove to be vain. This is the thing which throws man from the highest stage. Even prophets have to fight and to fight it. Know the danger of this path, and do not waste your time in falling into it. The one thing to rely upon is God's favor. Build neither on your study nor on your meditation, although they both help you. Build your dependence not even on your murshid but on God, Seek Him, trust Him. In Him lies your life's purpose, and in Him is hidden the rest of your soul.*

THE SUPPLEMENTARY PAPERS - CLASSES FOR MUREEDS - CLASS FOR MUREEDS I - Mureedship

Note

The last several sentences have been rearranged to improve the conveyance of the meaning from: "Do not build neither on your study nor on your meditation, although they both help you. But you are dependent on God, not even on Your murshid. Seek Him, trust Him. In Him lies your life's purpose, and Him is hidden the rest of your soul."

Gayan #354 - Chala #33 - Vanity is the crown of beauty, and modesty is its throne.

When love is for the human being it is primitive and incomplete, and yet it is needed to begin with. He can never say, 'I love God', who has no love for his fellow-man. But when love attains its culmination in God, it reaches its perfection.

Love creates love in man and even more with God. It is the nature of love. If you love God, God sends His love evermore upon you. If you seek Him by night, He will follow you by day; wherever you are, in your affairs, in your business transactions, the help, the protection and the presence of the Divine will follow you. The expression of love lies in silent admiration, contemplation, service, attention to please the beloved, and precaution to avoid the beloved's displeasure. These expressions of love on the part of the lover win the favor of the beloved, whose vanity otherwise cannot easily be satisfied; and the favor of the beloved is the only aim of the lover, nor is any cost too great a price for it.

The nature of beauty is that it is unconscious of the value of its being. It is the idealization of the lover which makes beauty precious, and it is the attention of the lover which produces indifference in the beautiful, a realization of being superior, and the idea, 'I am even more wonderful than I am thought to be'. When the vanity of an earthly beauty is thus satisfied by admiration, how much more should the vanity of the beauty of the heavens be satisfied by His glorification, who is the real beauty and alone deserves all praise. It is the absence of realization on man's part that makes him forget His beauty in all and recognize each beauty separately, liking one and disliking another. To the sight of the seer, from the least fraction of beauty to the absolute beauty of nature, all becomes as one single immanence of the divine Beloved.

Spiritual Liberty - Love, Human and Divine – The Moral of Love

Gayan #355 - Chala #34 - Without modesty beauty is dead, for modesty is the spirit of beauty.

'Hay' is the finest feeling in human nature, which is called modesty. Modesty is not necessarily meekness, or humility, or selflessness, or pride. Modesty is a beauty in itself, and its action is to veil itself; in that veiling it shows the vanity of its nature, and yet that vanity is a beauty itself. Modesty is the life of the artist, the theme of the poet, and the soul of the musician. In thought, speech, action, in one's manner, in one's movement, modesty stands as the central theme of grace. Without modesty beauty is dead, for modesty is the spirit of beauty. Silence in modesty speaks louder than bold words. The lack of modesty can destroy art, poetry, music, and all that is beautiful.

And if one asked, "What is modesty?", it is difficult to explain in words. It is a feeling which rises from a living heart; a heart which is dead has not got the taste of it. The modest person compared to the immodest one is like a plant standing by the side of a rock. If the heart of the immodest is like the earth, the heart of the modest one is like the water. Modesty is life itself; a life which is conscious of its beauty yet inclined to veil it in all its forms is modesty. At the same time modesty is the proof of sincerity and of prudence. The cracker cries aloud, "I am the light," and is finished in a moment. The diamond, shining in its light constantly, never says a word about its light.

ESOTERIC PAPERS - GATHA III - MORALS - Hay (Modesty)

Gayan #356 - Chala #35 - All beauty is veiled by nature, and the greater the beauty the more it is covered.

All beauty is veiled by nature, and the higher the beauty the more it is covered. That makes it easy for a wise person to find the difference between a true prophet and a false prophet, for one beats his drums and the other tries to keep in the background, if only his work in the world would let him keep back. It is his efforts in accomplishing something that bring him to the notice of the world. However, his longing is to be unknown, for the one who really deserves to be known is God alone.

RELIGIOUS GATHEKAS - Degrees in the Spiritual Hierarchy

Gayan #357 - Chala #36 - The beauty which modesty covers, art gently uncovers; while respecting the human tendency. it unveils the beauty which human conventions hide.

But there is a still higher significance of the cross which is understood by the mystic. This significance is what is called self-denial, and, in order to teach this moral, gentleness, humility and modesty are taught as a first lesson. Self-denial is an effect of which self-effacement is the cause. This is self-denial, that a man says, "I am not, Thou art"; or that an artist, looking at his picture, says, "It is Thy work, not mine"; or that a musician, hearing his composition, says, "It is Thy creation, I do not exist." That soul then is in a way crucified, and through that crucifixion resurrection comes. There is not the slightest doubt that when man has had enough pain in his life he rises to this great consciousness. But it is not necessary that only pain should be the means. It is the readiness on the part of man to efface his part of consciousness and to efface his own personality which lifts the veil that hides the spirit of God from the view of man.

ESOTERIC PAPERS - GATHA I - SYMBOLOGY - The Symbol of the Cross

Gayan #358 - Chala #37 - Modesty is the veil over the face of the great, for God Himself is most modest, who is seen by none except those intimate with Him.

Modesty is not necessarily timidity or cowardice. The bravest can be modest, and it is modesty which completes bravery. Modesty is the veil over the face of the great; for the most modest is God Himself, Who is not seen by anyone except those intimate with Him. Beauty in all its forms and colors, in all its phases and spheres, doubles itself, enriches itself by modesty. Modesty is not something that is learnt. It is in nature, for it is natural. Modesty does not only cover what is beautiful but amplifies the beauty and covers all that is void of beauty, in this manner fitting it into all that which is beautiful.

ESOTERIC PAPERS - GATHA III - MORALS - Modesty

Gayan #359 - Chala #38 - God lives in nature and is buried alive under the artificial forms which stand as His tomb, covering Him.

The question which arises in the mind of every thoughtful person is, what was the reason, what was the purpose of the creation of this world? The answer is, to break the monotony. Call it God, call it the only Being, call it the source and goal of all; being alone, He wished that there should be something for Him to know. The Hindus say that the creation is the dream of Brahma. One may call it a dream, but it is the main purpose. The Sufis explain it thus: that God, the Lover, wanted to know his own nature; and that therefore through manifestation the Beloved was created, in order that love might manifest. And when we look at it in this light, then all that we see is the Beloved. As Rumi, the greatest writer of Persia says, 'The Beloved is all in all, the lover only veils Him; the Beloved is all that lives, the lover a dead thing.'

ALCHEMY OF HAPPINESS – The Purpose of Life (1)

Gayan #360 - Chala #39 - Nature is the very being of man; therefore, he feels at one with nature.

What appeals to us in being near to nature is nature's music, and nature's music is more perfect than that of art. It gives us a sense of exaltation to be moving about in the woods, to be looking at the green, to be standing near the running water which has its rhythm, its tone and its harmony. The swinging of the branches in the forest, the rising and falling of the waves - all has its music. Once we contemplate and become one with nature, our hearts open to its music. We say: 'I enjoy nature', and what is it in nature that we enjoy? It is its music. Something in us has been touched by the rhythmic movement, by the perfect harmony which is so seldom found in this artificial life of ours. It lifts one up and makes one feel that it is this which is the real temple, the true religion. One moment standing in the midst of nature with open heart is a whole lifetime, if one is in tune with nature.

THE MYSTICISM OF SOUND AND MUSIC - MUSIC - The Music of the Spheres

Gayan #361 - Chala #40 - In the country you see the glory of God; in the city you glorify His name.

Those living close to nature in the solitude, or peasants living in the country, have greater intuition than intellectual people who live in the midst of worldly life. This shows that the life we live today in large towns is an unnatural life, lived in an artificial atmosphere, eating artificial food, adopting artificial ways. So one loses that heavenly quality, the divine heritage of man which is shown in the intuitive qualities.

THE ALCHEMY OF HAPPINESS - Communicating with Life

Gayan #362 - Chala #41 - True art does not take man away from nature; on the contrary, it brings him closer to her.

When one is alone with nature, near the sea, on the river bank, among the mountains, in the forest, in the wilderness, a feeling comes over one which is never felt among a crowd, not even if one were in the crowd for years. In one moment a feeling becomes born, as soon as one is face to face with the true art of God. It then seems as if the soul had seen something which it has always admired and worshipped. The soul now begins to recognize One Whom she has always silently worshipped, and now the presence of that mighty Creator, that Artist, is realized through seeing His art. Many experience this, but few will express it. None can come back from such an experience without a deep impression, without something having been awakened to consciousness through having seen the divine art.

This shows that this creation, this manifestation which is before us, has not been made mechanically, has not been created blindly or unconsciously; but as a great poet of Persia, Sa'adi, says, "The more one looks at nature, the more one begins to feel that there is a perfection of wisdom, a perfect skill, behind it, which has made it, and it will take numberless years for mankind to imitate that art. In fact mankind will never be able to attain it perfectly."

Whoever studies the kingdom of flowers, of vegetables, of minerals, the birds, the insects, the germs, and the worms, the animals and their forms and colors, and the beauty which each form suggests, will surely recognize as did the prophets of old that the world is created by the Spirit, that divine Spirit Who has created it with eyes wide open; and showing perfect wisdom behind it, and perfect skill in it, and a sense of beauty so perfect that man must always be incapable of achieving it. But now the question comes, "What is man?" Man is the miniature of God, and man has inherited as his divine inheritance the tendency to art.

THE SUPPLEMENTARY PAPERS - ART AND MUSIC IV - The Divinity of Art

Gayan #363 - Chala #42 - A good reputation is as fragile as a delicate glass.

When learning concentration, it is most essential to know first upon what to concentrate. If one thought, "Anything may do, as long as I exercise my mind," he must know that the object he keeps in his mind has a great deal to do with his life. If in his mind there is love, at least an attachment for an individual, it may be for his good or perhaps for his ill; it may perhaps not be the right thing. If it is hatred for someone, it may rebound and destroy all the affairs of the one who concentrates. If it is wealth, there is no doubt that one could become wealthy, but if it worked against one's health or one's friends or comfort, or peace in life, what would wealth be without peace? If it is fame upon which one concentrates, one may have to hold with both hands an empty reputation, which might fall down at any moment, like a piece of glass.

ESOTERIC PAPERS - GITHA III - CONCENTRATION - The Effect of Concentration Upon One's Life

Gayan #364 - Chala #43 - A good reputation is a trust given to a man by other people, so it becomes his sacred duty to maintain it.

Humility has its place, pride has its place in life. In the place of pride, humility cannot be fitted. Once the Nizam of Hyderabad was walking in the country, and a knight happened to see a thorn stuck in his shoe. He rushed, before the attendant had seen it, and took out that thorn from the king's shoe. The king looked back and said, "Were there no attendants present? It was for them, not for you," said the king, "and since you have taken this work, you can no longer continue to be my knight. Please retire." It is the sense of honor expected by his surroundings that makes a king a true king.

For a Sufi the sense of honor is not for his personality, he does not give his person a greater place than dust and the central theme of his life is simplicity and his moral is humility. Yet remember that the Sufi breathes the breath of God, so he is conscious of the honor of God. His pride is greater, therefore, than the pride of every man. It is in the intoxication of this pride that he proves to be God-conscious.

ESOTERIC PAPERS - GATHA III - MORALS - Ghairat (Honor)

Gayan #365 - Chala #44 - Either take good care of your reputation, or do not care for it at all.

We think little things so important: dignity, ill-treatment, insults, reputation; and what do they matter in the end? Do we not see people praised and raised up high in vanity and greatness one day, and next day they are quite forgotten? Before the revolution every shop in Moscow had a picture of the Czar in one window, and of Jesus with the Virgin in the other. Within three years, what a change there was! Even a whole race will change its attitude in a moment's time.

Praise, honor, love, kindness, are they lasting, are they dependable? Are we not seeking after wealth, or fame, or love, or kindness, or some help from morning until evening? However evolved we may be with our education and experience, yet what are we really seeking? Things from which we cannot derive any lasting gain. From these false things we gain the experience that the things to which we have hitherto attached importance and which we have valued are things that do not last. We learn at length that it would be wise to remember that all these objects and ideals and aspirations which we have in life should be judged according to whether they are dependable or not, lasting or not.

After we have perceived the truth that this or that is not to be depended upon, we find that it is not necessary to renounce them all, to give up everything in life. We can be in the crowd just as well as in seclusion in the wilderness. We can have all good things, wealth, friends, kindness, love to give and love to take, once we have learned not to be blinded by them, learned to escape from disappointment, learned to escape from repugnance at the idea that the things are not as we would want them to be. A man can still attend to business, he may attain wealth, he can carry out all those things, but now his eyes are wide open; before, they were blind.

This is the teaching of life. Thus it is that when we study life in the East, we will find that a Sufi may be a 'king or he may be a faqir. A Sufi means a seer; and a Sufi may still be a king. It is not the actual literal renunciation which counts, it is the personal abandonment of belief in the importance of transient things.

IN AN EASTERN ROSE GARDEN - Gain and Loss

Gayan #366 - Chala #45 - The man who has no reputation of his own has no regard for the reputation of another.

Sympathy is an awakening of the love element which comes on seeing another in the same situation in which one has been at some time in one's life. A person who has never experienced pain cannot sympathize with those suffering pain. In the same way a person sympathizes with someone whose honor or reputation has been harmed. The one who has no honor or reputation himself would not mind for he does not know what it is and what it is to lose it. A rich person who has lost his money may be laughed at by someone who has never had it. He can sympathize with him who has wealth, and still more can he sympathize with him who had wealth and lost it.

Very often the young imagine they love their mother and think they sympathize with their parents, but they cannot come to the full realization of their love until they reach that situation. Very often people think it cruel and unkind of their friends when they do not receive sympathy from them, but they do not know that to have sympathy does not mean having a warm heart only, but it means having that experience which reminds them of it, making them sympathetic. Sympathy is something more than love and affection, for it is the knowledge of a certain suffering which moves the living heart to sympathy.

ESOTERIC PAPERS - GATHA III - METAPHYSICS – Sympathy

www.ingramcontent.com/pod-product-compliance
Lightning Source LLC
Chambersburg PA
CBHW021759220426
43662CB00006B/117